Josephine Baker and Katherine Dunham

Dances in Literature and Cinema

HANNAH DURKIN

UNIVERSITY OF ILLINOIS PRESS
Urbana, Chicago, and Springfield

Manufactured in the United States of America
1 2 3 4 5 C P 5 4 3 2 1
∞ This book is printed on acid-free paper.

Library of Congress Cataloging-in-Publication Data
Names: Durkin, Hannah, author.
Title: Josephine Baker and Katherine Dunham: dances in literature and cinema / Hannah Durkin.
Description: Urbana: University of Illinois Press, 2019. | Includes bibliographical references and index. |
Identifiers: LCCN 2019002879 (print) | LCCN 2019019361 (ebook) | ISBN 9780252051463 (ebook) | ISBN 9780252042621 | ISBN 9780252042621 (cloth: alk. paper) | ISBN 9780252084454 (paperback : alk. paper)
Subjects: LCSH: Baker, Josephine, 1906–1975—Criticism and interpretation. | Dunham, Katherine—Criticism and interpretation. | African American women dancers—Biography—History and criticism. | African American women dancers—Biography. | Dance in literature. | Dance in motion pictures, television, etc.—United States. | Dance in motion pictures, television, etc.—Europe. | African Americans in motion pictures.
Classification: LCC GV1785.A1 (ebook) | LCC GV1785.A1 D87 2019 (print) | DDC 792.80922—dc23
LC record available at https://lccn.loc.gov/2019002879

Josephine Baker and Katherine Dunham

In loving memory of my mother,
Elizabeth Durkin (1956–2018)

Contents

List of Illustrations

Acknowledgments

This book would not have been possible without the financial support of the University of Nottingham and the U.K. Arts Humanities Research Council (AHRC). Overseas study grants from Nottingham, the AHRC, and the British Association of American Studies (BAAS) also helped to fund a crucial visit to the following archives: the Missouri History Museum Library and Research Center; the Morris Library Special Collections Research Center, Southern Illinois University Carbondale; the Manuscript, Archives, and Rare Book Library, Emory University; the Moving Image Section, Motion Picture, Broadcasting and Recorded Sound Division, Library of Congress; and the Beinecke Library, Yale University. I would also like to thank BAAS and the Eccles Centre for American Studies for providing a travel grant that allowed me to spend several weeks at the British Library. The advice of individual archivists has been invaluable and I am incredibly grateful to the staff at the above institutions, who all went out of their way to help. Molly Kodner at the Missouri History Museum even took time out of her busy schedule to show me surviving Katherine Dunham dance company costumes.

Nor could this book have been completed without the support of countless colleagues, mentors, and hugely supportive friends at the University of Nottingham and Newcastle University. I owe a particular debt of thanks to Professor Dave Murray, who helped to steer me in the direction of the original research project on which it was based and guided it through its early stages; Professor Sharon Monteith, who took over from Professor Murray in helping to shape it; and Professor Celeste-Marie Bernier, who supported my work tirelessly from start to finish and continues to be a key pillar of inspiration and advice. They have been more helpful and encouraging than I could ever have hoped and it has been an incredible privilege to learn from them. I would also like to thank Professors Judie Newman and John Howard for reviewing the manuscript at a crucial phase and for their generous thoughts and comments, and Professor Richard King, Dr. Ian Brookes, Dr. Nick Heffernan, and Dr. Graham Taylor, and other members of the University of Nottingham Music Listening and Race on Film groups for their endless ideas and encouragement.

Professor Alan Rice and Dr. Fionnghuala Sweeney have been friends and informal mentors since I started out in academia and I would be lost without their guidance. My scholarship has also been shaped by the expertise of the Institute for Black Atlantic Research at the University of Central Lancashire, of which Professor Rice is a director, and I owe a particular debt to Professor Lubaina Himid CBE, Dr. Raphael Hoermann, and fellow Josephine Baker expert Jade Montserrat for their exceptional knowledge and friendships. I would also like to thank the many audience members who listened and responded to ideas from this book at conferences, symposia, and workshops, not least the organizers and fellow members of the University College Dublin Clinton Institute Summer School and Heidelberg Center for American Studies Spring Academy, who took the time to comment on the project in its early stages.

I had the tremendous good fortune to have Dawn Durante as my editor at the University of Illinois Press and benefited hugely from her expert guidance, patience, and support. I am also incredibly grateful to the many other staff members at the University of Illinois Press who have worked really hard and patiently on this book, including Jennifer Argo, Kevin Cunningham, Alison Syring, and copyeditor Nancy Albright. Thanks too to the anonymous readers for taking the time to evaluate and comment on my work and for making this a better book.

Finally, I would like to express my profoundest gratitude to friends and family outside of academia. Catherine and Helen have been pillars of support for the duration of this book and for years beyond. Last but not least, I thank my parents Liz and Gerry; my siblings Frances, Joe, and Sam; their respective partners Rob, Gonia, and Jen; my aunt Mary; and my niece Lily.

None of my work would have been possible without their love and encouragement. Whenever I encountered hurdles, they always found ways to help. This book is dedicated to them.

An earlier version of part of chapter two was published as "Dance Anthropology and the Impact of Haiti on Katherine Dunham's Scientific and Artistic Consciousness," *International Journal of Francophone Studies* 14.1–2 (2011): 123–42.

Introduction

In an interview during the making of the French film *Zouzou* (1934), U.S.-born Black dance icon Josephine Baker declared that, "I sometimes think that it is my own life that's unfolding on the set," self-consciously positioning the film as autobiographical.[1] By connecting the picture with her own experiences, Baker pointed to ways in which the European imaginary conflated its exotic fantasy with her offstage identity while underscoring the production's debt to her artistry. Fellow international Black dance icon Katherine Dunham's films also drew on her fame as a choreographer to the extent that narratives were centered on her art and she even showcased her own company in rehearsal on screen. That Baker and Dunham's movie appearances were openly autobiographical highlights connections between their life stories and film narratives and the value of both in uncovering their contributions as Black women to twentieth-century transatlantic culture. Cinematic and literary spaces were for Baker and Dunham sites of mediation and marginalization in which they shared authorship with white men. Their interventions across both forms highlight the distortions and exclusions of racist cultural imaginaries on both sides of the Atlantic in the three decades prior to the civil rights era. Yet they are also rare visual and textual records of Black women dancers' midcentury artistry and authorship.

This study investigates Baker and Dunham's self-inventions on screen and in writing to map the intellectual underpinnings and visual impact of their art. By scrutinizing Baker and Dunham's choreographic practices and narrative voices, I shed new light on the ways in which they were received on both sides of the Atlantic and how they engaged personally with dominant critical interpretations of Black performance as crude and innate. My study evidences both women's extensive contributions to cinema and the memoir form and shows how they sought to challenge racist paradigms by constructing celebratory visions of Black womanhood in literature and cinema. Most of Baker and Dunham's work took place on the stage rather than on the page and screen. Nevertheless, their authorial interventions across both mediums were prolific and radical. Baker was the first Black woman to enjoy a starring role in mainstream cinema and Dunham was the first Black film choreographer to be credited for her work. Equally, they were the first well-known African American women to produce multivolume accounts of their lives, and their writings serve as valuable firsthand documents of African American women's interwar experiences. Their literary and cinematic careers demand collective attention for several reasons. On the page, they gave voice to the challenges of navigating interwar global spaces as young Black women and their narratives shed vital light on the origins and purpose of their art. Their writings also evidence their lifelong commitment to international egalitarianism. On the screen, they claimed the right to stardom while at the same time retaining some artistic autonomy and even shaping their films' aesthetics.

Why did Baker and Dunham enjoy such groundbreaking literary and cinematic careers? What do such careers tell us about the challenges and opportunities that they encountered as Black women seeking to navigate midcentury geographical and cultural boundaries? Why did they turn to life writing and the screen and on what terms were they able to engage with these mediums as Black women? How in turn did they seek to resist the limited terms of their engagement with these cultural forms? How did contemporary Black screen audiences receive their work? More broadly, where do Baker and Dunham's films and writings fit within African American literary and cinematic histories and why are they largely absent from these histories? This book investigates these questions. In so doing, it uncovers the cultural significance of Baker and Dunham's films and writings and interrogates their performances within them to recover their authorship. Both stars built on wider Black Atlantic performance traditions. Analysis of their literary and cinematic legacies therefore is vital not only for recovering the artists' individual struggles and achievements, but also for shedding light on a wider history of racism and creative resistance in twentieth-century transatlantic culture. Baker and Dunham's films and writings serve as records of how they wanted their artistry to be understood. They provide detailed case studies of—and give voice to—the battles for authorship that Black women artists endured in the mid–twentieth century, as well as their creative contributions to cinema, dance, and literature despite these battles.

Born just three years apart in Missouri and Illinois, adjoining states in the U.S. Midwest, Baker and Dunham were both remarkable for the decades-long global fame that they achieved as Black women artists. Baker began performing on the U.S. vaudeville stage before achieving teenage stardom in 1920s Paris, where she initially drew attention for her opening night "*danse sauvage*" and later for appearing onstage in nothing more than a skirt of bananas. She was held up as the physical embodiment of European primitivist conceptions of exotic "Blackness," and she became a muse to modernist artists and writers, including Pablo Picasso and Ernest Hemingway, who would call her "the most sensational woman anybody ever saw."[2] Simultaneously, Baker cultivated a glamorous persona and her cropped hair, avant-garde clothing, and African American vaudeville-derived dance movements set the pace of Parisian fashions. Her individualistic performances proved appealing to middle-class French women who, although still politically disenfranchised, were enjoying a new status of social and economic independence precipitated by World War I.[3] As Ean Wood notes, "To many young women, she became a symbol of liberation."[4]

Baker's European career endured for fifty years, during which time she worked as a dancer, singer, French Resistance spy, and humanitarian. She was honored with the *Croix de guerre* and *Chevalier de la Légion d'honneur* for her contribution to France's military intelligence service during World War II, a role that involved charming officials at diplomatic functions to obtain information about German troop locations. She also used a tour of Portugal and South America as a pretext for smuggling to London military secrets, which were hidden in invisible ink on the back of her sheet music.[5] After the war, she adopted and raised twelve children from around the world in an effort to establish her home, Les Milandes in Dordogne, as what she called *La Capitale du monde de la fraternité* (The World Capital of Brotherhood). She spoke alongside Martin Luther King Jr. at the March on Washington for Jobs and Freedom rally in 1963 and Coretta Scott King offered her the unofficial leadership of the civil rights movement following King's assassination in 1968.[6] Baker was also the first Black actress to enjoy a leading role in a major motion picture when she appeared in *La Sirène des tropiques* (1927), although her film career did not extend to white U.S.

audiences. As this study shows, such contrasting treatment is highly revealing of midcentury transatlantic racial politics.

Like Baker, Dunham's career was marked by international critical and commercial acclaim as well as an enduring devotion to antiracism. She established and ran the earliest self-supporting predominantly Black dance company, which was one of the earliest modern dance troupes to enjoy international success. Alongside Baker, Dunham was one of the first African American performers to be taken seriously by white dance critics, and she enjoyed close friendships with leading twentieth-century writers and intellectuals, including art critic Bernard Berenson, psychologist Erich Fromm, and Senegalese President Léopold Sédar Senghor.[7] Together with Baker, she appeared at the First World Festival of Negro Arts in Senegal in 1966, which was a key symbolic event in celebrating and developing a Pan-African artistic consciousness.[8] Dunham believed that providing dance education to deprived communities such as in East St. Louis would teach young people the value of their artistic and cultural heritages, in turn providing them with a sense of confidence and self-respect that would help to lift them out of poverty. Dunham was also a political activist who fought against lynching and segregation. In 1992, at the age of eighty-two, she embarked on a forty-seven–day hunger strike to protest against the U.S. Government's expulsion of Haitian refugees who were fleeing the military coup that brought down Jean-Bertrand Aristide's government. She was also one of the first African American women to conduct anthropological fieldwork and the first anthropologist whose chief purpose was to explore the function of dance in rituals and community life. Her observations of dance rituals while working as a graduate researcher in the Caribbean in the 1930s played a formative role in her choreography.

Baker and Dunham provide vital insights into Black women artists' representations and self-representations in transatlantic culture across the first half of the twentieth century. They are particularly appropriate for comparative study; they were contemporaries and remarkable for the prolonged and profound international impact of their careers. As light-skinned Black women, their performances and writings drew attention to the arbitrary nature of racial categorization. They both experimented with a rich history of African diasporic forms of artistry to reshape European and Euro-American conceptions of modern dance. Baker cultivated a highly idiosyncratic dance technique rooted in Black vaudeville during a period in which women on the popular stage were increasingly arranged in regimented routines, and she helped to popularize jazz styles such as the Charleston in Europe. Dunham developed a choreographic method that combined Caribbean cultural forms with ballet and performed both in concert halls and vaudeville theatres. Her work influenced leading choreographers of the twentieth century, including Agnes de Mille, Jerome Robbins, and Alvin Ailey. Baker and Dunham both worked with Balanchine and their collective influence may have inspired him to become the first U.S.-based dance master to incorporate into his choreography African diasporic dance styles, including angular arms, turned-in legs, and bent knees. Beth Genné makes the convincing case that Baker, who was Balanchine's first U.S. muse, provided inspiration to the choreographer by shaping his conception of the twentieth-century ballerina. Noting Baker's physical similarity to Balanchine's prima ballerinas, she asserts that, "It could very well be that Baker's long legs and lithe body not only fit Balanchine's ideal but also helped to create it."[9]

Dedicated practitioners and academics such as Ruth Beckford, Albirda Rose, Joyce Aschenbrenner, VèVè A. Clark, and Joanna Dee Das have worked to keep alive Dunham's choreographic legacy.[10] Kate Ramsey, Halifu Osumare, Yvonne Daniel, and the contributors to Elizabeth Chin's *Katherine Dunham: Recovering an Anthropological Legacy, Choreographing Ethnographic Futures* (2014) have also sought to excavate Dunham's pioneering contribution to dance anthropology.[11] Baker's association with the popular stage means that her contribution to dance has received less serious attention, for as Julie Townsend observes, "Baker is absent from many jazz and modern dance histories; and, a few recent examples excepted, if historians mentioned her at all, they tended to dismiss her as a mere entertainer."[12] Nevertheless, a number of dance scholars including Ramsay Burt, Brenda Dixon Gottschild, and Felicia McCarren have worked to uncover her contributions to the art form.[13] This study is indebted to their findings. However, Baker and Dunham's writings, which provide vital insights into their artistic philosophies, are rarely included in mainstream literary histories. Equally, they have not been considered seriously as film stars, despite their authorial contributions to the medium as Black women actors, dancers, and choreographers. Nor have such careers been scrutinized in a transatlantic context, despite the diverse receptions that their work enjoyed across international cultural frameworks.

A number of factors have helped to obscure Baker and Dunham's contributions to the page and screen, not least the long-running difficulties in accessing their literary and film archives. Their writings have been out of print for decades. Many of their films were low-budget, shown only in Europe, and unavailable for public viewing until their restoration and recirculation on DVD in the late 1990s and 2000s. Some of Dunham's screen work, the German film *Die Große Starparade* (The Great Star Parade) (1954) and the Mexican productions *Primavera en el corazón* (Spring in the Heart) (1956) and *Música en la noche* (Night Music) (1958), still await such recuperative treatment.[14] Only fragments remain of Baker's first known film, *La Folie du jour* (1927). She might first have appeared on celluloid in African American director Oscar Micheaux's *A Son of Satan* (1924), but the film is lost and with it any trace of her presence.

Baker and Dunham's careers on the stage have overshadowed their work on the page and screen. However, their films and writings also fall outside of mainstream literary and cinematic histories. Black women, not least celebrity memoirists, traditionally have been excluded from literary canons. Baker's writings have also been obscured because they were written in French, coauthored, and one of her works was published posthumously. Yet she was the first African American woman to produce several volumes of her life story. Anthropologists and dance specialists have so far undertaken the labor of recuperating Dunham's writings. But Dunham was a skilled author who deserves serious recognition for her place in Black women's autobiographical history.

Equally, the challenges of navigating historical film industries and audiences across national borders mean that studies of midcentury African American cinema typically adopt a U.S. focus. Yet the inter- and postwar European screen offered creative opportunities and roles to African American artists that were not available back home. As this study acknowledges, Baker was the first Black woman to star in a major motion picture, an achievement that was only possible outside of the United States given the nation's exclusionary racial codes. There was no centralized film industry in Europe and no censorship laws permitting Black and white characters from appearing alongside each other ostensibly as equals. Jazz singer Alberta Hunter, who performed in Europe for four decades between 1917 and the mid-1950s, remarked on the exceptional opportunities that were afforded to African American artists there: "The Negro artists went to Europe because we were recognized and given a chance. In Europe they had your name up in lights. People in the United States would not give us that chance."[15]

Baker and Dunham's omission from literary and cinematic histories therefore reflects the challenges of conducting research across disciplinary and national boundaries. However, their treatment also recalls a wider history of mythic artistic hierarchies, in which Black dance was positioned as "exotic" and "raw" material readily available for appropriation rather than as innovative artistry and an important component in the development of twentieth-century artistic movements. Black expressive practices represented valuable sources of cultural borrowings throughout the early and mid–twentieth century and the Black female dancer became a key symbol of physical freedom and pleasure during the interwar period. Yet Black women were rarely credited for their artistry; rather, their work was typically dismissed as crude and instinctive. As Jayna Brown notes, "'New women' embraced black expressive forms, adopting racialized gestural vocabularies to shape and redefine their own bodies as modern. Yet black women performers are seldom recognized as agents of these new physical vocabularies."[16] For example, Ethel Williams provided unacknowledged training for the Ziegfeld Girls and Irene Castle, who with her husband Vernon popularized ragtime dances such as the fox trot for white cultural consumers. Likewise, Edna Guy, an accomplished dancer, was relegated to the role of seamstress in the pioneering Denishawn School of Dancing and Related Arts. Although Elida Webb's Charleston choreography for Broadway show *Runnin' Wild* (1923) is now thought to have sparked the U.S. craze for the dance, James Weldon Johnson gave credit to the show's producers, Aubrey Lyles and Flournoy Miller, which shows that even Black contemporaries were ignorant of Webb's art.[17] Euro-American performers and choreographers such as *Ziegfeld Follies* dance director Ned Wayburn also claimed to have first staged the dance.[18] As Daphne A. Brooks summarizes, social marginalization and exclusion worked to deprive Black women of the right to self-representation, dehumanizing them in the process: "Having little access to the culture of property, to the culture of naming, or to patriarchal wealth, the mythically rendered black body—and the black female body in particular—was scripted by dominant paradigms to have 'no movement in a field of signification.' Born out of diasporic plight and subject to pornotroping, this body has countenanced a "'powerful stillness.'"[19] My research seeks to counteract such "stillness" by examining in detail the performative images generated within Baker and Dunham's films and writings.

To help rectify such silencing of Black women's artistry, this study widens the scope of literary and film analysis beyond traditional geographical and generic confines. It also blurs disciplinary boundaries by adopting a joint focus on film and literature as important sites of authorship. It places Baker and Dunham's own accounts of their lives and artistry alongside key visual records of their performances in order to shed new light on the artists' choreographic legacies. The ephemeral nature of stage performance means that films, photographs, and textual accounts are the only surviving firsthand records of Baker and Dunham's international stage careers. A collective analysis of these materials therefore represents the most systematic method of interrogating not only the racial frameworks that they negotiated but also their creativity within such confines. Baker and Dunham's writings give intellectual voice to the performances that we see on screen. Baker's memoirs also record her responses to her films. Equally, there are extensive autobiographical references in Baker and Dunham's screen work. Baker's European films dramatize her rise to fame. Dunham played herself on screen and her European productions feature her dance company in rehearsal. More than simply fictions that happened to feature these artists, Baker and Dunham's films therefore tell us a great deal about their public identities as midcentury Black women performers. Moreover, their contributions to the cinema serve as tools for countering ongoing tendencies in film studies to ascribe authorship to a typically white male director to the extent that women's and minority voices are still largely absent from mainstream screen histories. Instead, this study asks, what happens when we attribute authorship to the gestural strategies of moving bodies on the screen and page?

Central to my investigation in this regard is the way in which dancing bodies function as fluctuating signifiers and destabilizing transmitters of cultural identities. Through these readings, I extend Jayna Brown's suggestion that "we think about the body not as a *tabula rasa*, as a passive or powerless terrain upon which dominant ideologies etch their claims indelibly" but instead should "unthink this rigid version of the individual body as produced discursively." Brown reasons that, "Discursive claims compete, conflict, and are never complete. Racialized bodies wriggle through, around, with, and against these claims."[20] My study engages with the dancing body as a nonlinguistic representational strategy, exploring Dunham's own claim that "the arts, visual and performing, are, because of their freedom from language barriers among the most effective agents of contact, communication and persuasion."[21] In this way, it builds upon Jane Desmond's argument that, "To keep our broader levels of analysis anchored in the materiality and kinesthesia of the dancing body, we need to generate more tools for close readings . . . expanding understanding of the ways in which the body serves both as a ground for the inscription of meaning, a tool for its enactment, and a medium for *its continual creation and re-creation*."[22] Locating Baker and Dunham's dancing bodies as sites of disjuncture, I position their films and writings as cultural terrain on which historical struggles for control over meanings were played out. Baker and Dunham's innovative, idiosyncratic, and self-reflexive performances and narratives challenged artistic and cultural binaries. They were complex and visually evocative aesthetic statements that defied easy consumption and commodification.

Issues of agency and authorship, and Baker and Dunham's responses to those cultural hierarchies that were reluctant to credit them for their artistry, are indivisible from the structures of power in which they worked. Baker was not credited as a film author, but her dance scenes owed everything to her stage work, meaning that she should rightfully be understood as the coauthor of these scenes. Her stagings of Black womanhood on the screen were unruly and unrestricted; her rapid gestures seemed to resist an ordered pattern and appeared spontaneous rather than choreographed. By repeating a range of dance moves and styles over and over rather than adhering to a predetermined routine, however, Baker can be held to be the author of her work; her interpretation of the music was idiosyncratically her own. By contrast, Dunham was recognized for much of her artistry onscreen. She was the first Black American, and the first woman, to achieve credit, albeit unremembered, as a choreographer in Hollywood. I show that Dunham enjoyed extensive authorship over her performance scenes and that her artistry even helped to shape the aesthetics of two of her films, *Carnival of Rhythm* (1941) and *Mambo* (1954).

This study turns first to Baker and Dunham's writings to foreground the dancers' authorial voices and to highlight the intellectual and autobiographical underpinnings of their art. Together, Baker and Dunham were the first African American women to produce multivolume accounts of their lives. On the surface, their publications are profoundly different. Baker's texts are celebrity memoirs that describe—and were devised to capitalize on—her European stardom. Conversely, a key concern of Dunham's books was to record the sacred and creative practices of Caribbean peasant cultures. Such texts make few allusions to her fame. Baker was just twenty, had little formal education, and could not speak French when she began compiling her memoirs, which were coauthored by white men. Dunham writes from a scientist's socially privileged perspective; her work stemmed from a student field trip. Yet Baker and Dunham's texts share a concern with Black women's cultural experiences across international borders and were published at a time when such encounters—and African American women's life stories more generally—rarely appeared in print. Their writings are especially valuable for documenting the origins of dance practices that led them to global stardom and show how both women engaged self-reflexively with their public identities.

The chief goal of my analysis is to recover the autobiographical significance of such writings, which are still largely absent from African American literary histories. Close scrutiny of these texts reveals Baker and Dunham's pioneering contributions, as Black women writers, to the memoir form. As T. Denean Sharpley-Whiting notes, writing in this genre "represents a critical oppositional space where black women have been able to redefine, indeed reinvent, themselves. The act of writing allows for a return to the self, an exploration of the self. Through 'writing,' according to French feminist antitheory theorist Hélène Cixous, 'women will return to the bodies which have been more than confiscated from [them].'"[23] Indeed, as with their screen performances, this study argues that Baker and Dunham's writings were acts of self-invention and reinvention, as they defied rigid racial frameworks. Their memoirs are as fraught as their dance stagings with problems of mediation and misrepresentation, yet they reveal much about them as artists and as individuals. Most notably, they show how both women used dance to intervene in midcentury racial and gender ideologies. Their extremely frank portrayals of Baker and Dunham's formative experiences shed light on the problems of artistic autonomy and authorship faced by Black women during this era, while also foregrounding their intellectual contributions to midcentury literature, dance, and cinema.

The historical significance of Baker's writings has been overlooked in large part because they are collaborative texts and it is difficult to separate her narrative voice from those of her white male coauthors. Yet as she did in her screen and stage work, Baker found ways to shape her narratives, which reflect on the racism that she encountered in the United States and Europe and reveal an enduring frustration both with her exoticizing treatment by white male critics and with broader racial injustices. Dunham has gained belated recognition for her pioneering interventions in the field of anthropology, but her contributions as a midcentury Black woman autobiographer have still to be fully appreciated. Dunham's book-length ethnographies record her personal experiences in mid-1930s Jamaica and Haiti, including her initiation into Vodou. As with Baker's work, dance is at the heart of these texts, and like Baker's writings they document the challenges that she encountered but also the freedoms that she enjoyed as a Black woman traveling for the first time across interwar cultural and national borders.

This study then turns to Baker and Dunham's films, which are vital visual records of their dance practices. They evidence the international cultural visibility that the two artists enjoyed while at the same time revealing how their work was translated, and frequently misrepresented, within midcentury transatlantic racial imaginaries. As the first Black women to enjoy major international screen careers, a comparative investigation of Baker and Dunham's films therefore is invaluable for understanding Black women's early cinematic mistreatment but also their creative achievements on celluloid. Together, Baker and Dunham's European films, all of which capitalize on the dancers' perceived exotic Otherness, highlight the persistence of racist paradigms in the midcentury European imagination. Conversely, such films help to recover European cinema's importance in affording African Americans early screen opportunities by revealing the freedoms that Baker and Dunham enjoyed as dancers and choreographers in productions not beholden to Hollywood racial codes. In particular, they serve as visual records of the cross-cultural artistry that both women employed to disrupt dominant racial and gender configurations and create celebratory visions of Black womanhood.

This study locates Baker's silent roles as the starting point, not simply of Baker's screen career, but of mainstream Black female film stardom more generally. For the first time, films aimed at white audiences were conceived specifically to capitalize on a Black dancer's fame, and the success that Baker achieved facilitated and directly informed the idolization that Dunham enjoyed in postwar Europe. These early productions also shed light on links between colonial and ethnographic ideologies and the development of commercial filmmaking.[24] Noting the temporal parallels between Baker's early career and the emergence of colonial films, Elizabeth Ezra argues that Baker's screen work served as evidence of colonial obsessions in the interwar French subconscious. Ezra asserts that Baker's films "seem to celebrate the mixing of cultures, but they actually seek to preserve the exotic as such—that is, to keep it literally outside."[25] Similarly, Terri Francis points up temporal overlaps between Baker's films and popular ethnological entertainment in 1920s and 1930s France. She allows that, "Older than cinema, ethnological entertainment is also a mass amusement form, whose influence can be seen in Baker's film roles."[26] Baker's cinematic roles reinscribe popular colonial narratives in which Black women were positioned as the self-sacrificing, but ultimately unsuitable, love interests of European men. However, the films are often deliberately playful, and even oppositional, insofar as they enable Baker to articulate her choreography on screen. Even if the cinematic frameworks are discriminatory, there is a distinction between the plots and dance sequences that allows for her performance to be read as a contestation and even interrogation of the narrative.

Cinematic footage of Baker's work therefore has value in helping to visualize a much older Black artistic and intellectual tradition. As Jayna Brown has shown, there was nothing especially unique about the performance style that launched Baker to European fame. Instead, her unruly movements merely adhered to a tradition of "improvisatory disobedience" developed in previous decades by Black child performers such as Ida Forsyne, Louis Douglas, and Ethel Williams, who performed regularly in Europe before World War I. That Douglas oversaw *La Revue Nègre*'s choreography underscores such cultural linkages. This observation is not meant to undermine Baker's artistry and the strategic ways in which she employed it, but rather to recover the African American artistic roots of a performance style marketed and read as "primitive."

Equally, Anthea Kraut and Susan Manning have identified Dunham's stage work as a key site through which white spectators began to recognize the artistic significance of African diasporic dance forms.[27] But her artistry has yet to be situated within midcentury African American cinema histories.[28] My work on Dunham builds on the writing of Roy Thomas, whose 1978 article, "Focal Rites: New Dance Dominions," remains one of the few analyses of Dunham's cinematic legacy. He suggested that Dunham's involvement in commercial film resulted in her artistry being "seen by millions of viewers on both sides of the Atlantic Ocean," arguing in turn that the cinematic articulation of her artistic vision opened up opportunities for subsequent African American choreographers to construct new Black identities in Hollywood.[29] In Thomas's view, film acted as a medium through which Dunham was able to construct a new pictorial vision of African diasporic experiences that resisted homogenizing framings of Black women. Thomas does not account for the racist cinematic frameworks in which Dunham performed, an issue that will be addressed in this study, but his single article is significant for the fact that he is alone in contextualizing her film image.

This study adopts a methodological approach that involves close engagement with twentieth-century performance and cultural history as well as detailed literary and film analysis in order to scrutinize and contextualize the personas that Baker and Dunham presented on the page and screen. I also draw on a wide range of primary sources to shed light on the ways in which Baker and Dunham's films were received on both sides of the Atlantic and how the performers engaged personally with critical interpretations of their identities as dancers and choreographers. Newspaper reviews and commemorative programs dating back to Baker's 1925 Parisian debut facilitate an examination of her promotion and international reception. Although her

European fame was largely unremarked on by mainstream U.S. newspapers, reports in the Black press show that Baker continued to hold an important place in the African American public consciousness after her relocation to Paris. My work with Dunham is based on video sources, including interviews, dance seminars, and anthropological fieldwork footage from the Caribbean and elsewhere. I examine letters and contracts between Dunham and film producers, which reveal her efforts to challenge racist treatments of Black performers in 1940s Hollywood by demanding dignified screen roles and artistic control over her performances.

Six core chapters provide the scope to analyze Baker and Dunham's filmed dance performances and literary works collectively. I begin with their writings to chart their intellectual interventions in early-twentieth-century Black Atlantic dance and recover their significant contributions to an African American women's autobiographical tradition. My reading follows on from the work of Kwakiutl L. Dreher, who explores overlooked autobiographies by Black women celebrities, including Dunham's *Stormy Weather* (1943) costar Lena Horne and former Dunham company member Eartha Kitt, to make a case for adding them to the African American literary canon. Dreher seeks to liberate such women's voices from their static glamour portraits and show how their stories speak more broadly to African American women's experiences of racism. Unlike Dreher, I do not seek in Baker and Dunham's memoirs their "real stories," for such texts are as fraught as their dance stagings with problems of mediation and misrepresentation.[30] However, they reveal much about their performance strategies and humanist philosophies. They show how both women used dance to intervene self-reflexively in midcentury racial and gender ideologies. Their extremely frank portrayals of Baker and Dunham's formative experiences shed light on the problems of artistic autonomy and authorship faced by Black women during this era, while also signaling how they envisaged dance as a site for intercultural exchange as well as personal legitimization. I unearth ideologies of exoticism that impinged on both women's work, but I also show how they engaged with the written form to challenge such misrepresentations. Although their narrative perspectives are very different, with Baker sharing authorship over her memoirs and Dunham approaching life writing from a scientist's perspective, the challenges that they voice as Black women narrators exemplify the strength of dehumanizing attitudes to Black people across midcentury transatlantic culture. Their responses to such social positioning are also strikingly similar: both women adopt self-reflexive narrative voices and explore dance to communicate radical narratives of Black female subjectivity. My readings therefore situate the memoirs as important companions to Baker and Dunham's films that together foreground their authorial interventions within such confines.

Chapter one focuses on three of Baker's memoirs, *Voyages et aventures de Joséphine Baker* (1931), *Une vie de toutes les couleurs* (1935), and *Josephine* (1978), to recover her intellectual voice and liberate her from exoticizing abstraction. The memoirs aid in Baker's commodification insofar as they were cowritten by white men and their publications were timed to capitalize on specific Baker shows and films and, finally, on her death. Yet disjunctures between the main narrative and sections written expressly by her white male coauthors suggest that she played a significant role in their creation. I apply scholarship on emancipatory narratives and highlight engagements with U.S. racism to evidence Baker's authorial influence and establish the memoirs' value as rare literary accounts of an African American woman's early-twentieth-century transatlantic experiences. Baker's writings have particular value for helping to recover the intellectual underpinnings of her stage and screen persona. Instead of adhering to exotic fantasies of Black womanhood as set out by her coauthors, Baker depicts a body that is mistreated. The texts serve as self-reflexive critiques of the racial intolerance that she encountered in the United States and Europe and, as such, provide vital insights into psychological experiences that influenced her idiosyncratic artistic practice. The memoirs also contest colonial frameworks by presenting physical expression as a self-affirmative response to racial prejudice, a construction that would prove equally significant in Dunham's textual exploration of Caribbean dance cultures.

Chapter two examines Dunham's book-length ethnographies *Katherine Dunham's Journey to Accompong* (1946) and *Island Possessed* (1969). Much like Baker's writings, it shows that the texts should be recognized as autobiographical narratives that foreground corporeal experience and help to trace the genesis of Dunham's cross-cultural artistry. These texts recount Dunham's observations as a dance anthropologist in the Caribbean during the mid-1930s, shortly before she halted her academic training to pursue a career on the stage. Like Baker's narratives, both works are highly reflexive and ambiguous and thus deserve recognition within a history of Black women's autobiographical writing. They position Dunham as a self-conscious narrator who immerses herself physically in the cultural practices that she has been assigned merely to record. *Journey to Accompong* describes Dunham's participation in Koromantee war dances, while much of *Island Possessed* is devoted to her firsthand experience of a *lavé-tête*, a ritual marking the point of entry into the Haitian dance religion of Vodou. Dance enables her to take part in the rituals that she observes and to achieve a degree of cultural integration. Both texts therefore shed light on a much wider lifelong project, namely, Dunham's attempt to legitimize Caribbean cultures by incorporating their ritual dance forms into concert dance. In much the same way that Baker popularized early-twentieth-century Black Atlantic dance forms on the European stage, such an undertaking would undermine significantly perceived artistic and cultural binaries by ensuring the centrality of Caribbean cultural influence over North American concert and social dance throughout the mid–twentieth century. This chapter therefore positions these texts as valuable personal reflections on Dunham's development as an artist and activist. They show how she implemented dance material collected during her field trips to develop a cross-cultural choreographic practice that blurred artistic and racial boundaries.

Subsequent sections chart Baker and Dunham's creative contributions to U.S. and European cinema to recover their screen work as key sites of mid-century Black women's film authorship. Baker and Dunham's films evidence the strength and endurance of racist attitudes on both sides of the Atlantic. Equally, they serve as vital visual records of performances that intervened in these restrictive frameworks to upset racial and artistic hierarchies and create glamorous visions of Black womanhood. The performers' film experiences also show that they were able to enjoy much greater artistic freedom and recognition in Europe than was possible in classical Hollywood. Beginning with Baker's early silent films, I uncover the ways in which interwar French cinema provided a groundbreaking—albeit ambivalent—platform for her artistry. Chapter three examines constructions of Baker's dancing body in her two surviving silent productions, *La Revue des revues* and *La Sirène des tropiques* (both 1927). The two films are historically significant as visual documents of her performing style when she arrived in Paris in the mid-1920s. I consider Baker's intervention in interpretations of her body as a colonial commodity and demonstrate that physical expression and dance in particular also provided space in which Baker could cultivate witty, highly individual performative personae that disrupted contemporary race and gender constructions. In *Sirène*, Baker plays a colonial subject who is in love with her colonizer, which links her performance to French imperialist narratives. The film therefore appears to reinforce a fantasy of Black lives that Baker and Dunham's memoirs and choreography sought to break down. In these silent cinematic environments, however, Baker expresses agency through her ever-shifting body. This chapter shows that such individual expressiveness placed Baker at odds with chorus girl troupes whose emphasis on regimented movements worked to display women's bodies by mechanizing their performances into synchronized routines. I also consider the cultural impact of *Sirène*, which was the first mainstream film to star a Black actress and whose success with Black cinemagoers when it was imported to the United States in 1929 signals that they valued her achievements as an international star.

A seven-year gap separated *Sirène* and Baker's third feature-length film, *Zouzou* (1934). Chapter four examines *Zouzou* and *Princesse Tam-Tam* (1935) for the ways in which Baker retained the romanticized primitive role of her early films while simultaneously cultivating a fashionable star image. I also show that Baker brought significant individuality to her performance scenes to resist the films' racially subjugating narratives and assert her authorship. Continuing to adhere to her earlier dance style, by the 1930s Baker had transformed her stage persona, discarding the sexually suggestive banana belt with which she launched her career in favor of a look that more closely reflected her status as a member of Parisian high society. By this stage of her career, Baker had also adopted the stylistic methods of contemporary French music hall singers such as Mistinguett by singing *chansons*, or French ballads, including "J'ai deux amours" (I Have Two Loves), with which she would become associated. She learned how to dance *en pointe* and performed the title part in a revival of Jacques Offenbach's *opéra comique La Créole* (1934). She appeared on stage in gowns by Paul Poiret, Christian Dior, and Coco Chanel, and she wore jewelry by Tiffany and Cartier, which helped to situate her as an influential fashion icon.

Baker's sound films are imbued with a sense of ambivalence: she is positioned as a cinematic subject of the French colonial imaginary but also as a glamorous film star to market her to the United States. For example, in her most famous number in *Zouzou*, she sits in a cage and sings of her love for her "lost" Haiti, which can be read allegorically as an imperialist lament for what was once Europe's most profitable slave colony; but in another scene in the film she is surrounded by adoring Frenchmen as she sings "C'est lui" (He's the One). Both films are formulated around contemporary colonialist and primitivist tropes, and yet Baker's exaggerated gestural performances and "star" image are very much at odds with this dominant view. In contrast to her disastrous reception in the United States in Broadway show *Ziegfeld Follies of 1936*, which this chapter also explores, the films enable her to be glamorous and idiosyncratic and thus to cultivate a self-reflexive, highly personal screen image.

Dunham's film career began shortly after Baker made a failed bid for Hollywood stardom with *Follies*. The elisions and degradations that Dunham endured reveal the futility of Baker's U.S. cinematic endeavor. But such roles nevertheless show how, like Baker, Dunham drew on Black Atlantic artistry to rupture crude cinematic representations of Black womanhood and assert her authorship on screen. Chapter five examines Dunham's scenes in three of her Hollywood films, *Carnival of Rhythm* (1941), *Star Spangled Rhythm* (1942), and *Stormy Weather* (1943), and reflects on the extent of her artistic influence over each performance. The productions were made at the height of Dunham's involvement in U.S. cinema. They provide key case studies of World War II–era Hollywood racial codes and reveal how Dunham negotiated these representations. In this chapter, I consider Dunham's attempts to challenge Black performance stereotypes in aesthetic terms, including her incorporation of Black Atlantic dance with ballet, as well as her use of sophisticated costuming. Dunham's screen experiences paralleled those of Baker in that her work was compromised by producers who depicted her all-Black dance troupe as exotic spectacles so that, superficially at least, she appeared to have enjoyed little control in Hollywood. Across her career, Dunham was limited by a production framework which had the power either to distance her performances from film plots, as in *Star Spangled Rhythm* and *Stormy Weather*, or to remove her altogether, as in *Pardon My Sarong* (1942). But tendencies to overlook Dunham's performances for their subjugated status obscure the ways in which she used cinema to showcase pioneering artistry that was rooted in her anthropological research.

Chapter six examines Dunham's interventions in French and Italian cinema during the 1940s and 1950s to highlight the substantial creative freedom that midcentury European cinema granted to a Black woman choreographer. Dunham's troupe was the first major U.S. dance company to perform in postwar Europe and its success recalled the stardom that Baker enjoyed in the 1920s and 1930s. Dunham and her company appeared in three feature-length European films, the French-Italian coproduction *Botta e risposta* (1950), the Italian film *Mambo* (1954), and the German musical revue *Die Große Starparade* (1954), which she hoped would provide correctives to what she perceived to be Hollywood's misrepresentations of her artistry. This chapter examines issues of authorship and racialization in *Botta e risposta* and *Mambo*, which, as internationally circulated films, demand attention as the sites through which her company was seen most extensively in Europe. Both were box office successes and played important roles in dictating how Dunham and her company were received. An undercurrent of primitivism is present in

Botta e risposta's staging of its African American performers and *Mambo* uses Dunham's dance material to invoke themes of atavism. And yet Dunham was afforded authorial control over her dance scenes to an extent not possible in Hollywood and, like Baker, used these scenes to present a culturally complex vision of Black womanhood that countered racist misconceptions. These films feature the only known commercial footage of Dunham's dancers in rehearsal and therefore shed vital light on Dunham's work-in-progress at the height of her performing career. I establish *Botta e Risposta*'s historical significance as a cinematic record of work by Dunham and other leading African American artists and argue that Dunham should be understood as a coauthor of *Mambo*, whose narrative is framed around her company and which situates her choreography as central to its aesthetics.

In her posthumously published memoir, *Josephine*, Baker recalled that, when she arrived in Paris, "For the first time in my life, I felt beautiful," and that she began to think of her body as an "instrument that I must care for."[31] Responding to a rumor that her legs had been insured for a million dollars at the height of her U.S. fame in the early 1940s, Dunham replied, "Well, that was the story. . . . A lot of people set more value on my legs than I did. I just never paid much attention to them, but they did apparently attract a lot of attention."[32] Baker and Dunham were indeed objectified as exotic spectacles. But they were also admired as glamorous performers and were influential women artists. Their work intervened in racist imaginaries on both sides of the Atlantic. In so doing, they presented visions of Black women's dancing bodies that challenged white and inspired Black audiences and had significant impacts on midcentury transatlantic culture. Across this study, I explore their literary and cinematic voices to reveal the complex identity conflicts at play in their work and to recover their major contributions to the page and screen.

CHAPTER ONE

The Dancer in Translation

Baker's Coauthored Narratives

In 1927, Baker appeared in her first starring feature film, *La Sirène des tropiques*. Around the same time, she worked with her secretary Marcel Sauvage on her first book, *Les Mémoires de Joséphine Baker*, which contained sketches by the artist Paul Colin. Colin claimed later to have launched Baker to fame by selecting her as the star of *La Revue Nègre*, her first Parisian show, and his posters for the production helped to cement her iconic place in interwar French culture.[1] Baker's work with Sauvage and Colin was captured in a short, silent film, in which Baker adopts exaggerated expressions to mime her life story as Sauvage records her actions and Colin sketches her. The thirty-second sequence is a cinematic advertisement for *Mémoires* that was filmed and presumably screened alongside *Sirène*. Such footage shows how white male promoters made possible Baker's early European success and how they cannily circulated her image on the page and screen—often simultaneously—to maximize her cultural impact.[2] However, her restless body shows that she was not a passive object of their multimedia representations. She leans over Sauvage's shoulder and directs his account as both men work to keep up with her energetic display (see figure 1). Her overstated movements reduce the scene to farce and point up the fantasies on which the men's depictions are based.

This sequence has important implications for how we perceive Baker's films and writings, which were filtered through a pseudo-ethnographic

FIGURE 1. Josephine Baker directing Marcel Sauvage's pen in the cinematic advertisement for *Les Mémoires de Joséphine Baker* (1927).

gaze but which depended on her idiosyncratic dance style for their success. Together, Baker's cinematic and literary works show how she experimented with a multifaceted and frequently paradoxical vision of Black womanhood. She drew on African diasporic dance forms to transgress cultural boundaries and create performances of physical self-expression even within an exoticizing framework. As we shall also see with Dunham's works, Baker's interventions in both forms point up the negotiations, translations, and consequently the ambiguities of corporeal expression across racial, national, and artistic boundaries. Baker and Dunham's memoirs help to unearth the interior significances of performances that were frequently dismissed as erotic and exotic. Although they adopt contrasting viewpoints, with Dunham acting as a cultural observer and Baker describing dance as part of a lived experience, both women's writings foreground corporeal experience. They engage meaningfully with the psychological and cultural significances of African diasporic forms of artistry to fracture colonialist narratives. They show how geographical relocation enabled both women to experiment with performance vocabularies and formulate international visions of Black subjecthood. Baker's memoirs situate her as an impoverished and abused child who finds in dance an escape from hardship. Consequently, they generally complicate her public construction as an exotic commodity, and their concern with racial injustice anticipates and helps to explain the humanitarianism that would define her post–World War II career.

This chapter closely analyzes such memoirs. Baker was the first well-known African American woman to tell her life story across several volumes, preceding by four decades her fellow St. Louisan Maya Angelou, who previously has been credited with this pioneering literary achievement.[3] Yet Baker's writings continue to occupy a marginal place in African American literary history and with the exception of *Josephine* (1978) have not been translated from French.[4] I apply scholarship on emancipatory narratives and highlight engagements with U.S. racism to establish Baker's coauthorship of texts that are still read as the work of white writers. In so doing, I recover the human voice and evidence the intellectual interventions of a dancer who, as Brent Hayes Edwards argues, has too frequently been positioned as "a sort of inconsequential stage alien, untethered to the world around her," and thus as a passive subject of twentieth-century racial and gender ideologies rather than an active player in the changing status of colonial subjects and women in interwar Europe.[5] I explore the texts to trace the psychological origins of Baker's dance style and to position the antiracism that defined her post–World War II life as a lifelong concern. I also identify the memoirs' significance as rare literary accounts of an African American woman's early-twentieth-century transatlantic experiences.

Joanne M. Braxton has suggested that a partial recovery of the "lost ground" of Black women's autobiography can be achieved by "taking a serious look at works of performers and entertainers often written in collaboration with a second party."[6] While remaining sensitive to their authorial complexity, Braxton identifies such writers as significant but overlooked contributors to a Black women's literary tradition. This chapter suggests a method for approaching such mediated texts. Baker's memoirs were shaped by white male writers, published in French, and designed to capitalize commercially on Baker's notoriety. They require us to shift across geographical and generic boundaries and develop analytical tools that acknowledge their limitations as sources. Yet despite such challenges, detailed exploration of such texts provides a way to foreground the voice of, and more meaningfully recover, the artistry and humanity of Baker and the lived experiences of pre–civil rights era working-class Black women more broadly.

Baker arrived in Paris as a nineteen-year-old dancer with African American vaudeville troupe *La Revue Nègre* in the autumn of 1925; by 1927 she was one of the highest paid stars in Europe. Her fame coincided with a period in French history marked by rapid economic and social change as well as transatlantic cultural exchange engendered by World War I. Hundreds of thousands of colonial soldiers and workers were recruited from the Caribbean and West Africa to aid in the war effort, and African American soldiers also arrived in France, creating a sizable Black expatriate community. The music brought by African American military bands, most notably James Reese Europe's 369th Infantry Regiment (Harlem Hellfighters) Band, sparked a Parisian craze for jazz music. Baker's entry into French culture also occurred at the height of *Negrophilia*, a movement closely related to primitivism that arose initially in the Parisian art world at the start of the twentieth century in which, according to James Clifford, "a series of stereotypes [of Black people] long associated with backwardness and inferiority acquired positive connotations and came to stand for liberation and spontaneity, for a simultaneous recovery of ancient sources and an access to true modernity."[7] Baker's performances also spoke to France's *mission civilisatrice*, a doctrine that sought to "uplift" colonial subjects through a process of "assimilation," in which citizenship rights would be granted to those who adopted Christianity, European dress styles, and the French language, together with a post–World War I fear that such a doctrine would threaten the French "race."

Baker's risqué costumes and physically expressive dance routines also recalled a wider history of pseudo-ethnographic display stretching back to Sara Baartman, a Khoikhoi woman who was exhibited in London and Paris in the early nineteenth century and whose supposedly oversized genitalia were kept on display at the *Musée de l'Homme* until the mid-1970s.[8] Universal Expositions and the developing science of anthropology, both of which were exploited to "evidence" pseudoscientific racial classifications in order to justify France's colonial ventures, amplified fascinations with an imagined Other throughout the late nineteenth and early twentieth centuries.[9] Baker's arrival in Paris in 1925 coincided with the foundation of both the *Institut d'ethnologie*, the first French organization whose chief purpose was to provide professional fieldwork training and produce ethnographic scholarship, and Paris's *Exposition internationale des arts décoratifs et industriels modernes* (International Exhibition of Modern Decorative and Industrial Arts).[10] Paul Colin connected Baker directly to the "art deco" movement that the Exposition engendered by applying its style to the posters that he designed to advertise her. Thus, as Ramsay Burt asserts, "Baker achieved a status that has gone down in history because initially she was the right person in the right place at the right time."[11]

However, a key concern of this study is to explore ways in which Baker and Dunham used dance to engage self-reflexively with and even disrupt early-twentieth-century racial ideologies, and how they articulated their practices on the page and screen. The important role that early-twentieth-century racial imaginaries played in Baker's success should not be overlooked. But her achievements also rested on complex physical artistry that built on a history of Black performance and reshaped European conceptions of modern dance. In her posthumous autobiography, *Josephine*, Baker recalled that originality, self-discipline, and craftsmanship were central aspects of her persona. Likening her body to artists' and musicians' tools, she wrote that, "I *had* to succeed. I would never stop trying, never. A violinist had his violin, a painter his palette. All I had was myself. *I* was the instrument that I must care for [emphases in original]" (58). Baker's recognition of the cultural capital attached to her body points to her awareness of her own commodification as a pseudocolonial spectacle. However, her admission that her body was an instrument acknowledges the technical complexity of her performances. Such a statement provides vital insights into Baker's dance practice. It shows that she self-reflexively narrated her memoirs and highlights their importance in shedding light on the psychological and philosophical underpinnings of an artistic practice interpreted within a European colonial gaze and yet rooted in a history of Black Atlantic performance. In turn, it points to the texts' broader value as rare firsthand documents of the racism that Black women artists endured on both sides of the Atlantic during the interwar period, as well as the creative practices that they developed to negotiate and often subtly to critique such frameworks.

Baker's writings were deliberately engineered to publicize her performances and to bolster her star image. The books were compiled by European men and with the exception of *Josephine* were effectively "as told to" discussions with the star. Baker's lack of formal schooling means that the level of direct authorship that she enjoyed over her early memoirs remains highly debatable. *Les Mémoires de Joséphine Baker* (1927), the subject of the short film discussed at the start of this chapter, was conceived shortly after Baker arrived in Paris and shows little evidence of her direct intervention. Seeking to capitalize on Baker's commercial success, the text combines fleeting descriptions of her young life with fan letters, recipes, and beauty tips, effectively situating her as an exotic Other for the amusement of a European readership. The *Baltimore Afro-American* condemned the book as "journalism at its worst" and a "worse than useless" means of comprehending the dancer.[12] Baker was listed as the coauthor with her personal secretary Marcel Sauvage, but had no role in the text's genesis; according to Jean-Claude Baker, Sauvage came up with the concept and Colin encouraged him to act on his idea by promising to provide illustrations.[13] Baker's lack of authorship is underscored by the fact that, at such an early stage in her career, she was only semiliterate in English and could not speak much French. *Mémoires* therefore was subject to a double mistranslation: English to French, and the spoken word to the literary form. The star did not see proofs of the text because she could not read them; instead, her entourage approved them. Sauvage confesses in the preface that the act of translation risked descending into misinterpretation: "At first, I was accompanied by an interpreter, then Miss Baker learned enough French to try to speak it, so it was quite amusing—sometimes very difficult."[14] Consequently, the literary voice of Sauvage, who was both a poet and a journalist, is evident. As biographer Jean-Claude Baker observed, phrases such as "'an indigestion of snakeskin' requir[e] a command of language the teenager did not have."[15]

Nor should Baker's ultimate frustration with her literary representations be overlooked. In 1959, she refused an opportunity to work with Charles T. Samuels, who had coauthored *His Eye Is on the Sparrow* (1950), the autobiography of Baker's former Broadway rival Ethel Waters. Baker cited her displeasure that her French Resistance comrade Captain Jacques Abtey had written *La Guerre secrète de Joséphine Baker* (The Secret War of Josephine Baker) in 1948 without her authorization. She stated that, "I am not considering a book [about my life] to be written at the moment. I must have time to think all this over quietly because so far people have done bad jobs and I feel a little disappointed."[16] Although Baker referred specifically to an unofficial biography to register her displeasure, her response reveals her skepticism that even an authorized work would present a satisfactory portrait of her life. Her choice of words—"I am not considering a book to be written"—is a telling indication that she did not expect to be allowed much direct authorial control, a self-conscious acknowledgment that efforts thus far had been set down by French writers. Her frustration with written accounts of her life would later be articulated without irony in her final memoir, *Josephine*, in which she wrote that, "Books tried to package experience. I like my living fresh" (99).

However, Baker's repeated engagements with the memoir form reveal an enduring hope that life writing could serve as a corrective to unauthorized narratives purporting to document the star's life. Bouillon asserts early in *Josephine* that her final goals were to write a book, make a film, and establish a museum to tell her life story.[17] Her effort to persuade Langston Hughes to script films about her and her family, as discussed at the end of this chapter, evidences this claim. Nor should the books be dismissed because they were orally transcribed for, as Sidonie Smith and Julia Watson point out, many nineteenth- and early-twentieth-century life narratives were produced in this way.[18] All of Baker's memoirs contain prefaces and such paratextual additions, which were designed to "authenticate" the subject's tale but which resulted in texts with multiple authorial voices, were also common in nineteenth-century writings, such as emancipatory narratives.[19] Although *Mémoires* capitalized on Baker's pseudo-ethnographic image, her next three texts, *Voyages et aventures de Joséphine Baker* (1931), also cowritten by Sauvage; *Une vie de toutes les couleurs* (1935), which was coauthored with another French journalist, André Rivollet; and *Josephine*, compiled posthumously by her ex-husband Jo Bouillon, deserve careful attention as more personal portraits of the star.[20] Biographers such as Lynn Haney, Phyllis Rose, and Jean-Claude Baker have used the texts to interpret Baker's early life, and their level of detail and factual accuracy suggest that they are based on the star's recollections.[21] Baker biographer Bennetta Jules-Rosette, who remains one of the few scholars to discuss the memoirs' content, makes the case that the performer helped to author the texts because, "Although it is not always possible to determine the exact extent of Baker's participation in her early projects, her voice was evident in every piece."[22]

Although their different purposes and circumstances should not be overlooked, recent critical approaches to orally transcribed emancipatory narratives provide a useful starting point by which to approach Baker's texts. They can help us to recover the historical and literary value of such works and, by extension, other coauthored Black entertainer autobiographies such as those by Ethel Waters, Lena Horne, and Billie Holiday. Structural similarities mean that Baker's writings can be likened to the "mediated" memoirs of former enslaved women such as Sojourner Truth and Harriet Tubman. For as Jean McMahon Humez asserts, although such texts involved mediation by a white writer and editor and to notable alterations in the women's stories, "Valuable oral historical material . . . has been embedded within this framework."[23] Humez calls for a careful examination of such narratives, suggesting that, "A critical awareness of how the texts were created allows us to understand just what kind of truths these texts can tell."[24] Like Truth and Tubman's narratives, Baker's memoirs provide insights into her relationship with her white associates and the power relations that dictated her public persona, but they are also rare firsthand accounts of an African American woman's transatlantic interwar experiences. Their personal insights invite us to reflect on, and can even serve as correctives to, the distortions and elisions of mainstream histories. In particular, they reveal the psychological origins of her idiosyncratic performance style.

Much like her films, Baker's narratives are selective accounts of her life that were engineered and assembled by white men. But as in her films, Baker intervenes in these literary frameworks to assert her authorship. Evidence of her voice can be found throughout the texts, in which she engages self-reflexively with her status as a cultural commodity. She critiques career mistakes and the misinterpretations of audiences and critics with a frankness that runs counter to the texts' commercial intentions. In *Josephine*, she even takes revenge on a white suitor for crimes against her forebears: "I ordered the young man to his knees and planted him by my bedside. Then I left for the theater. Unkind? Perhaps. But looking back on it now, I wonder if the ghost of an African ancestor humiliated by an arrogant plantation owner hadn't been lurking someplace under my well-oiled scalp" (58).

The memoirs' thematic concerns and narrative continuities also demonstrate that Baker enjoyed significant authorial influence. Most of these books describe Baker's deprived St. Louis childhood, revealing a sophisticated understanding of U.S. racism and intraracism rooted in firsthand experiences of physical abuse and sexual danger. They give voice to the antiracist activism to which she would devote her life. Jennifer Anne Boittin agrees with Jules-Rosette that, "Baker can be considered an author of all the books upon which she collaborated," but ultimately interprets the dancer's early writings as a "tool furthering her colonial reputation, a method allowing the French to enter a supposedly savage fantasy world."[25] Yet Baker's second and third memoirs critique racial prejudice; at times they diverge quite profoundly from colonial and even primitivist framings of the star. For example, Baker's second memoir *Voyages* was written as a response to European and South American xenophobia and defends her against such attitudes by creating a literary vision of a dedicated and self-sacrificing performer. Like Dunham's memoirs, which are discussed in the next chapter, the text provides a candid account of a Black woman's experiences across national boundaries and details powerfully Baker's sense of fear and psychological dislocation in unfamiliar and frequently hostile landscapes.

Voyages recounts the artist's two-year journey through Europe and South America as part of her first international tour, and it describes her perspective on social and political unrest in her host nations. *Voyages* is historically significant as a firsthand account of an African American woman's international travels in the late 1920s and early 1930s. Like Dunham's *Journey to Accompong* and *Island Possessed*, which describe an African American woman's Caribbean experiences in the mid-1930s, it articulates some of the challenges of traversing geographical, racial, and gender boundaries that Black women faced during the interwar years. By comparing attitudes to Baker across international locales, the memoir accentuates the contradictions of racist mind-sets, and the text reveals a self-reflexive staging of self in opposition to such attitudes in which Baker is situated as the innocent victim of racial prejudice. It also helps to pinpoint the beginnings of Baker's antiracist humanitarian work, which, although centered on U.S. discrimination rather than French attitudes toward colonial subjects, would lead her to devote much of her career to an international fight against racism.

Voyages was published in 1931 and like *Mémoires* was based on interviews by Sauvage, although by this stage Baker was fluent in French and no longer relied on a translator. The book coincided with Baker's starring role in *Paris qui remue* (1930–1931) at the Casino de Paris and also acted as publicity for her forthcoming sound films, *Zouzou* and *Princesse Tam-Tam*. The text concludes with an allusion to these two productions: "Now, I just have to get ready to shoot the two great films that I must shoot. Goodbye then, and see you soon."[26] Such a statement positions the text as an extended film advertisement. But the book also includes a revealing critique of *Sirène* as a crude misrepresentation of Caribbean cultures and of Baker's art. She admits to "a little bitterness" that the production had "lots of mistakes," and criticizes "the negligence and disregard for good sense that we should have had . . . I frolicked around the Tropics in a fur coat" (141). She also despairs at journalists' false gossip about her on-set behavior, which "sometimes saddened me and often made me laugh," and which hints at a wider frustration with her treatment by white male critics (144). Such writers, she notes, are "full of imagination" (148). The memoir engages self-consciously with Baker's public identity to refract such cultural misconstructions. In so doing, it evidences her authorial influence.

Voyages is a self-reflexive account of the performative nature and hence the distortions of Baker's public identity that highlights the contrast between her public and private selves. She is expected to "amuse people . . . pull old men's beards, tickle the fat ladies, and make their long coats and stiff clothes dance" (14). Baker complicates such a role by positioning it as tedious, reducing it to a listlike series of duties that appear monotonous, repetitive, and one-sided in their capacity for pleasure. Her statement, "And they thought that it amused me, of course," is telling (14). The text gives some insight into Baker's awareness of and feelings toward her status as a pseudo-ethnographic spectacle. Recalling that, "it was a very painful job to be a curiosity" (14), Baker makes plain the primitivist framework in which she finds herself and critiques such a reductive reading of her identity by affirming that, "People imagine that I just left the jungle," and "The white imagination sure is something when it comes to Blacks. And the prejudices, the same everywhere" (16).

Echoes of *Mémoires*' sensual representation of the performer do recur. Baker encounters a thunderstorm during an outdoor concert in Bucharest. She resolves to perform her banana dance nevertheless to prevent financial disaster for the organizers. Her water-laden banana skirt soon falls to the floor, leaving her completely naked. The audience's delighted reaction points up the titillating appeal of Baker's performances. The same incident is described completely differently in *Josephine*, indicating either that Sauvage distorted Baker's remembrances or that Baker willingly played up erotic readings of her work early on to enhance her fame. In *Josephine*, Baker dances dutifully for her fans because the impresario had "no intention of reimbursing his audience" (76). By the end of her act she "felt completely nude," and her discomfort undercuts the performance's perceived sensuality (77). Such a feeling is compounded by the reaction of Baker's lover-manager Giuseppe "Pepito" Abatino, whose muttered one-word response—"Charming"—suggests that he considered Baker's performance to have descended into vulgarity (77). Yet references to Baker's body are otherwise rare in *Voyages*, which is concerned chiefly with the contrasting cultural habits and racial attitudes of the various European and South American countries on the artist's tour.

Evidence that Baker's firsthand experiences of the growing xenophobia in interwar Europe precipitated a more serious literary engagement with racial politics in contrast to *Mémoires*'s playfulness can also be found in *Mon sang dans tes veines* (1931), a novel produced in Baker's name that was published at the same time as *Voyages*. *Mon sang* was authored by Abatino and the writer Felix de la Camara, and it can be read as a play on the "tragic mulatta" narrative of nineteenth-century literature as it depicts a Black woman who dies after donating blood to a white man.[27] The female protagonist expires to render unequivocal her social exclusion, as is typical in such a text, but she interrogates pseudoscientific racist thought by enacting a "communion" of blood with her unrequited lover.[28] Although Baker did not write the story, it was subtitled "after an idea of Josephine Baker" and she contributed its preface, which she signed to assert her authorship, and in which she declared, "What is color! . . . Blood? . . . always we are told this . . . As if the different bloods were fighting each other and could not mix," before acknowledging that "the hazards of life had put in my veins a blood of three colors. My father was white; and Aunt Elvara, Indian."[29] That such a statement represented Baker's own literary voice is substantiated by a later humanitarian speech, in which she declared, "I think they must mix blood[;] otherwise the human race is bound to degenerate. Mixing blood is marvelous. It makes strong and intelligent men. It takes away tired spirits."[30]

Unlike Baker's early memoirs, *Mon sang* was poorly received; however, it established an antiracist rhetoric running through Baker's narratives from *Voyages* onward that helps to situate them as early articulations of her later humanitarian goals. The novel's protagonist is called Joan, a play on "Josephine" that can also be read as an Anglicized reference to French heroine Jeanne D'Arc (Joan of Arc) and therefore as a deliberate attempt to associate the artist's plight with martyrdom. Jules-Rosette identifies the text as the origin of a Marian, or Madonna, motif of self-sacrifice and self-idealization that Baker would later draw on when attempting to construct an international brotherhood centered on her Rainbow Tribe.[31] What is striking about such a trope is that it can be read as a conscious rewriting of the "tragic mulatta" narrative in which self-sacrifice is envisioned not as the ultimate outcome of a life in which one has no place in society but instead as a means of breaking down racial barriers. The "tragic mulatta," invariably childless, has no future in society. By contrast, Baker took on the role of mother to twelve children from around the world to imagine a future without racism. Not only did her life story serve as an inspiration for *Mon sang*, but she also drew on *Mon sang* to shape her own life narrative.

Voyages builds on *Mon sang*'s Marian motif by presenting the star as an innocent target of xenophobia. The text serves as further evidence of Baker's lifelong commitment to antiracism. *Voyages* comments on the different kinds of racial prejudice that Baker encounters in Europe and South America, which vary from adulation to condemnation. Such conflicting views call attention to the subjective nature of racist thought as they are demarcated along national boundaries, with responses to Baker ranging from widespread praise in Scandinavia to vitriolic hatred in Austria. The contrasting description of Germany given in her 1927 memoirs with that of *Voyages* four years later underscores the fickleness of racist mind-sets by demonstrating that they diverge over time as well as physical space. In *Mémoires*, Baker's reception in Berlin is "A triumph!", she receives "an incredible number of love letters," and acclaimed director Max Reinhardt offers her a three-year contract at the Deutsches Theater.[32] Although Baker is generally welcomed on her return to the country, *Voyages* records that she is not allowed to dance in Munich because the authorities deem her to be "immoral" (101), and she discovers that in Central Europe more generally she represents a "scarecrow" or "flag" around which fears of social and moral decline have come to circulate (35).

The authorities are Baker's most vocal opponents, and they inflame local prejudices: "The old Catholic parties pursued me with a Christian hatred, from station to station, from city to city, from one location to another. There were brawls, battles, injuries" (35). Baker exaggerates Central Europe's negative response to her arrival, recalling that, "I have seen . . . police charge, swords drawn, and men run in front of me, revolver in hand" (36). Although hostile crowds greeted Baker in Vienna, her arrival did not provoke violence. She therefore uses hyperbolic language to emphasize the irrationality of such hatred toward her, a mere "dancer" (63). Such self-presentation reinforces the text's Marian motif of innocent sacrifice and serves as a pointed critique of intolerance by underscoring the tragic potential of such misguided beliefs.

Baker attributes city chiefs' reactions to her dance style but also to her "color" (36) to suggest that audiences were objecting as much to her complexion as to her performances. In Austria, Baker encountered such a negative response from students and the Catholic Church that she was placed under police guard for her own protection.[33] Posters featuring an almost naked Baker were distributed to discredit her and press accounts described her as a siren and devil. She lost the backing of her original performance venue and was forced to postpone her visit by a month. A priest at a church opposite the Johann Strauss Theater where Baker eventually performed expressed a fear of "nègres blancs" (white negroes) (66), a term sometimes used to describe Europeans who danced the Charleston, implying that Baker's presence would lead to racial contamination. The Austrian Parliament also debated whether she should be allowed to perform in Vienna. According to the *New York Times*, the Parliament "commented, mostly unfavorably, upon her black body and figure" and listed Baker's most vocal opponents as the "organization known as the Hakenkreuzlers, which formerly attacked only Socialists and Jews."[34] Lynn Haney asserts that the students and political parties that opposed Baker "would supply the moral force for Nazism."[35] Such linkages emphasize the extensive xenophobia that Baker encountered in Austria.

However, the memoir also shows that Baker used corporeal expression to challenge intolerance and point up her humanity. When she is finally permitted to perform in Vienna, she undermines audience expectations by appearing onstage in modest dress. Noting that she has generated "a second of great silence and surprise," she sings a slave lament with a "fearful and beating heart" (66). In so doing, she connects herself to a wider history of enslavement and racial injustice and rebukes her vilification as "the revelation of the devil" (66). By recalling the event in the text, she uses the same persuasive technique on the reader. It is unclear if many members of Baker's German-speaking audience understood the song's lyrics, but her emotive performance won over her critics. She notes in her memoir that she is met with great applause and she uses the moment to emphasize the inclusivity of her art by dancing, "as I have always danced, as I will always dance, *without thinking either of good or evil*, but of my dance, of true, sincere, pure dance, which must testify, before men and before God, *who is God of all men whether white, black, yellow or red* . . . that there is a free, eternal youth, always and forever, despite everything, a simple and great joy of living which is sufficient in itself [emphases added]" (67). Superficially, the statement reaffirms primitivist perceptions of Black dance as a liberating contrast to European sterility. However, it refracts the xenophobic discourses that have come to surround her work by making the case for the spiritual equality of all humankind. In *Josephine*, Baker echoes this sentiment, declaring, "Now I could dance anything I wanted, any way I liked, expressing the joy and love which, despite what the priests might say, were surely recognized in paradise" (75), which provides further evidence of her lifelong commitment to humanitarianism and her influence over both memoirs.

Nevertheless, the threat of physical violence that Baker initially faced in Vienna, and which forced her to travel under armed guard, provides insights into the challenges that she faced as a Black woman navigating interwar European cultural and national boundaries. In *Voyages*, only after appeasing her audience can she explore the city as a "tourist" (72). Baker's social constraints are again dramatized through dance. She finds herself performing to 8,000 people in the Great Hall of the Lucerna Palace in Prague. She is overwhelmed by the immensity of the venue and describes herself as "lost" in "An immense room" that is "long, deep and cold" (53, 55). Her singing voice gets "los[t] in the distance" and she is forced to "danc[e] from the extreme right to the extreme left" to fill the vast stage space (55–56). Baker is also tormented physically by the orchestra's hurried tempo. She emphasizes the conductor's "white hands," his "ghost hands," in pointed critique of European men's control over her work (56). The scene challenges primitivist conceptions of Baker's art as effortless to show how such misinterpretations served to obscure her humanity. The audience is oblivious to her struggle to interpret physically the orchestra's fast-paced rhythms, reading as deliberate a fall that "tore off all the skin of my arm and elbow" (57).

This event can be read allegorically, as the recollections of a performer trapped within the dictates of a controlling and demanding performance framework and an audience that is ignorant of her art. But it also reveals how Baker fought to maintain individuality and retain some agency, both on stage and in writing. Resolving that "I have to *win*" [emphasis added] (53), Baker's dance becomes a psychological battle of wills in which she attempts to "exhaust the orchestra" (58). She becomes "like a skinned dancer, a picture of blood" (58). By the end of the performance, she burns "like a torch," but through physical wit and determination she has "exceeded" the orchestra, which "seemed to deflate" (58–59). Baker sinks "deep into my fatigue, my exhaustion, my pain" and describes herself as "dead" (59). The star again uses hyperbole to position her work as self-sacrificing. She lies on the floor with her arms crossed; like *Mon sang*'s Joan, she has become a martyr to ignorant racial attitudes. The scene emphasizes Baker's status as a victim of unsympathetic power structures that exploit and depersonalize her while simultaneously pointing up the technical skill of her work and her determination to refute readings of primitive mindlessness. Consequently, it serves as evidence both of Baker's authorship over the memoir and of her effort to assert her artistry on stage.

If *Voyages* represents a striking depiction of the injustices and absurdity of Central European interwar intolerance, then *Une vie* describes its variant across the Atlantic. *Une vie* is Baker's most detailed account of her formative years and is a significant firsthand literary record of the life of an impoverished Black woman growing up in the U.S. Midwest at the height of the Great Migration. The text reveals the psychological impact of both racism and intraracism on Baker's early life. It enables her to construct a triumphant narrative in which she is the central agent of her artistic identity and whose concern with prejudice and childhood neglect would come to serve as central themes of her humanitarian career. The formative encounters with physical abuse that the text describes provide insights into the psychological and intellectual underpinnings of Baker's pseudo-exotic yet parodic performance style. It shows that her dance technique was the strategic consequence of racial abuse and that her performances destabilized racial identities even as they appeared to reinforce them because they relied on idiosyncratic gestures that challenged white audience expectations of Black performance.

Like Sauvage's texts, *Une vie* is a mediated account of Baker's life. The star's remembrances are filtered through the writing of French journalist André Rivollet, whose preface abounds with primitivist fantasies. Situating her arrival in Paris against the fad for chorus girls with "automatic movements," Rivollet asserts that, "The sensuality of the black world burst upon us."[36] Rivollet marked the text's publication with a lecture and gala evening celebrating the influence of jazz, and especially Baker as its "exteriorization," on French culture.[37] He remarked on her current role in Jacques Offenbach's *opéra comique La Créole*, which, like the memoir and Baker's sound films, was intended to cement her status as a European artiste. But Rivollet's praise rested on an assumption that Baker's art was untutored. In *Une vie*'s preface, he describes her *La Créole* performance as follows: "Always with the same ear, without even knowing the values, the musical notations, Josephine, transformed into a Creole, sings by instinct as before, when she improvised her Louisiana yodeling" (18). Rivollet's construction of Baker as unschooled undermines her artistry. His conflation of St. Louis with the Southern state of Louisiana also reiterates a popular tendency to misrepresent Baker's birthplace as what Carole Sweeney terms a "fictional new-world geography of plantation and slaves filtered through a nostalgic archive of New Orleans" rather than the industrialized, ghettoized, and segregated reality. The association of Baker with Louisiana recalls racist imagery surrounding the Cakewalk, which enjoyed popularity in Paris at the turn of the twentieth century, in which both artists and the press concocted a plantation fantasy image of "la Louisianne" to symbolize the dance craze's birthplace.

However, Rivollet does signal that the text will provide a concrete history for Baker and locate her, not as an exotic primitive, but as a member of a deprived Black community in the U.S. industrial Midwest. Rivollet admits that it is Baker "the woman" and "her hidden childhood, her youth, her development . . . that I wanted to know," and that her preface to *Mon sang*, in which "she evokes the so troubling question of the races," drove him to find out more about her early life (10–11). Consequently, the text privileges the corporeal and biographical but in a manner that disrupts sensuous readings. It foregrounds the child and teenage Baker's abused and neglected body, which is at times too dark and at others too light. The personal nature of these experiences, which include vivid descriptions of urban poverty, and their thematic contrasts with the preface suggest that Baker exercised significant authorship over the memoir. The narrative does still resort to archetypal characterizations. Baker's moccasin-wearing Aunt Elvara is a "fearsome Indian" (27) whose "anger shook the whole neighborhood" (21). Left alone, Elvara performs "a dance of the Checkecree [*sic*] tribe"; at other times, she smokes a "peace pipe" (27). Equally, Rivollet infantilizes the star by suggesting that she acts out and scribbles down her recollections with what his friend, dramatist Jean Giraudoux, calls "childish sincerity" (18). But the text also draws on Baker's early life to critique simplistic identity constructions. It points to an enduring concern with racial inequality and childhood exploitation that would inspire Baker to form a Rainbow Tribe symbolizing international egalitarianism. In particular, it provides insights into the comic ugliness that she cultivated in her performances by showing how she adopted an idiosyncratic performance style to deflect her sense of racial inferiority.

Baker's body as described in *Une vie*, far from being sensual and exotic, is neglected, beaten, and exploited. At a very young age, she is forced into a life of domestic service, an experience that highlights her poverty and reflects the economic limitations that Black women living in the interwar Midwest endured. For such women, Baker's occupation was typical. As late as 1930, more than 80 percent of Black women in the workforce in nearby Chicago were employed as personal servants and domestics.[38] Their exclusion from semiprofessional occupations was such that, between World War I and the beginning of the Depression era, only 5 percent of Black women in Chicago occupied these roles.[39] Baker describes in vivid detail the hardships of her life as a domestic worker, an occupation that she endures from the age of seven:

Here is the work timetable:

> Go to the market in the morning, peel the potatoes, light the fires, empty the night pots, wash them, wash the spittoons, air the beds, scrub the steps at the front and back of the house, sweep the rooms and, once a week, wash my clothes. At night I slept downstairs with the dog, in the cellar where she [Baker's mistress Mrs. Keiser] kept her coal and wood (42).

Baker is subjected to arduous physical labor despite her extreme youth. Forced to inhabit the cellar with an animal, she is spatially and socially degraded.

In such a world, nudity is associated with abuse, not sensuality. After stripping her to protect her clothes from damage, Mrs. Keiser beats Baker viciously when she thinks she has not cleaned the house: "I was laid bare; she beat me until I had blisters on my back and my behind" (42). Mrs. Keiser drags Baker out of bed by the ears when she wakes up too late and pulls her nose so hard for using too much washing-up soap that, "I could not breathe through my nose, only through my mouth" (42). As a final punishment, Baker is made to plunge her hands into boiling water so that "All the skin and nails were boiled, ready to fall off" (43), an action that puts her in the hospital and finally brings an end to her employment.

Baker is also forced to navigate a world of sexual danger. Although she is too young to understand his fascination, the eight-year-old Baker becomes a source of carnal desire for Mr. Mason, her second employer's husband. Chillingly, her sexual predator is only caught when he "slowly and gently, enters my bed" (52), which underscores her vulnerability to abuse. Nor is this an isolated incident. She provokes her mother's violent fury by refusing the sexual advances of a financially generous employer, "Mr. Dad," who the text describes as "a man of fifty who loved to have little girls live with him" (67–68). Baker once again is stripped and beaten: "Mother removed my clothes and beat me until the skin came off. She threw a chair on my face and beat me with a cat o' nine tails. I could stand no more and I ran into the street, naked. The more I ran, the more I wanted to die, ashamed, as a ten-year-old girl, to be seen naked" (68). In this scene, nudity is associated with humiliation and vulnerability, dispelling primitivist readings of sexual uninhibitedness and evidencing Baker's authorship over the memoir. Rather than exoticizing Baker's body, such textual recollections emphasize the hardships and threats of physical and sexual violence that were present in her young life.

Baker's complexion attracts particular abuse. She claims to be the product of her mother's brief affair with a white man and learns as a child to associate her light skin with dishonor. She is told that her darker-skinned half-siblings are "too good for me" (46). One Christmas, her inebriated mother beats her, making her feel "ashamed" that she is a "bastard" (47). *Une vie*'s sensitivity to skin tone divisions refracts exotic European fantasies. Her experiences corroborate studies such as St. Clair Drake and Horace R. Cayton's *Black Metropolis* (1946), a sociological examination of late 1930s Chicago that records the social and psychological impact of skin color prejudice on interwar Black families, particularly women.[40] *Une vie*'s knowledge of skin tone politics in a Midwestern Black household once again evidences Baker's authorship and highlights correlations between skin tone and one's perceived place in U.S. society, serving as a pointed critique of the social restrictions imposed on early-twentieth-century African American women. Such a narrative evokes the "tragic mulatta's" Otherness. However, like *Mon sang*, the text reworks the trope's significations through an emphasis on geographical and physical liberation and by focusing on the fluidity of identities to expose such a trope as a reductive construct.

The text therefore provides rare firsthand insight into the economic limitations, internalized self-hatred, and sexual dangers that Black working-class women faced in the early-twentieth-century United States, and it also communicates the rare opportunities that stage performance offered to such women. Baker runs away from home at thirteen to join the traveling vaudeville troupe, the Dixie Steppers. As well as providing an escape from physical abuse, exploitation, and her mother's intraracial prejudices, the stage affords her a measure of economic and spatial freedom. Hazel Carby cites Baker's memoirs as an example of women entertainer biographies that show that, "joining a touring vaudeville troupe or tent show was an important avenue of geographic mobility for young black women. . . . In addition, being a member of a vaudeville show or performing in a nightclub was not attractive primarily because it offered a mythic life of glamor but because it was a rare opportunity to . . . reject the life of a domestic servant."[41] However, vaudeville offered no escape from racism. Known widely as "Tough on Black Asses," the Theatre Owners' Booking Association (TOBA) established a national circuit for African American performers but was run mainly by white people and provided little protection from financial exploitation. Racist violence reached its height during the 1910s and early 1920s, which made traveling in the South hazardous. There was also a growing trend of hiring light-skinned chorus girls as Black producers sought to appeal to white audiences and compete with the mainstream theater industry. Victims included Ida Forsyne, an international star and creative forerunner to Baker who found that "I couldn't get a job because I was black, and my own people discriminated against me" when she returned to the United States in 1914 following an acclaimed nine-year tour of Russia.[42] When the fifteen-year-old Baker first auditioned for the Broadway musical *Shuffle Along*, producer Noble Sissle quickly dismissed her as "Too small, too thin, too ugly" (85). Baker recognized his statement's racial undertones: "He needed the prettiest Creoles in America. I was too dark: I cried" (86).

According to *Une vie*, Baker managed to secure a chorus spot in *Shuffle Along*'s second company. However, in *Josephine*, she suggests that she was hired initially as a dresser and gained an onstage role only by learning the chorus line's routines and then persuading the manager to accept her as a replacement when a dancer fell ill.[43] She was able to retain this role not because she conformed to European standards of beauty but because she adopted idiosyncratic stage mannerisms, attaining notoriety as "the mischievous girl on the end of the [chorus] line."[44] Baker used comedy to deviate from the chorines' display, achieving creative freedom at the same time that she played up her physical difference and perceived inferiority. As Sweeney affirms, "The circumstances of Baker's apparently subversive minstrelsy for a young uneducated Black woman was likely an act of show business survival. Too dark for true erotic appeal, she needed to distinguish herself somehow."[45] In *Une vie*, Baker claims to dance "without knowing": "The first night, I begin the steps without knowing what I'm doing and I act the comic. The audience applauds" (85–86). Similarly, she describes herself as "like crazy" when she first performs in Paris (98). No longer hearing the music and moving increasingly faster, she recalls that, "I jumped, I leaped, I threw up my arms and legs" (98). Such statements encourage contradictory readings by reinforcing notions of primitive mindlessness that obscure the Black vaudeville performance material on which Baker drew. However, they also promote a more thoughtful understanding of her bodily behavior by positioning it as an economically and psychologically strategic response to perceived physical nonconformity.

This self-invention story is repeated in *Josephine*, which encompasses her life from her childhood to her death. The text explores the practical purposes of her performances and attempts to reconcile them with her humanitarian agenda. As in *Une vie*, Baker situates her work as unrehearsed. She describes her opening night dance in *La Revue Nègre* as follows: "Driven by dark forces I didn't recognize, I improvised, crazed by the music, the overheated theater filled to the bursting point, the scorching eye of the spotlights. Even my teeth and eyes burned with fever. Each time I leaped I seemed to touch the sky and when I regained earth it seemed to be *mine alone* [emphasis added]" (52–53). Baker capitalizes on primitivist readings to paradoxically emphasize her authorship. As Anthea Kraut observes, "Adopting the rhetoric of involuntariness and invoking metaphors of inebriation, Baker implies that she could not be held accountable for her body's actions. . . . In the process, she gives herself license to 'wrest the composing voice' away from the nominal creator."[46] Baker's assertion of agency suggests that, within a European production framework that commodified her image and constructed her as an exotic Other, she was able to retain creative independence. This is significant because it insinuates that her routines adhered to her U.S. dance style, which built on vaudeville traditions to create parodic corporeal displays. Borrowing the term *alienation effect*, a common translation of Bertolt Brecht's theatrical technique of *Verfremdungseffekt*, Daphne A. Brooks describes the performative strategies of nineteenth- and early-twentieth-century African

American and racially ambiguous actors and celebrities such as Sojourner Truth, Adah Isaacs Menken, and Ada Overton Walker as "Afro-alienation acts."[47] She suggests that such figures "critically defamiliariz[ed] their own bodies by way of performance in order to yield alternative racial and gender epistemologies" and to "intervene in the spectacular and systemic representational abjection of black peoples."[48]

Brooks's thesis is an invaluable aid to understanding Baker's and, as we will see, Dunham's careers as it shows how individual performers could and did interrogate racist paradigms by devising innovative artistic strategies that forced audiences to re-see Black identities. However, there is a risk of overstating the transformative potential of performances caught within exploitative frameworks and whose intentions and receptions were thus profoundly complex. In an article on Baker that builds on her "Afro-alienation acts" claim, Brooks speculates that her body "perhaps *re-oriented* the spectacular attention directed at Black female bodies in public spaces and potentially *disabled* the kind of exploitative spectatorship that circumscribed Sara Baartman."[49] Such acts still had white producers and *Une vie* and *Josephine* signify that Baker's onstage displays were sites of mediation as much as contestation. Both texts acknowledge that Baker's work intervened in a European racial imaginary. Yet she still found space within this framework to present a highly idiosyncratic stage image that challenged white audience expectations of Black performance and called attention to the constructed nature of her art.

Throughout *Josephine*, Baker claims with pride that her dancing and singing are "Unschooled" (38), and she locates her style's origin to her early childhood, a period prior to any formal training.[50] In reality, Baker enjoyed an apprenticeship in St. Louis vaudeville, which attracted Black performers from across the United States. Her idiosyncratic routines recalled a history of burlesque and African American child performances. As Jayna Brown points out, "The precedent . . . had already been set by women such as Ethel Williams, but Baker does not mind taking credit for the picaninny conventions that made her name."[51] The perceived originality of Baker's practice should be disregarded; rather than being celebrated as a novelty, her work should rightfully be understood as inheriting and building on a tradition in which Black performers developed distinctive gestural strategies to negotiate crude and occlusive cultural environments. Black performers were largely consigned to minstrel shows when they first gained a prominent stage presence after the Civil War. Within this constraining framework, they developed improvisatory techniques that became central components of jazz dance and whose liberating structures challenged social norms that restricted bodily behaviors, affording them a measure of self-expression. Baker's memoirs highlight the psychological significance of such practices, and as we will see, her films are equally valuable as rare visual documents of them.

Josephine was edited and published posthumously by Jo Bouillon, one of Baker's husbands and father to her Rainbow Tribe of adopted children. The only memoir to draw from Baker's own writings, it was constructed from three hundred pages of an incomplete draft that she began in the early 1960s together with personal correspondences and family and acquaintance recollections. As Bouillon notes in the preface, "Wherever there was information lacking, I turned to Josephine's friends, her sister Margaret, our children and my own memory to fill the gap" (xiii). Bouillon takes over the narrative at the end of World War II, when he met and married Baker. As with her earlier memoirs, the star's recollections are mediated by a white male writer. Disturbingly, despite Bouillon's fourteen-year marriage to Baker, he describes her in the text as an "Amazon" (ix) and "civilized and wild by turn" (145) and reveals pseudoscientific racist attitudes to his own children. He emphasizes the "Nordic fairness and stamina" of his Finnish-born son Jari and "innate equilibrium" of the French-born Jean-Claude (x), suggests that the "mixed blood" of his two eldest sons Akio and Janot "soon made them bigger and quicker than their Japanese brothers" (195), and deems Luis, from Colombia, an "ex-savage" (202). He also turns to two key architects of Baker's original French persona, Paul Colin and Théâtre des Champs-Élysées manager André Daven, for a firsthand account of her arrival on the Paris stage. Colin reiterates primitivist mind-sets, describing *La Revue Nègre* as a "colorful, raucous group" that "Leap[t] onto the stage like children at play," and "broke into a frenzied tap dance" (49). For Daven, Baker was "eroticism personified," and the apparent "simplicity of her emotions, her savage grace, were deeply moving" to him (51).

Matthew Pratt Guterl denounces *Josephine* as a "book that is presented as an autobiography but is really a carefully edited selection of memories . . . meant to make money, or to make it possible to make money in some other way; it was never meant to be full, robust, or honest."[52] Yet the first half of the text, which comprises chiefly Baker's narrative voice, still has value as it demythologizes her public image and engages self-reflexively with her status as a cultural commodity. Baker highlights European men's manipulation of her persona. Reluctant to undress and made to feel like a "storefront dummy on display" (49) when sketched by Colin for the first time, she concludes that Colin "obviously saw me as an object; not a woman but something to be painted" (50). As in *Voyages*, she lists activities that she was expected to perform: "Paris was in a giddy mood, eager for pleasure. I supplied the amusement it craved, patting my gentlemen customers' heads and pulling their beards, flattering the women and teaching them the Charleston" (68). At times, she felt trapped by her role: "Birds are free. They can fly where they like. If only I could do the same" (59). As in *Voyages*, she also points out the inaccuracies of journalists' accounts, noting that, "Articles in which I barely recognized myself continued to fill the press" (54). Recalling Pierre de Régnier's review of her opening night performance in *La Revue Nègre*, which likened her body to "a cross between a boxing kangaroo and a racing driver," a "snake," a "dipping saxophone" and a "young giraffe," and which Sauvage claimed in *Mémoires* triggered his fascination with the star, Baker asserts that she received such reviews with "astonishment" (55).[53] However, she maintains that she gained the upper hand over her critics by using their reviews as "French textbooks" (53). She also distances herself from Expressionism, an early-twentieth-century European art movement whose debt to so-called "primitive" art meant that she was frequently associated with it, dismissing it as "whatever *that* meant [emphasis in the original]" (59).

Baker claims that she sought to disrupt her erotic persona by proving that she was a dignified and intelligent woman offstage. She states that, "Since I personified the savage on the stage, I tried to be as civilized as possible in daily life" (55). She also complicated her public image by attempting to present onstage a body that looked as light as possible: "I spent thirty minutes every morning rubbing my body with half a lemon to lighten my skin and just as long preparing a mixture for my hair. *I couldn't afford to take chances* [emphasis added]" (58). Throughout the first decades of the twentieth century, beauty companies that targeted African American women unanimously endorsed light skin and straight hair, an approach that was widely criticized by Black newspapers and church leaders who felt that such a look pandered to a Eurocentric beauty ideal. Brenda Dixon Gottschild contends that Baker's adoption of a bobbed, oiled-straight hairstyle was an attempt to subvert gender and racial conventions, and she points out that hair straightening in parts of Africa predates colonialism.[54] However, the obsessiveness of Baker's skin regime suggests that it was also driven by a fear of being seen as too dark. Such behavior signals that she believed that her status in Paris depended on her ability to adhere to Eurocentric beauty notions and that she sought to distance herself from her more exotic image to achieve meaningful inclusion in French society. Surrealist writer and ethnographer Michel Leiris later insisted that Baker might not have been so readily embraced had her skin tone been darker.[55]

Nevertheless, Baker admits that she created a frequently paradoxical stage image and engaged pragmatically with her persona by playing into readings of exoticism. Arriving in Berlin for the first time in 1926, she states that, "There were rumors that the show [*La Revue Nègre*] was indecent, an impression I may have strengthened when a reporter asked me to describe my ideal world. One where we can all go naked, as in paradise, I replied" (58). In so doing, Baker denies a comfortable reading of her image. She also juxtaposes such sexual self-confidence against negative attitudes to her body in the United States. She recalls the "disgust" of her fellow chorines, who labeled her as a "monkey" when she achieved attention for her unruly performances in *Shuffle Along* (29). In response to their taunts, and in a notable contrast to her seminaked European performances, she "took to dressing in the bathroom" (29), a space where she could conceal skin deemed to be too dark. As in *Une vie*, Baker's evocation of this incident situates her devotion to racial equality as the consequence of early encounters with racial prejudice and intimidation. It allows her negatively to contrast U.S. intolerance with European primitivist fascinations with Black bodies and to defend and reconcile the nudity of her early performances with her later humanitarian actions by asserting that they were sites of self-affirmation.

Une vie and *Josephine* situate Paris as a socially and physically liberating alternative to the United States. As chapter six of this study will show, Dunham also contrasted her European experiences with her treatment in the United States. *Une vie* emphasizes Paris' lack of racist social structures, insinuating that Baker's transatlantic journey affords her not only fame but also freedom from the racial prejudices that she has endured in the United States. The star describes Paris as "like in a dream, like in a new world, so far, so far from America" (92). In a pointed critique of U.S. segregation, she describes how she expected to be turned away from a wagon-restaurant because white people were eating there. Instead, she discovered that, "To my great surprise, I was greeted very nicely even though there were many white people. I was so happy to be treated on the same footing as them!" (92). She contrasts public displays of physical expression with the U.S.'s puritanical attitude to sexual behavior, affirming that the men and women that she witnesses "kissing in the street" would be "sen[t] to prison" back home (93). In *Josephine*, she notes how Parisian women's bodies "moved freely" and declares France to be a "wonderful place!" (42). Baker's depiction overlooks the voyeuristic fascination with Black bodies that played a key role in her early Parisian success, yet it enables her to situate the city as a site of artistic and psychological rejuvenation.

By contrast, *Josephine* emphasizes U.S. racial intolerance. The narrative begins with the East St. Louis Race Riot of 1917, which by official estimates was the bloodiest race riot in U.S. history and an event that Baker declares "marked me, first unconsciously, and later all too consciously, for life" (1).[56] The performer describes the terrifying event as the "Apocalypse" and the "ultimate catastrophe" (2). The incident is followed by a silence "punctuated by whimpers, sobs and moans rising from the shadows," which underscores its horror, and Baker is told later that a man's eyes have been ripped out and a baby torn from its mother's womb (3). She recalls watching as a "white man, his face contorted with hatred, was savagely beating a figure kneeling before him" (3). She asserts that, "The only way I could tell that his victim was black was by his raised hands; the rest of him was wet with blood" (3). The figure's bowed position highlights his defenselessness and evokes *Mon sang*'s Marian victimhood motif to elicit readers' empathy; his ambiguous identity undermines racial differences and points up the senselessness of such bloodshed.

Baker claims that this incident triggered her antiracist activism: "Because of a lie, men and women of color had suffered and died. Surely such injustice would someday end since God, although he was white, had said we all were brothers. I swore that day from the bottom of my heart that I, Tumpy [Baker's childhood nickname], would somehow help to make this change occur. I would remember the massacre all my life" (5). Such a statement enables Baker to negate the problematics of her place in a European primitivist imaginary and in fact to justify it as part of a wider campaign for equal rights by situating her Parisian reception as a positive contrast to U.S. violence.

The riot represented a narrative that Baker was keen on telling at the end of her life, and she repeated it to Henry Louis Gates Jr. in a 1973 interview. When Gates asked Baker why she left the United States, she replied: "I left in 1924 [*sic*], but the roots extend long before that. One of the first things I remember was the East St. Louis Race Riots. . . . All the sky was red with people's houses burning. On the bridge, there were running people with their tongues cut out. There was a woman who'd been pregnant with her insides cut out. That was the beginning of my feeling."[57] In this recollection, the horror is intensified: the dead pregnant woman is not just heard about but seen. In reality, Baker was not caught up directly in the riots as she lived in St. Louis, which is separated from East St. Louis by the Mississippi River.[58]

So why did she mention them? Mary L. Dudziak speculates that, "The stories of the riots were seared in Baker's memory; so horrified was she that she remembered the riots as if she had been there herself," implying that she was so struck by its devastating impact on the neighboring Black community that she later believed that she witnessed the bloodshed firsthand.[59] In fact, Baker may have felt the terror of the event as it occurred as her sister Margaret claimed sixty years later to have seen Black people fleeing across the river.[60] Like Baker, Margaret also recalled a mother whose "stomach [was] cut open with baby in her" and other babies who were thrown in the river "like rats."[61] By situating the event as the "beginning of my feeling," Baker therefore is identifying the need for racial equality as an enduring concern rooted in a real childhood trauma. Even if much of her remembrance is imagined or based on secondhand information, it still records a devastating personal awakening to the threat of racist violence. It allows her to impress upon the reader the psychological and physical consequences of racial intolerance while humanizing victims of such hatred and underscoring the irrationality of prejudice. Such a recollection may have had a pragmatic purpose too. In her interview with Gates, Baker referred to the riot to justify leaving the United States, an action for which she would be criticized during the civil rights movement. Young African Americans accused her of joining in the struggle when the "hard part of the battle was over" and of being a "beneficiary of others' pain and blood."[62] By connecting her life to a history of racial violence, Baker was able to identify herself with victims of inequality at a time when she wanted to gain credibility as a spokesperson for civil rights.

However, this should not obscure Baker's lifelong commitment to challenging U.S. racism, of which her memoirs should be seen as important articulations. Although her work is largely forgotten, Baker was a key player in the civil rights movement. Returning to the United States for the first time in twelve years in 1948 and appalled at segregation policies that led to her exclusion from thirty-six New York hotels, she decided to travel incognito through the U.S. South, reporting on the incidents of discrimination that she experienced for a French magazine. She was invited to give a lecture on U.S. race relations at Fisk University in Nashville, Tennessee, where she contrasted the racist treatment that she endured in her birthplace with the adulation she had enjoyed in Paris. She claimed that, "There is no such thing as race prejudice in France" and promised to dedicate her life to campaigning for African Americans' rights.[63] Baker used her position as a leading Black performer to overturn segregation policies. In 1951, she refused to perform at the Copa City Club in Miami on the basis that, "I cannot work where my people cannot go. It's as simple as that."[64] Her action caused the club to change its policy and the National Association for the Advancement of Colored People (NAACP) commended her success.[65] Her pride at appearing before an integrated audience at the club caused her to declare, "This is really my first appearance in this, my native land in 26 years. The other times didn't count."[66]

Baker also imposed a nondiscrimination clause in her nightclub contracts, succeeding in integrating accommodation and audiences in Las Vegas, and she turned down the opportunity to perform in Atlanta when three hotels refused to change their segregationist policies. She campaigned on behalf of Willie McGee, a Black man from Mississippi whose execution for allegedly raping a white woman was a key inspiration for Dunham's protest ballet *Southland*, as well as the Trenton Six, African American men accused of murdering a white shopkeeper in New Jersey.[67] She also attempted to integrate the whites-only soda fountain at Hecht's Department Store in Washington, D.C., and pressured Chicagoan and San Franciscan business leaders to hire more Black workers. Her efforts led the NAACP to declare May 20, 1951, "Josephine Baker Day" on the basis that she "exemplifies both in her artistic and personal life the principles for which the NAACP, with all good Americans and people of good will everywhere, stand—'Equality, security, and freedom for all.'"[68]

But Baker's work against U.S. segregation was quickly restricted. Five months after receiving her NAACP accolade, she implicated the influential newspaper columnist Walter Winchell in discriminatory practices by accusing him of failing to come to her aid when New York's prestigious Stork Club restaurant refused to serve her. Winchell responded by publicly labeling Baker a "Communist" and suggesting that she had helped to incite the 1949 Peekskill Riots against Paul Robeson, while also noting that she had voiced support for Mussolini during Italy's invasion of Ethiopia in 1935. Winchell wrote to Federal Bureau of Investigation Director J. Edgar Hoover to investigate her alleged Communist sympathies, prompting the bureau to keep a file on her. The State Department feared that Baker's outspoken criticism of U.S. race relations would prove damaging internationally and attempted to silence her, as they would similarly police Dunham, who was also monitored by the FBI and who would claim to have been denied overseas government sponsorship because of her antilynching ballet *Southland*. Unable to remove Baker's passport as it had with Paul and Eslanda Goode Robeson and W. E. B. and Shirley Graham Du Bois due to the French citizenship that she received upon her 1937 marriage to industrialist Jean Lion, the U.S. embassy prevented the star from appearing in Peru, Columbia, and Haiti, and she was arrested as a suspected Communist in Cuba in 1953. As Dudziak observes, "following World War II she was a superstar with international appeal. Once she began criticizing American race relations, she lost valuable markets for her performances—both in the United States and, owing to the efforts of the embassies, in other countries sensitive to American influence."[69]

Baker finally returned to the United States to give a speech at the March on Washington in 1963, although the U.S. government's earlier efforts to silence her undermined her power to act directly as a figurehead for the civil rights movement. Nevertheless, Baker's commitment to racial equality endured. Beginning in 1954, she adopted twelve children from around the world as part of a decades-long attempt to turn Les Milandes, her chateau and surrounding village in the Dordogne, into *La Capitale du monde de la fraternité* (The World Capital of Brotherhood) and performed onstage until the end of her life to fund her utopian project. When Les Milandes was declared bankrupt in 1968, she sought instead to set up a *Collège universitaire de fraternité universelle* (University College of Brotherhood), an independent secondary and tertiary education system, to counter pseudoscientific racist thought. As with Dunham, who, as we will see, spent much of the 1960s and 1970s running a Performing Arts Training Center for deprived young people in East St. Louis and also sought to turn her Haitian home into a school and medical center, Baker's work should be viewed as a significant international antiracism project. Both women promoted education as part of a global humanitarian mission to counter prejudice.

In 1958, Baker wrote to Langston Hughes, a fan of her antiracist activities, to follow up his positive response to her suggestion that he write films about her and the Rainbow Tribe.[70] Baker wanted the productions to promote her humanitarian agenda, believing that they could even "serve as an encouragement to those in North America who believe in brotherhood."[71] Baker raised the matter again with Hughes at the First World Festival of Negro Arts in 1966, prompting him to discuss it with fellow writer Arna Bontemps. Hughes died one year later, and the projects remained unrealized, yet they demonstrate the extent to which Baker had come to perceive of her life story as a public articulation of her humanitarian project. Together, Baker's memoirs show how she developed a narrative in which she conceived of her life story as a tool by which to challenge U.S. racism. Despite neglect of the memoirs in light of their ambiguous authorship, the texts do not simply reinforce racist paradigms but instead present complex and highly personal critiques of intolerance. They should thus be taken seriously as extremely rare firsthand literary accounts of a working-class Black woman's experiences of interwar racism. They also reveal the psychological origins of an idiosyncratic performance style that played up readings of spontaneity to paradoxically advance Baker's agency and situate it as a necessary means of overcoming perceived social and racial inferiority. Together, *Voyages*, *Une vie*, and *Josephine* serve as valuable articulations of Baker's voice that reveal her lifelong preoccupation with racial injustice and show that she engaged with bodily experience to intervene self-reflexively in dominant racial ideologies.

CHAPTER TWO

The Dancer as Translator

Dunham's Ethnographic Memoirs

In her childhood memoir *A Touch of Innocence* (1959), Dunham travels with her stepmother and a family friend to Baker's hometown of St. Louis. The group reacts to this new environment by feeling like "foreigners" who "didn't belong *here*."[1] Dunham's class-conscious stepmother, although Black herself, sees only social degeneration brought by the Great Migration, taking "personal offence at the decline of Chouteau [Avenue], which had always had a bad reputation, but which had certainly suffered terribly from the influx of southern Negroes since her own young girlhood."[2] However, Dunham embraces the scene, leaning her face "as far into the street as she could" and thinking that she had "never before seen in people such abandon and naked joy and fullness of meaning."[3] Dunham's romantic view of an impoverished neighborhood points up her social distance from Baker, whose childhood home resembled those of Chouteau Avenue. However, Dunham's observation also reveals a formative concern to explore the artistry and social bonds of deprived Black communities, which would become a key feature of her performance practice. She describes the scene with what Ramsay Burt calls an "ethnographic understanding of detail," and he asserts that she incorporated such experiences into her choreography.[4] Midwestern Black neighborhoods, such as Chouteau Avenue and State Street in Chicago, in fact inspired some of her most famous works, including *Barrelhouse* and *Floyd's Guitar Blues*.[5]

Although unlike Baker, Dunham merely witnesses a deprived St. Louis street, such a scene speaks to both women's lifelong concern to revalue the cultural achievements and psychological experiences of Black subjects.

The incident encapsulates Dunham's anthropological and humanitarian approach to art. When she arrived in neighboring East St. Louis in 1967 after being appointed as a professor at Southern Illinois University in nearby Edwardsville, she was struck by the "hopelessness, apathy, and utter despair" of the community.[6] In response, she established a Performing Arts Training Center to educate local disadvantaged youths in dance and teach them the value of their artistic heritages. She declared that, "As an anthropologist and a humanist I felt that I could give something, make individuals aware of themselves, their environment, and create a desire to be alive."[7] Much of *A Touch of Innocence* was written in Tokyo at the end of a company tour. However, the text's final page is marked "Habitation Le Clerc—Port-au-Prince, Haiti," which became Dunham's second home following a research trip to the island in the mid-1930s.[8] Dunham later admitted that she signed and dated her manuscript in Haiti to bring recognition to the nation, foregrounding its importance to her life and work.[9] As with Baker, geographical peregrination and social concerns were central to Dunham's career. Like Baker, travel provided her with an opportunity for self-discovery and also enabled her to explore the artistry and psychological significance of African diasporic dance forms.

Like Baker's writings, *A Touch of Innocence* has tremendous literary and cultural value as a rare firsthand document of an interwar African American girlhood. Dunham enjoyed a more economically secure upbringing than did Baker, but both women's works call poignant attention to the challenges of navigating a society marked by racism, intraracism, and the threat of sexual abuse. However, as the incidents described in *A Touch of Innocence* predate Dunham's dance career and as the key goal of this study is to show how Baker and Dunham formulated their art on the page and screen, the central focus here is on her two other major literary works, *Katherine Dunham's Journey to Accompong* (1946) and *Island Possessed* (1969), which record her ten-month anthropological trip researching Caribbean dances in the mid-1930s. These texts serve as extensive literary reflections on her cross-cultural encounters and intellectual growth, which positions them like Baker's memoirs as important contributions to an African American women's autobiographical tradition. Such works hold particular historical significance because they are highly personal reflections on Dunham's contribution as a Black woman dancer to midcentury transatlantic culture.

This chapter investigates *Katherine Dunham's Journey to Accompong* and *Island Possessed* as autobiographical narratives that shed light on the genesis of Dunham's cross-cultural artistry. Dunham's writings are largely absent from autobiographical histories even though she was only the second African American woman after Baker to publish multiple volumes of her life experiences. Daphne Lamothe connects Dunham to the New Negro movement, while recent work has spotlighted her involvement in the Illinois Writers' Project and Black Chicago Renaissance more generally.[10] Yet as Stephanie Leigh Batiste observes, Dunham "rarely receives the credit she deserves as a skillful writer."[11] Ivette Romero-Cesareo suggests that, as a Black woman travel writer, Dunham has been "lost in the undefined spaces of overlapping fields and genres."[12] Dunham does feature in the *Oxford Companion to African American Literature* and the *Cambridge Companion to African American Women's Literature*.[13] In the latter, Joanne Braxton reflects on *A Touch of Innocence*'s ongoing neglect while reading it as a forerunner to Maya Angelou's *I Know Why the Caged Bird Sings* (1969). That she does not mention Dunham's other books shows the extent to which they are still classified as ethnographies, not memoirs. As chapter one revealed, Baker's French language texts are similarly resistant to easy inclusion within an African American women's autobiographical tradition. Yet although they adopt different narrative perspectives, with Dunham taking on the role of observer and Baker drawing from her own background, Dunham's ethnographic works mirror Baker's memoirs as personal reflections on international racist paradigms. The texts explore physical expression and bodily translation in particular to highlight the subjective underpinnings of racial, artistic, and geographical categories and point up their ambiguities. Like Baker's writings, they shed autobiographical light on Dunham's dance philosophy, by which she sought to realize an artistic and cultural legitimization of the Caribbean by incorporating its ritual dance forms onto the concert dance stage. Such an undertaking positioned her like Baker as a leading antiracism campaigner throughout the 1950s and 1960s. In particular, Dunham's work situated her as a key participant in the Black Arts Movement and ensured a significant Caribbean influence over North American dance practices throughout the mid–twentieth century.

Dunham arrived in the Caribbean with the then unusual goal of researching local dance patterns. Although fieldworkers such as Melville Herskovits and Zora Neale Hurston had already begun to investigate dance's cultural significance, Dunham was the first anthropologist to make it the primary focus of her investigation. She visited Martinique and Trinidad but spent most of her time in Jamaica and Haiti because these islands were believed to have maintained some independence from colonial domination and retained some African traditions. Dunham's work in Haiti should also be understood in light of longstanding U.S. fears of and fascinations with the nation as a primitive Other. As Kate Ramsey acknowledges, "Since the late eighteenth century, Haiti had been constructed in the West as an imaginative space signifying atavistic magic, savagery, and sensuality."[14] A particularly notorious example of such literature was Sir Spenser St. John's *Hayti: Or, the Black Republic* (1884), which imagined communities consumed by "fetish worship and cannibalism."[15] Such associations were exacerbated in the U.S. imagination following the country's occupation of the island in 1915. One of the earliest and most influential ethnographic tracts on Haiti was William Seabrook's *The Magic Island* (1929), whose lurid illustrations of its sacred practices had an immediate and lasting effect on U.S. popular culture. Drawing on work by Gérarde Magloire and Kevin Yelvington, Millery Polyné refers to an "anthropological imagination" of Haiti rooted in colonial and neocolonial ethnography, in which "Africa," "voodoo," and "Race" became key symbols, and he identifies dance as the central image of these associations.[16]

However, Dunham's firsthand engagement with Caribbean rituals led to a profoundly different articulation of the islands' dances and their practitioners. By literally embodying the performances that she observed, Dunham developed a close physical relationship with her subjects that contested traditional scientist-subject hierarchies. *Journey to Accompong* and *Island Possessed* record the memories of these interactions. In these texts, Dunham expresses a sense of intimacy with her subjects as dance enables her to take part in rituals and achieve cultural integration. Her arrival in the Caribbean can be read as the beginning of a rich mutual exchange in which the host nation resists its status as scientific subject by claiming power and influence over the scientist. This sense of communality through dance is particularly relevant to studies of Dunham's wider cultural impact because critics have read her choreography as an important site of cross-cultural amalgamation and exchange. For example, Ramsey asserts that Dunham developed a "modernist concert dance idiom based on Afro-Haitian and Caribbean forms . . . that not only contributed to widespread interest in and travel to Haiti in the 1940s and 1950s but also ensured that elements of African diasporic performance came to permeate North American concert dance."[17] Her narratives therefore serve as extensive literary reflections on the Caribbean roots of an art form dedicated to promoting Black Atlantic dance traditions.

Dunham's first memoir, *Journey to Accompong*, is a detailed account of the month that she spent with the Maroon community of Jamaica's Accompong region in 1935. The Maroons were descendants of several communities of formerly enslaved men and women who had escaped their captors and held onto their freedom during British colonial rule. The text was Dunham's second book-length work after her master's thesis, "Dances of Haiti: Their Social Organization, Classification, Form, and Function" (1947), and the first to be published.[18] In a letter to Dunham, anthropologist Harold Courlander commented on an early draft of *Journey to Accompong*. He underscored the book's creative approach to ethnography by noting that, "The times are perhaps against it, but times change, and it will be wanted a little later."[19] Courlander was impressed by Dunham's conversational style and intimacy with her hosts. He encouraged her to add as much color into her account as possible and even to embellish her observations of her Jamaican subjects. He wrote, "you ought to allow yourself a little more liberty with getting inside these people. If you don't know what they think, guess. It will give them more depth, and enrich the book."[20] Courlander's praise shows that he recognized the book's value as a vivid record of a lone woman's experiences in an unfamiliar country. But he dismissed its significance as ethnography, suggesting that, "The book isn't technical or academic anyway."[21]

Courlander's interpretation of the text solely as a subjective account of a woman's experiences within a Caribbean community condescendingly dismissed Dunham's observations as too overtly confessional to be serious research, drawing a clear division between scientific study and personal experience. His letter hints at the rigidity of midcentury anthropological hierarchies, in which, in order to maintain the interpretative authority of the almost invariably white, male fieldworker, acknowledgments of self-doubt and uncertainty were deemed inadmissible from the ethnographic record. Courlander recognized the text's significance as a confessional narrative, but he reinforced a dichotomy between anthropology and autobiography that undermined its cultural significance.

Dunham was a student of Melville Herskovits, one of the first scholars to recognize the importance of African survivals in the Americas, and one of her research objectives was to identify African dance traditions in the Caribbean. Herskovits prepared her for this role by instructing her in his anthropological method. He showed her how to be unobtrusive by acting as an unassuming presence in the community, thereby maximizing her chances of achieving cultural inclusion. However, Herskovits's training was intended to generate detailed research, not meaningful interaction. Dunham's Caribbean project was founded on achieving scientific integrity; her interpretations were meant to be authoritative descriptions of the subjects she had been assigned to observe. James Clifford notes that, in classical ethnography, "the author's personal voice is seen as a style in the weak sense: a tone, or embellishment of the facts."[22] Thus, "States of serious confusion, violent feelings or acts, censorships, important failures, changes of course, and excessive pleasures are excluded from the published account."[23]

Herskovits also instructed Dunham to read her observations as evidence of an African past rather than as dynamic cultural practices with an ongoing social purpose and meaning. Pioneering anthropologists such as Herskovits and Franz Boas were more interested in the African origins of Black diasporic cultures than in reading them as ongoing intellectual processes or as psychological responses to present circumstances. Herskovits encouraged Dunham to visit Accompong because it was considered to be the last surviving trace of independent settlements established by escaped slaves. Accompong was held to be a particularly rich research site because it was believed that, as an unusually independent and insular community, it held substantial African cultural retentions. Although Herskovits had visited the community for a few hours, he believed that Dunham would be the first outsider to spend more than a night there. Similarly, Dunham suggested that Haiti was chosen as the central focus of her investigation because it was believed that "the preservation of authentic and original forms was more characteristic of Haiti than of other islands of the West Indies."[24] Herskovits read cultural practices in historical terms, helping to reinforce an illusory concept of cultural purity and disregarding the Black Atlantic as a key site of modernity.

Unlike Herskovits, Dunham was attentive to the ongoing significance of dance practices in the Black new world. As Joyce Aschenbrenner asserts, "Dunham's objective was not merely to record dances and make good films but also to understand the social role of dance."[25] Dunham expressed dismay when Herskovits read her film recording of a Koromantee war dance, a practice that she believed to hold cultural and historical significance, as "that picture where men are hopping about very fast."[26] Much of Dunham's success in Caribbean society was made possible by her willingness to transgress many boundaries, including the class, gender, and cultural differences that separated her from her hosts. In choosing to experience firsthand a Koromantee dance in Jamaica and a Vodou *lavé-tête* rite in Haiti, Dunham acted out a level of interaction that would now be termed "participant observation," a method of cultural immersion in which the participant nevertheless retains the role of scientific recorder.[27] Although this method of anthropological analysis predates Dunham's work, Halifu Osumare asserts that her adoption of this approach through firsthand experience of a Vodou initiation was unusually embracive. Osumare writes, "Although the cultural-relativist, participant-observation technique had been the theorized anthropological method since Boas, her professors were clearly taken aback at the fervor in which she employed participatory fieldwork techniques."[28] Specifically, Osumare refers to a 1936 letter from Herskovits, in which he expresses concern over Dunham's level of cultural immersion and writes, "*I am a little disturbed . . . at the prospect of your going through* canzo *ceremony* [a trial by fire that marks the participant's initiation into the second stage of Vodou], *and I am wondering if it would not be possible for you to attend merely as a witness* [author's italics]."[29]

Dunham's immersion method is enacted most explicitly via bodily experience, most notably through ritual and dance. Clifford argues that, "Participant observation obliges its practitioners to experience, at a *bodily* as well as an intellectual level, the vicissitudes of translation."[30] The observer's experiences are channeled through shared bodily expression, and subjective physical sensation becomes a site of interpretation. In this context, Ursula Rao and John Hutnyk contend that anthropological texts "originate from the memory of bodily participation in dialogue and reflect the knowledge that it generates."[31] Klaus-Peter Köpping suggests that anthropological understanding is only truly possible when it is based on meaningful two-way embodied communication, in which anthropologists self-consciously confront their position of Otherness or alienation within the community and give in to their inferior social status. He maintains that, "the writing of ethnography should not degenerate into the mere technology of translation but must be a creative act. It can only be so if there was true corporeal dialogue."[32] By bodily participating in her hosts' community through active engagement in Koromantee and Vodou ceremonies, Dunham abandons traditional methods of scientific detachment in favor of meaningful cultural inclusion.

In *Journey to Accompong*, Dunham develops a self-questioning narrative voice that decenters the anthropologist's traditional position of authority, and which remains sensitive to the social complexities of 1930s Accompong. Jamaica marked Dunham's first point of prolonged contact with the Caribbean, and the text is an autobiographical account of the fear, self-doubt, and euphoria of a young woman venturing abroad for the first time. As in Baker's memoirs, in which Paris functions as a curative contrast to an alienating United States, Dunham finds Accompong to be psychologically liberating. One of Dunham's early mentors, Robert Redfield, described an early draft of the book as "a vivid record of a personal experience," and Dunham recounts her feelings of trepidation and excitement as she begins her journey.[33] She writes that, "somehow this was me. And as I looked back at that thin little thread trailing down into the lowlands, I couldn't help but feel a strange ecstasy as though all of the steel-mill drabness of Joliet, Illinois, and the dark winter pinch of Chicago, and the confusion and bewilderment of New York City were sliding rapidly downhill and right off Kingston Bay into the ocean."[34] Dunham's candid description of her feelings destabilizes the text's narrative authority. By accentuating her sense of excitement and uncertainty, Dunham emphasizes the personal and subjective nature of her experiences. In so doing, she problematizes the anthropologist's interpretative authority and interrogates the boundaries between scientific description and life writing.

Journey to Accompong is divided into thirty sections, each giving an impression of Dunham's daily observations and changing attitudes toward her environment and hosts. The text's diarylike structure connects it strongly with traditional memoir form and underscores the fact that much of the work was written while Dunham was actually present in Accompong. As early as 1949, dance critic Margaret Lloyd recognized the intimacy of Dunham's ethnography, noting that, "The text, in the casual form of day-by-day notes and comments, imparts the feeling of actuality, of being there."[35] As Lloyd observed, the overriding authorial voice is that of a young woman who has left home for the first time and is discovering how to conduct anthropological research in the Caribbean while also forming human relationships for which Herskovits's scientific training has provided little guidance.

As a perceptive engagement with a modern Black consciousness, *Journey to Accompong* recalls Baker's memoirs. It also parallels the work of one of the few other Black American anthropologists of the period, Zora Neale Hurston. Hurston made recordings of Bahamian dances as early as 1929, several years before Dunham visited the Caribbean, and her translation of such practices to the stage predated Dunham's research-to-performance method.[36] However, as she never received the formal support that would enable her meaningfully to explore her dance observations on the page and there is no surviving footage of her dance recordings or stagings, the focus here is on another significant parallel between the two women's work.[37] Both Dunham and Hurston conducted research in Jamaica and Haiti in 1936, and as David Murray notes, Hurston's literary record of her experiences in the Caribbean in *Tell My Horse* (1938) reveals an unusual self-reflexivity: "Her use of fictional techniques, variously combined with the standard forms of objective ethnography, has been seen as anticipating the 'reflexive' anthropology of later years."[38] Like Dunham, therefore, Hurston's uncertain and ambiguous narrative voice can be read as a self-conscious questioning of the ethnographer's authority.

However, *Journey to Accompong* is much more explicitly self-conscious than Hurston's ethnographic writings. Not only does it demonstrate a radically self-reflexive approach to anthropology, but it also deserves meaningful recognition within a Black women's autobiographical tradition. In her consideration of Hurston's account of Jamaican marriage rituals in *Tell My Horse*, Joanne M. Braxton argues that, "her work assumes a tone that is clearly autobiographical."[39] Yet Braxton admits that Hurston "attempts to assume the role of the passive observer-recorder, subduing her narrative voice," and "there is no assertion of autobiographical intent."[40]

In *Journey to Accompong*, on the other hand, Dunham provides explicit personal detail. She writes that the "very African" food does not agree with her, and she finds it hard to sleep on the "noisy mattress of banana 'trash'" (5). The rural nightscape brings "blackness entirely new," she finds the language "almost unintelligible," and she is left "feeling very much alone" (5). The text is extremely candid about Dunham's status as a community outsider and of her sense of geographical and cultural displacement. Unlike Hurston's writings, it is openly autobiographical, and, much like Baker's memoirs, it draws on themes of alienation to position Dunham's experience as a journey of self-discovery. Braxton argues that Black women writing in the 1940s rejected the self-sacrificing thematics of emancipatory narratives to "extend the quest for a dignified and self-defining identity to include a search for personal fulfillment."[41] For Braxton, Black women writers of this period used autobiography to celebrate Black women's subjecthood. *Journey to Accompong* fits into this assessment in its adoption of an autobiographical perspective to describe in detail one woman's voyage of self-discovery and search for community acceptance. However, Dunham uses her experience not only as an act of personal fulfillment but also to explore the social and cultural complexities of Jamaican lives. Like *Voyages* and *Une vie*, *Journey to Accompong* is an early textual exploration of international Black subjecthood and as such sheds light on Dunham's intercultural dance practice. Like Baker's memoirs, which reworked "tragic mulatta" narratives as part of a wider concern to highlight the fluidities of racial identities, *Journey to Accompong* serves as a formative articulation of Dunham's fight against racism.

In his introduction to *Journey to Accompong*, eminent midcentury anthropologist Ralph Linton recognized and applauded Dunham's unusually self-reflexive method. He noted that, "while Miss Dunham's observation is that of a trained anthropologist, her method of approach was that of a sympathetic participant . . . while many ethnologists go to a primitive group seeking proof for previously conceived theories, Miss Dunham seems to have been completely open-minded" (viii). As a cultural relativist, Linton's conception of primitivism centered on a notion of folk cultures not as less complex but simply as distinct from European and U.S. societies. Linton was a pioneer of psychological anthropology, which adopted Freudian theory to explore the relationship between cultural practices and mental processes. His praise for *Journey to Accompong* demonstrates that he perceived the text to be an extension of his own anthropological method, which sought to shift the focus from cultural practices onto practitioners themselves in order to explore further the complexities of human civilizations. As he writes, "Miss Dunham presents [the Maroons] as friendly and delightful people . . . In this book one gets not only a picture of an interesting and unusual society, but of warm and living personalities. This component is often missing from accounts of fieldwork that are tailored to fit academic requirements" (viii). Linton's reading shows that Dunham's interest in the villagers as people reconfigured traditional ethnographic accounts that dehumanized their subjects as mere conduits of rituals and cultural practices. However, what Linton failed to perceive was that *Journey to Accompong*'s reflection of physical interaction breaks down self-Other binaries, querying the very notion of cultural distinctiveness that even his more thoughtful understanding of primitivism continued to uphold.

Journey to Accompong illustrates that Dunham set aside prior beliefs about the Accompong community, and implicitly much of her anthropological training, allowing the villagers to act as her tutors. Osumare argues that the text combines contemporary ethnographic practices with modern self-reflexivity and community interaction. She writes that, "We know from *Journey to Accompong* that she utilized a functionalist theoretical frame by recording the various social institutions in relationship to each other . . . Yet, she had come there 'to study and take part in the dances.'"[42] Dunham's biographer Joyce Aschenbrenner describes her approach as that of a "neophyte who was there to learn" and who "put the Maroons in the role of teachers to a benighted African American from the United States, one of a class of people whom they knew to be ignorant of their heritage."[43] Dunham's account acknowledges the limits of her perspective and relegates the historically omniscient scientific observer to both participant in and student of Jamaican culture. Betraying cultural biases and ignorance during her first meeting with the Accompong community, Dunham writes that she is "dying to hear wild exotic native music and watch weird ceremonies," only to be forced to spend her first night listening to her own jazz collection (4). Having taken charge of her phonograph, the village chiefs subject her to an "inspection" before accepting her (4). Treated with suspicion, she is placed in a position of inferiority that suggests the roles of anthropologist and subjects have been reversed. Dunham's recollection acknowledges that her social standing was not necessarily voluntary and that, rather than being merely the passive targets of Dunham's scientific project, her hosts played an active role in dictating her place in and shaping her understanding of Accompong.

Later, Dunham admits defeat in her attempt to comprehend community members' behaviors and gain a definitive understanding of Maroon culture. Describing a trip away from Accompong, she notes how she "felt extraordinarily gay as I left behind me Maroontown and these strange people who are so graciously simple at one moment and so unfathomable at the next" (96). Dunham therefore undermines traditional subject-observer hierarchies, as well as scientific claims to omniscience. At one stage, she refers to the unwieldiness of her camera equipment and by extension her role as anthropologist in Accompong's mountainous environment. As she walks along a path with a local woman, she describes her acquaintance as, "skipping ahead like a nimble little ewe down the path, and I lumbering along, my camera slung over one shoulder and banging against my hip as I try to keep up with her" (59). By drawing attention to her incongruity, Dunham underscores the impracticality of fieldwork and unsettles the anthropologist's perceived position of authority, intimating that, in order to draw nearer to and understand her subjects, she must give up her camera and consequently her role as scientist.

Hurston reviewed *Journey to Accompong* for the *New York Times* and reserved some praise for the work, describing it as a "lively and word-deft account," and an "entertaining book."[44] But she challenged its legitimacy by dismissing it as a fleeting foray into Caribbean culture, suggesting that, "thirty days in a locality is not much in research and hardly affords time enough for the fieldworker to scratch the surface."[45] Hurston's critical reading was motivated by animosity that developed between the two women as rival anthropologists in the Caribbean in the mid-1930s. In her unpublished memoir "Minefields," Dunham recalled how she felt "offended" when Hurston published on Jamaica and Haiti, and that it would be "some time" before she allowed herself to "appreciate" Hurston's writing.[46] By focusing on the temporal brevity of Dunham's trip, however, Hurston overlooked *Journey to Accompong*'s significance as a personal revelation of extensive cultural participation, which Dunham achieves through close physical contact with community members and particularly through dance.

In a lecture at the University of California at Los Angeles in 1942, Dunham employed her dancers to demonstrate scenes from her theatrical staging of social rituals *Rites de Passage* (1941) to show how her Caribbean fieldwork had inspired the production. She recalled how she realized the potential of dance as an interpretative method while studying at the University of Chicago in the 1930s: "It occurred to me . . . that someone who could actively participate in this activity [dance] would be able to arrive much more clearly at the function of the dance in a specific community than the field worker who depended primarily on observation."[47] Consequently, Dunham's most meaningful point of contact with the Maroon villagers occurs when she engages in community dance performances. *Journey to Accompong* therefore serves as an extensive literary reflection on the origins of her dance practice. In so doing, it sheds vital light on the psychological and philosophical underpinnings of an artistic practice interpreted like Baker's work within a primitivist gaze and yet rooted in a history of Black Atlantic performance. It highlights the value of both women's writings for understanding the origins of their art and for helping to situate their performances within a wider African diasporic dance tradition.

Hoping to discover "native" dances early on in her visit, Dunham instead finds social practices that are based heavily on the Quadrille, a European-derived couple dance, which draws her attention to dances as ongoing cultural processes rather than as artifacts. The Quadrille eventually gains pace and becomes the Shay-Shay, or Mento, a much livelier, more intimate, and less formal dance that she concludes must be a "Creole improvisation" (26). Dunham at first believes that the Shay-Shay is deliberately erotic but on taking part in the dance discovers that elderly members are still dancing after she and other younger participants have been forced to retire. She concludes that the dance has no sexual intent but is a means for the most highly skilled to show off. She writes that, "the Maroons seem to dance purely egotistically, for the thrill of the perfection of art" (26–27). Through her participation in Accompong social dances, Dunham discovers that erotic movements in the dances she witnesses do not necessarily have sexual purposes but instead can be used to reaffirm generational hierarchies and celebrate individual artistry.

Dunham also discovers that such actions can have ritual significances. Her greatest concern during her stay is to witness and record the dances of Koromantee, Obeah religious rituals with roots in the practices of the Asante peoples of what is now Ghana. Dunham spends most of her trip trying unsuccessfully to persuade community members to demonstrate such customs. She concludes that her failure is due to the village leader's attempts to eradicate the practices. However, Erin Mackie refers to the text in a study of Caribbean countercultures to speculate that, "one might surmise that these traditions were being purposively withheld from the eyes of a foreigner," and the villagers' secretiveness suggests that Dunham struggled to overcome her outsider status.[48] Nevertheless, the day before departing, Dunham encounters a Myal dance, an Obeah ritual in which a shaman draws village grandmother Mis' Mary into a trance to entice out of her a "duppy," or evil spirit. Dunham notes the erotic overtures of the dance, in which the shaman's pelvis moves with an "unmistakable sexual purpose" to awaken the duppy (133). But she also realizes that his action leads to a reversal of gender roles, and that the "doctor was afraid . . . of this woman whom he had raised from the dead" (133). Overwhelmed by the dance's hypnotic intensity, Dunham decides that she "must close her eyes for a moment" before the ritual ends abruptly (133). Unable to comprehend the performance's meaning, she is told by village elder Ba' Teddy that it is best if she "fergit" it and admits to being "almost relieved to be thus reprimanded" (134). She engages self-reflexively with her failures as an anthropologist as she admits that the scene remains beyond her interpretative powers.

Nonetheless, Dunham seems to have tried to re-create the performance, as similarities between the Myal dance and the *Fertility* section of *Rites de Passage* have been detected. John O. Perpener contends that, "Whereas the myal dance used sexual movement to evoke curative powers, Dunham used similar movement to represent the fecund power of a mating ritual."[49] But Perpener also observes that Dunham's dancers adopt hypnotic states to offset the erotic readings of the scene even as they engage heavily in pelvic movements: "By having the dancers create a feeling of detachment, Dunham commented upon the serious nature of the events occurring on stage and drew attention to interpretations of the movement that were different from those that were familiar to American audiences."[50] By witnessing the Myal dance, Dunham discovers that seemingly sexual gestures can play fundamental roles in religious rituals by serving as physical acts of spiritual rejuvenation and community cohesion. She employed pelvic gestures in her choreography to reenact these processes with the purpose of reconfiguring associations of Black identities away from exotic sexuality and toward sensual and communal experience.

Following the Myal ritual, Dunham is allowed to take part in a Koromantee dance. As she joins in the practice, she remarks on its fierce energy. It begins "much like the warming up of an athlete," and she finds herself part of a "melee of leaping, shouting warriors," before switching to "'bush fightin,' crouching down and advancing in line to attack an imaginary enemy" (135). According to Ruth Beckford, "Koromantee is a dance of preparation for war, and contains movements that stimulate aggressive behavior. Women shake rattles and men swing sticks at imaginary enemies. Occasionally a woman grabs a man's shoulders and shakes them, trying to arouse in him even more hostility."[51]

Dunham reads the dance as an invocation of human bravery and resilience. Caught in close bodily contact with Mis' Mary, the village elder who endured the Myal ritual, Dunham is shocked into recognition of the dance's historical significance. She writes that, "At one stage of the dance Mis' Mary and I are face to face, she no longer is a duppy, but a Maroon woman of old days, working the men up to a pitch where they will descend into the cockpit and exterminate one of His Majesty's red-coated platoons" (135–136). Such recognition is based on reading the dance not as an African survival, but as a physical reenactment and thus as a reassertion of resistance against enslavement. Dunham here anticipates her later devotion to the arts as education by considering how dance might function psychologically for the Maroons as an imaginative re-creation of community heroism and freedom from bondage, suggesting dance's possible purpose as a way for Black people to reconnect with historical achievements.

Dunham also notes that the dancers are no longer self-conscious about her presence, construing that "I might not have come at all, for the difference that it has made. I was accepted and one of them" (132). After the dance, she concludes that, "Now I had the delicious thrill of accomplishment . . . of belonging completely" (137). By engaging physically in the rituals that she has been assigned merely to record, Dunham reframes traditional scientist-subject binaries to achieve inclusion in her hosts' community and gains insights into the cultural significances of dances that her mentor Herskovits perceived as historical artifacts. Dunham's decision to translate these encounters into her performances shows that such interactions played a key role in shaping her ongoing choreographic practice. *Journey to Accompong* therefore is an important autobiographical account of the formation of her dance practice that charts the debt that such work owed to 1930s Accompong society.

Journey to Accompong presents a bold, original account of culture shock and intercultural education and is an important record of the philosophical underpinnings of Dunham's choreography. Dunham borrowed heavily from Black Atlantic dance cultures during her performance career, but like Baker she reworked them. Instead of framing them as static artifacts of an African past, she drew attention to their enduring social relevance and transatlantic links. When she returned from the Caribbean in 1936, for example, she was struck by the similarities between the Lindy Hop, then at the height of its popularity in the United States, and the Shay-Shay, which she interpreted as a "Creole improvisation" when she observed it at a social dance in Accompong. She wrote that, "it was apparent to me that almost the entire pattern and certainly many of the specific movements were very similar to those . . . which I had just been recording."[52] *Journey to Accompong* therefore serves as a significant firsthand account of the international experiences of an early Black woman scientist. The text reveals the self-reflexivity and dynamism in Dunham's approach to cultural encounters and underscores the ways in which she used dance to highlight and develop international dialogues of physical artistry.

Dunham's second memoir, *Island Possessed*, is an even more confessional narrative that positions her Caribbean experiences at the forefront of her dance philosophy and artistic legacy. The text recounts her stay in Haiti. As well as describing her interactions with key political figures, including future Haitian presidents, Dumarsais Estimé and François "Papa Doc" Duvalier, the text recalls her engagement with religious and community rituals, including a Mardi Gras ceremony and the spirit transfer of a bocor (Vodou priest). Much of the text is devoted to Dunham's firsthand experience of a *lavé-tête*, a ritual marking the point of entry into Vodou. In this regard, *Island Possessed* represents a textual extension of Dunham's master's thesis, "Dances of Haiti," in which she discusses Haitian dance rituals and evaluates their religious and psychological significance. Dorothea Fischer-Hornung has described "Dances of Haiti" as "among the founding texts on the anthropology and aesthetics of Vodoun."[53] She asserts that, like Hurston and filmmaker Maya Deren, Dunham "attempted to decipher the meaning of Vodoun . . . for the community of practitioners, for non-practitioners, as well as for themselves in the context of their lives as scholars and artists."[54]

But *Island Possessed* goes even further than "Dances of Haiti" in its engagement with Vodou. Written in Senegal during the 1960s and published in 1969, more than thirty years after and thousands of miles from the experiences that it describes, its dislocation from its setting and narrative experiences help to situate it as a highly self-reflexive text. Dunham wrote *Island Possessed* after returning from Haiti to enjoy a lengthy international dance career and also at the end of the U.S. civil rights movement, a period during which she fought personal battles against racial injustice. Like Baker's social protests in the 1940s and 1950s, Dunham's stance against racial segregation and injustice in fact preceded the civil rights movement. On October 19, 1944, she protested before a segregated audience at Memorial Auditorium, Louisville, Kentucky, and in 1950 and 1953 she staged *Southland*, a ballet about lynching. In 1950, she filed a lawsuit against a Brazilian hotel when it refused rooms to her company. The publicity that her case generated led to the passing of national legislation that prohibited discrimination in public places.

In *Island Possessed*, Dunham's original observations are augmented, and even challenged, by the reflections of an older and arguably wiser self. For instance, the narrator confronts her youthful self's familial and admiring relationship with Estimé by considering his decision prior to his deposition in 1950 to praise the violent actions of his supporters. She concludes that, "Concerning Dumarsais Estimé I am left in doubt about many things."[55] Dunham's thesis minimizes the observer's positionality and favors scientific language; it represents a deliberate adherence to scholarly discourse that situates Dunham's Haitian trip as an observational project. By contrast, *Island Possessed* adopts an autobiographical narrative strategy by presenting a candid account of Dunham's experiences on the island and her immersion in Vodou. While on the one hand, "Dances of Haiti" is a key scientific contribution to the island's dance rituals, on the other hand, *Island Possessed* incorporates the author into practices she is meant simply to document, highlighting the text's significance as autobiography. In so doing, she positions Caribbean community rituals as sites with profound psychological and social significances to their adherents.

Dunham arrived in Haiti in 1935, just one year after the island emerged from a nineteen-year U.S. occupation, and the same year that Aimé Césaire coined the term *Négritude* to describe the international Black ideology that was being developed in response to French colonial racism. Dunham claimed that, although she took her "guidance in political thinking and intellectual and conscious awakening for granted" (46) and did not realize it at the time, Estimé introduced her to the concept of *Négritude*. At the time of writing *Island Possessed*, she disowned the term for "so easily bordering on nationalism" (47), concluding that "I do not admit to a spiritual or cultural poverty in Black people which would make it necessary to coin a word or system of thinking of oneself outside the human division" (4–5). Yet she admits to having been influenced by Estimé's thinking. She writes, "I must have practiced, preached, and lived [*Négritude*]" (4), and she describes Estimé's influence on her growing racial awareness, noting how his outlook had succeeded in "awakening a conscience which had been selfish, not social" and therefore in imbuing her scientific mind with social consciousness (42). Likening Estimé to Haitian independence hero Toussaint Louverture, she writes, "It was now up to me to turn this thirst for knowledge to a way to service, as Estimé's ambition was not for self, but for service. . . . Gradually, I began to see the things around me with his eyes, with his evaluations, though never losing the intense preoccupations with what I had come to Haiti for, the *vaudun* and the complex surrounding it" (42). As *Island Possessed* illustrates, Estimé's social consciousness inspired Dunham to contemplate the humanities of her subjects and to treat her presence on the island as a long-term commitment both to individuals and to complex cultural rites. Estimé's influence shows the extent to which 1930s Haiti served for Dunham as a space not merely for scientific but also psychological growth, which underscores *Island Possessed*'s autobiographical significance.

Like *Journey to Accompong*, *Island Possessed*'s firsthand description of Haitian rituals bears a striking resemblance to Hurston's *Tell My Horse*. David Murray suggests that *Tell My Horse*'s close engagement with Vodou was unusually immersive for its time and, in this regard, foreshadowed more recent forms of anthropology: "Anthropology has tended to deal with native belief in magic, witchcraft, and the like from outside rather than phenomenologically, and one of the significant ways in which Hurston anticipates later ethnographies is her direct involvement in hoodoo and voodoo practices."[56] Dunham's participation in Haitian customs had even greater cultural significance—and articulated an even more explicit cultural sensitivity—than Hurston's work, however. For as Murray also observes, unlike Hurston whose experience in Haiti was ultimately fleeting, Dunham's fieldwork was "the beginning of a long association with Haiti and a whole series of initiations."[57] Far exceeding her position as scientific observer of Vodou rites, Dunham became permanently entrenched in Haitian cultural life, later achieving the rank of mambo (priestess) in the religion and purchasing Habitation Leclerc—the former home of Napoleon's sister Pauline Bonaparte Leclerc—as a second home in the late 1940s. Unlike her colonial predecessor, Dunham sought to use the site for public good by setting up a medical facility and attempting to establish a school there. A lifelong campaigner for Haitian rights, in 1992 the then eighty-two-year-old embarked on a forty-seven-day hunger strike to protest the injustices of the U.S.'s forced repatriation of Haitian refugees who were fleeing the military coup that overthrew President Jean-Bertrand Aristide. Lamothe asserts that, "Hurston seemed unable or unwilling to get close to any individuals other than the urban elite and American expatriates that she relied on as her informants."[58] In stark contrast, Dunham enjoyed close friendships throughout postoccupation Haiti's lower-class community, demonstrating a deliberate social flexibility that she emphasizes in *Island Possessed.*

Early in the text, Dunham describes an almost effortless cultural integration into Haiti. As an American scientist but also as a light-skinned Black woman, she discovers that her social standing is adaptable and finds herself at times treated as an outsider and at other times as an insider, despite Haiti's many racial divisions. Reflecting on her fluctuating status, she writes: "Of my kind I was a first—a lone young woman easy to place in the clean-cut American dichotomy of color, harder to place in the complexity of Caribbean color classifications; a mulatto when occasion called for, an in-between, or 'griffon' actually, I suppose; most of the time an unplacable, which I prefer to think of as 'noir'—not exactly the color black, but the quality of belonging with or being at ease with black people when in the hills or plains or anywhere and scrambling through daily life along with them" (4). By situating her identity as ambiguous, Dunham here destabilizes racial and cultural categories by contrasting Haiti's system of racial classification with the United States' polarized conceptualizations of "Blackness" and "whiteness." In so doing, she reveals a flexibility of identity on the island—which she hints would be impossible in the United States—that enables her to occupy several social positions at once and not only to observe but also to immerse herself in various different social groups and keep meanings and subject positions circulating.

This observation is not intended to overlook Haiti's complex caste system, in which a person's social standing was determined largely by skin tone and whose discriminatory effects Dunham delineates in detail in chapter one of *Island Possessed.* Instead, it is to suggest that Dunham's illumination of an alternative perception of racial difference from that practiced in the United States—as well as her inability to fit comfortably within it—highlights the subjective and arbitrary nature of racial categorization. In *Island Possessed,* Dunham is highly conscious of the limits of her powers as a scientific observer, as she engages self-reflexively with her narrative authority to contest cultural hierarchies. By exploring firsthand a range of roles, Dunham indicates an awareness of the fluidity of identities, a slipperiness of social positioning that, like Baker, she would later explore physically through dance.

Draft manuscripts of *Island Possessed* spell out the complex relationship between the text's scientific themes and its self-reflexive focus on shifting constructions of identity. A very early synopsis of chapter three dating back to July 1963 lists as intended topics "Analysis of Vaudun and its importance in the life of the Haitian peasant; influence in life of entire island," but also "Self examination; how much was in the spirit of scientific investigation."[59] These notes reveal that as early as her first draft, Dunham planned for her text to function as a scientific work but also as a personal account of her Haitian experiences. In the 1950s, art critic Bernard Berenson encouraged Dunham to write for publication. Psychologist Erich Fromm had previously suggested that she consult biographical and autobiographical writings as a cure for depression. Dunham began writing as catharsis and used the written form as a means of dealing with personal trauma, which included her firsthand experiences of racism, a troubled relationship with her father, and the institutionalization and early death of her brother. In an early draft of *Island Possessed*, Dunham recalled that the themes of *A Touch of Innocence* were so personal that when she wrote it, "it had to be after the deaths of each immediate member of my family."[60] Likening her Vodou experiences to the confessional nature of this memoir, Dunham referred to her initiation as "an experience which I had never intended to write about . . . [but] I cannot wait for Haiti to die because Haiti will never die."[61] Dunham's unwillingness to write about Vodou underscores the secretive nature of its rituals and the sacred trust that enabled her to experience them at the same time that it highlights her emotional investment in them. By writing about her initiation, Dunham emphasizes intersections between the private and public in her work, challenging self-other binaries by creating a written confession of an encounter that had a profound psychological effect on her life and indeed her career.

Dunham interrogates her anthropological authority from the very beginning of *Island Possessed*. Describing her arrival on the island in the opening paragraph, she writes, "It was with letters from Melville Herskovits, head of the Department of Anthropology at Northwestern University, that I invaded the Caribbean—Haiti, Jamaica, Martinique, Trinidad . . . then Haiti again for the final stand for the real study" (3). This statement establishes Dunham first and foremost as a scientist, whose reputation has been authenticated by close association with a preeminent white male authority figure. Dunham is recalling her rigorous training to draw attention to the fact that she was sent to Haiti to conduct dispassionate research, not to get to know its people. Dunham's choice of terminology insinuates a self-reflexive querying of her position as scientist, however. By choosing to suggest that she has "invaded" the Caribbean, Dunham engages with Haiti's troubled history as a former slave colony, also hinting at the United States' recent controversial occupation of the island, which she later criticizes for having "very little consideration for the customs, desires, and habits of the people themselves, and with no wish, until the harm was done, to find out what the national character was like" (24). By positioning herself as an invader, too, she queries the authority of her trip and the moral sanctity of her research. By comparing her anthropological work to an invasion, Dunham blurs the boundaries between scientific intervention and territorial expansion and conquest. She hints at the role that the rationale of "science" has historically played in defining and consequently in controlling colonial subjects. Dunham's insights represent the reflections of an older woman who has enjoyed a close and enduring relationship with Vodou, and she reveals a sense of ambivalence regarding her position as scientist that highlights the problematics of her place in a school of European American intellectualism, which had made her trip possible but which also inculcated blindness to lived human experience.

Dunham reconceptualizes the ethnographer as an uncertain translator of a culture whose complexities and contradictions are beyond her capacity to categorize, thereby destabilizing the narrative authority of anthropological inquiry by pointing to its inherently subjective qualities. For example, one of her earliest experiences was seeing a dead bocor move into the spirit world, which strained her powers of articulation. She allows that she has "tried to write up a coherent form of experience of the bocor's spirit transference, but until now it has remained elusive, something which comes back to me over and over but which isn't clear in detail" (40). When reflecting on the Haitian people's treatment of Estimé following his removal from power, she expresses concern about the island's collective mentality. She writes, "I knew how Estimé had been loved, was still loved, and the fact that his life would be in danger even outside the country turned all the years that I had known Haiti into a mockery. I had dreamed of, written about, acquired property in, spread the good word far and wide about *a country of which I really know nothing* [emphasis added]" (53). In such passages, Dunham fundamentally interrogates her outsider's view of Haitian lives. In rejecting the traditional authorial certainty of the ethnographer, she hints at the limitations of anthropological inquiry, which through scientific categorization risks failing to understand its subjects. This ambiguity is explored in detail in her complex relationship with Vodou, in which she finds herself on a "fringe border of belief and nonbelief" (105), an irreconcilable duality in which Dunham is both a skeptical observer and, by choosing to participate in a *lavé-tête* rite, an active and willing participant.

During her *lavé-tête*, Dunham once again acts out a form of participant observation based on physical engagement in a collective experience. Her study is enacted through shared corporal expression, as subjective physical sensation becomes a site of interpretation. Dunham emphasizes her physical and emotional state throughout the three-day ceremony. She describes an "aching from head to foot" as she lies on the "damp floor" (68); later, she expresses a sense of "revulsion" and of feeling "a little faint" (111) as she prepares for a ceremonial marriage to the Vodou snake spirit Damballa. These striking descriptions of her initiation heighten the intensity of the experience and also underscore its psychological impact. Working to destabilize scientific frameworks, Dunham relocates the subject of her observation from the cultural practice to the anthropologist's own body, thereby facilitating a shift from omniscient observation to autobiographical encounter.

Through the *lavé-tête*, Dunham therefore experiences a transition from detached scientific observation to active, indeed intense, membership of a collective, engaging with Haitian cultural experience through shared bodily immersion in religious ritual. Observing her fellow initiates, she writes, "I was beginning to feel at home with them, to sense the tie of kinship that must hold together secret societies the world over" (79). Moreover, it is through physical interaction that she achieves communal acceptance and cultural inclusion as a dance ceremony is the ritual climax of her indoctrination into Vodou. Dance is the subject that Dunham arrived in Haiti to study and it serves a ritual purpose in Vodou ceremonies, most notably by summoning up the loa (spirits), who serve as intermediaries between the worshippers and their god. During the dance ritual, she confesses that she finds herself in "harmony with self and others," concluding that "Now I was 'out and above and beyond myself,' dancing" (131).

At the height of the experience, Dunham feels "weightless, like Nietzsche's dancer, but unlike that dancer, weighted; transparent but solid, belonging to myself but a part of everyone else" (136). The frankness of Dunham's encounter here underscores *Island Possessed*'s significance as a firsthand literary record of the Caribbean origins of her dance practice. Kimerer L. LaMothe argues that, "Nietzsche uses 'dance' to represent a relationship to the body that revalues what he perceives as Christian hostility to bodily life" and suggests that dancers such as Isadora Duncan and Martha Graham borrowed Nietzsche's ideas to create performances of self-affirmation.[62] But

LaMothe's reading does not include Dunham's contribution in this regard or consider the strikingly similar purposes of practices developed by Black vaudeville dancers such as Baker. By engaging in a Vodou ritual, Dunham, like Duncan and Graham but also echoing Baker's eccentric performance strategies and a wider history of Black artistry that would have a profound influence on early-twentieth-century social conventions, explores dance to reconfigure standard Christian mores that physically restrict human behavior. Moreover, in Dunham's case, as in a great deal of African diasporic performance traditions, dance functions not only as a form of self-affirmation, but also to reclaim communal identity and draw attention to traditionally disregarded cultures.

Dunham's acceptance into Vodou was driven by her hosts' belief that her ancestry connected her to them, and it is possible to infer that the intimacy of her experience was facilitated by her perceived racial identity. Dunham notes the special attention that she received as a descendent of "Nan Guinée" (Africa) whose heritage had been lost but which could be regained through ritual contact with the ancestors via Vodou. She writes, "That I would come into their midst, able to worship these gods in dance, and knowing, if fragmentarily, the essences of the religion which had meant for them spiritual and, in periods of their history, physical survival . . . seemed to be of utmost importance to the cult itself—as it was important that I carry the meaning of the true vaudun to my people in that other country" (106–7). Dunham's immersion in Vodou was therefore at least partly made possible by her hosts' understanding that she would communicate its spiritual and cultural significance to African Americans.

Haitian dance rituals have historically functioned as physical expressions of psychological survival and as interpretative responses to the suffering brought about by enslavement. In her assessment of Vodou's social function, Colin (formerly Joan) Dayan reads the religion as a response to slavery's horrors rather than as an expression of African survivals. She suggests that: "For the 'possessed,' that dance is not a loss of identity but rather the surest way back to the self, to an identity lost, submerged, and denigrated. In the horrors of the New World, the ability to know the god in oneself meant survival, which is nothing other than the ability to keep *expressing* the self, and acceding, if only temporarily, to a form of power that defies compromise."[63] Dunham's physical engagement with Vodou enabled her to attain a remarkable degree of incorporation into her hosts' community, in turn providing her with a heightened understanding of a religious practice built on reestablishing communal ties and individual self-worth following the traumas of enforced separation and physical degradation. Through embodied communication in religious ritual, Dunham experiences a pioneering relationship with her anthropological subjects that breaks down traditional scientific hierarchies, as the observer must at least in part give in to the authority of her hosts and sublimate the gaze to the physical participation in dance ritual. Vodou ceremonies demand that their members submit to the loa, which imbues participants with an enhanced sense of community inclusion by providing an active and important role for the individual within the group.

At the climax of her initiation, Dunham takes part in what she describes as the "signature dance" of Vodou (135), the Yanvalou, an ecstatic movement dedicated to the serpentine loa Damballa in which the torso undulates like a snake and which leaves its practitioners in a "state of complete submission and receptivity" (ibid.). Under its "hypnosis," Dunham is drawn into such close physical contact with her fellow participants that her knees "pressed against the knees of someone else without even realizing the closeness" (ibid.). By abandoning scientific observation in favor of embodied participation, Dunham experiences intimate contact with her hosts, which enables her to experience cultural practices on a shared physical level. This egalitarian process of cross-cultural exchange based on shared bodily experience would later form the basis for Dunham's stage choreography, which collapsed perceived dance hierarchies to express the artistic and cultural significance of African diasporic dance forms. *Island Possessed* thus serves as an important literary account of Dunham's intellectual development and debt to Caribbean artistry.

Dunham used what she learned in Haiti and Jamaica to develop a dance technique that sought to resist crude distortions of Caribbean cultures by aestheticizing these practices and reading them as sites of continual re-creation and exchange. Dunham's initial efforts at bringing Haitian dance rituals before the nation's elites propagated enthusiasm for these forms around the world. Michael Largey asserts, "While Dunham herself was not initially involved with Haitian tourism, her efforts to bring the *yanvalou*, *kongo* and *mayi* dances to Haitian stages had the indirect effect of cultivating a taste for Haitian dance among Haitian and foreign audiences."[64] Kate Ramsey goes further, claiming that Dunham's public staging of Haitian folkloric dances both on and off the island served as the catalyst for the state's embrace of such forms as vehicles of Haitian cultural nationalism.[65] Dunham's research trip also inspired her to introduce Caribbean dance forms onto the concert stage as she positioned her performances as the products of her anthropological research.

Throughout her thirty-year international performing career, Dunham underscored the artistry of African diasporic dance forms by presenting them on the stage and screen. She challenged cultural hierarchies by combining Caribbean and South American rituals with European and Euro-American dance practices. She developed a distinctive style known as Dunham Technique, a complex blend of African and Caribbean movement patterns (flexible torso and spine, articulated pelvis and isolation of the limbs and polyrhythmic movement) integrated with ballet and U.S. modern dance forms. Dunham Technique adapted dance rituals that Dunham experienced in Haiti, such as Yanvalou and Zépaules, as training exercises, and one of her most famous performances was *Shango*, a staged translation of a Vodou ritual that formed part of her critically and commercially acclaimed four-year tour of postwar Europe. The artistic consequences of Dunham's Vodou-inspired choreography were widely felt both in Europe and in North America. For example, Robert Farris Thompson has examined the religious origins of the 1950s Mambo dance craze and suggests that one particular Mambo movement, a sudden action termed "the head," was borrowed directly from Dunham's ritual-inspired choreography.[66]

As with Baker, Dunham's career served as an important platform for an antiracist philosophy in which education was a direct means of achieving equal rights. During the years that Dunham drafted *Island Possessed* in the 1960s, she established an arts training program for young people in East St. Louis. As Joanna Dee Das records, her act turned one of the United States' most deprived cities into an "important hub" of the Black Arts Movement.[67] She was also employed as the U.S. representative to the First World Festival of Negro Arts in Senegal in 1966, an event that, like the Black Arts Movement, aimed to celebrate Black people's cultural achievements, and was asked to help develop the National Ballet of Senegal. The festival took place over twenty-six days and featured thirty nations and a wide range of leading Black thinkers and artists including Baker, Duke Ellington, Langston Hughes, and Wole Soyinka. As a key symbolic event in celebrating and developing a Pan-African artistic consciousness, as Penny Von Eschen maintains, "For many black American artists, the festival was more than simply a counterpart to African American art. Animated by the ideas of *Négritude* advocated by Senegal's poet-president Léopold Senghor, the festival was a celebration of the formal and spiritual connections between African and Afro-diasporic art forms, reflecting both the African inspirations and international resonances of developments in black American culture."[68] Although Dunham's cultural ambitions for Senegal were out of touch with contemporary West African concerns and ultimately unrealized, *Island Possessed* therefore should be read as a text that locates her firmly within the international context of the Black Arts Movement.[69]

In her speech before the First World Festival of Negro Arts, Dunham called for urgent attention to the cultural meanings of artistic expression, declaring that, "because of the complex surrounding it, dance becomes more than any other art form the expression of the life of a people."[70] Dunham used the performing arts as a means of achieving social amelioration. She believed that providing dance education to impoverished Black communities such as those in East St. Louis would teach young people the value of their artistic and cultural heritages, in turn providing them with a sense of confidence and self-respect that would help to lift them out of poverty. As Sara E. Johnson argues, "Dunham was thus an integral figure of the Black Arts Movement of the 1960s and 1970s, using cultural production as a way of linking local struggles to international ones."[71] Correspondingly, she sought to apply the Black Arts Movement's international cultural endeavors to local communities to create a dynamic process of intercultural education through the arts.

As well as being a key player in the festival and key contributor to the Black Arts Movement, Dunham should also be recognized as an instigator of the African cultural revolution that made the festival possible. In a study that seeks to expand the Black Arts Movement's traditional configuration as male, literary, and racially separatist, Julia Foulkes stresses that Dunham and fellow Black dancer-anthropologist Pearl Primus, who conducted fieldwork in West and Central Africa in the late 1940s, in fact preempted the movement by fostering cultural links with the continent.[72] During a 1965 audience with President Senghor in Senegal, Dunham was told that her touring dance performances in the late 1940s and early 1950s had inspired chiefs-of-state in sub-Saharan Africa to develop their own culturally celebratory artistic projects.[73] Biographer Ruth Beckford points out that, "In Senegal in 1966 she realized that she had aided in spearheading Africa's cultural revolution. Furthermore, she felt that she belonged to the African intellectual complex and wanted to understand and develop with the African country."[74]

According to leading Jamaican scholar and theater producer Rex Nettleford, when he first met Dunham in 1960 she was considering relocating her company to Jamaica to escape the racism they endured in the United States.[75] Around this period, Dunham attempted to establish a dance school at Habitation Leclerc, but political and economic circumstances combined with her limited time and resources prevented her from doing so.[76] Dunham then tried to transfer her vision in Jamaica, where she encountered resentment from local artists who felt threatened by her fame. In the 1980s, she again sought to create an institute for intercultural communication in Haiti. Dunham's plans were never realized, which hints at her ultimately tenuous social position as a U.S. citizen in the Caribbean. Yet her philosophy of intercultural exchange did have a significant indirect impact on the Caribbean's artistic identity. For example, Nettleford recalled how the "sheer excitement" of the Dunham company's performance in Jamaica in 1950 "pushed" future Martha Graham and Alvin Ailey dancer Clive Thompson to pursue a dance career.[77] It also convinced Nettleford, then a schoolboy, of the value of his burgeoning theater work, and that "the likes of us had something to say for ourselves in our music and our dance."[78] In a 2006 interview, he remembered being drawn by Dunham to the artistic and cultural values of Jamaican dance forms, as "It was Dunham who convinced me that there is something classic in the way we dance."[79] In 1963, Nettleford founded the National Dance Theatre Company of Jamaica, which like Dunham Technique worked to combine Jamaican cultural practices with European forms. As Vice-Chancellor of the University of West Indies, he ensured that Dunham's cultural philosophy was included in its teachings.

Dunham also fostered the international career of Haitian dancer Jean Léon Destiné, a leading exponent of the island's dance in the United States who was responsible for establishing a government-sponsored National Folklore Troupe in Haiti. Destiné befriended leading Black intellectuals such as Paul Robeson and Langston Hughes and worked on Hughes's and African American composer William Grant Still's Haiti-set opera *Troubled Island*, which was staged by the New York City Opera in 1949. Polyné asserts that, "The dancer's widespread popularity enabled him to entertain and educate U.S. audiences about Haitian folkloric dance . . . and also helped him continue to establish relationships with U.S. African American intellectuals and artists."[80] In 1953, another Dunham dancer, Lavinia Williams (sometimes referred to as Lavinia Williams Yarborough), founded the Haitian Institute of Folklore and Classic Dance and served as director of the island's Théâtre de Verdure, where she developed dance forms that were based on Vodou rituals. Williams also established national schools of dance in several Caribbean countries, was a faculty member at New York University, and helped to set up the National School of Dance of Haiti and the Ballet National d'Haiti. As Lynne Fauley Emery notes, "The contribution of Lavinia Williams Yarborough to Black concert dance is twofold: first, she has preserved the authentic folk forms of the West Indies; and second, she has prepared dancers, many of whom eventually perform on the stages of American theaters."[81]

Dunham shaped Destiné and Williams's careers and the roots of their achievements can be found in her work. Destiné spent two years with Dunham on her Broadway and international touring production *Bal Negre* (1946) before forming his own company. Noting that Williams's experience in Dunham's company "profoundly influenced her understanding of dance and the ethnology of dance in countries with people of African descent," Polyné argues that she developed a choreographic approach that emphasized the "form and function" of community dance practices to foster social cohesion and artistic appreciation of Caribbean cultures.[82] This method was remarkably similar to Dunham's internationalist and socially inclusive approach to dance, which sought to celebrate Caribbean performance cultures and facilitate intercultural exchange by pointing up the artistic and psychological significances of the islands' dance practices.

One final Dunham protégée who would make a substantial contribution to revaluing Caribbean dance rituals was avant-garde filmmaker and anthropologist Maya Deren. Deren worked as Dunham's personal secretary in the early 1940s and visited Haiti three times between 1947 and 1954 to document Vodou. Her anthropological account of Haitian life, *Divine Horseman: Living Gods of Haiti* (1953), remains a leading scholarly text on Vodou—Dunham herself described it as "one of the classics of Haitian folk and religious customs"—and the album and unfinished film that Deren made to accompany her book are important oral and visual records of its ritual practices.[83] Deren's engagement with Vodou formed the basis of a combined exploration of dance and cinema that downgraded the traditionally privileged human subject in favor of the wider significance of the filmic "ritual." As she explained in *An Anagram of Ideas on Art, Form and Film* (1946), "The ritualistic form treats the human being not as the source of the dramatic action but as a somewhat depersonalized element in a dramatic whole. The intent of such depersonalization is not the destruction of the individual; on the contrary, it enlarges him beyond the personal dimension and frees him from the specializations and confines of personality. He becomes part of a dynamic whole that, like all such creative relationships, in turn, endow its parts with a measure of its larger meaning."[84] In Vodou, Deren discovered a platform by which to further Dunham's efforts to highlight the arbitrary nature of social and cultural hierarchies. Like Dunham, she explored the fluidity of identities through communal interaction and exchange.

In the midst of writing *Island Possessed*, and at the height of the Black Arts Movement, Dunham outlined her plans for a dance academy on Gorée. She conceived of the project as a way to reappraise African dance forms by drawing international attention to the social and artistic lives of their practitioners, declaring that, "The arts, visual and performing, are, because of their freedom from language barriers among the most effective agents of contact, communication and persuasion."[85] *Journey to Accompong* and *Island Possessed* therefore shed light on Dunham's lifelong project to legitimize the Caribbean internationally by incorporating its ritual dance forms onto the concert stage. They are valuable articulations of Dunham's artistic philosophy, in which she used her anthropological knowledge of dance to enhance understandings of the complexities of Black Atlantic cultures. As ethnographic memoirs, they are deeply entrenched in problematizing scientific representations of Caribbean lives. In both texts, Dunham communicates a deeply ambivalent, disconcerting narrative voice that confronts its own uncertainties. By reconfiguring her role from a detached observer to that of an active participant who literally embodies the cultural rites of her hosts, Dunham blurs the boundaries between self and Other.

As with Baker's writings, Dunham's ethnographic texts uncover the intellectual and autobiographical underpinnings of multifaceted stage presentations that sought to rupture derogatory perceptions of Black women's bodies. The writings are frank, if complex, portrayals of the origins of their dance and show that both women engaged self-reflexively with the roles that white male mentors and managers expected of them. The very personal experiences that such texts describe highlight their significance as Black women's life narratives and provide insights into the emergence and development of the dancers' humanist philosophies. Yet, as we will now see, Baker and Dunham's performances were forced to navigate contradictory and frequently ambivalent racial imaginaries, as well as European and Euro-American production frameworks that sought to capitalize on the perceived eroticism and exoticism of their art. As rare records of their dance practices, their films shed light on such performances and demonstrate that they were sites in which mediation and transgression coexisted and in which racial ideologies were both reinforced and undermined.

CHAPTER THREE

Performing within Primitivism

Baker on the French Silent Screen

Just over a year after arriving in Paris, Baker appeared in her first motion pictures, the silent short *La Folie du jour* (The Day's Madness) and the feature-length *La Revue des revues* (Parisian Pleasures) (both 1927). Both films included color footage of the star in her first two shows at the Folies-Bergère music hall. Baker believed that a career in cinema would enable her to diversify her public persona. Instead, she found her formative experiences on celluloid to be physically arduous and creatively straitening. In *Josephine*, she described her early film work as "less fun than I'd anticipated. It involved doing exactly what I'd done for the past two years: getting into an egg decorated with marabou feathers, stepping out again, dancing with my bananas."[1] In *Voyages et aventures de Joséphine Baker*, she recalled being blinded by the heavy lighting used in early filmmaking: "The cinema is so dazzling . . . Eyelashes and eyebrows sizzle . . . I could not see anything. I was in the middle of a fire, all ablaze under the relentless spotlight beam."[2] Baker was tormented still further by the incessant demands of the filmmakers, who "spoke, commanded, shouted."[3] She likened her first experiences of cinema to being "trapped in a magic circle," and she claimed to have been left suffering for "days and days" by the experience.[4]

These memories highlight cinema's constraining effects on Baker. The brief surviving footage from *La Folie du jour* socially distances the artist from her audience by situating her as an exotic curiosity. Baker emerges from jungle undergrowth clad only in a bra and skirt of bananas and dances suggestively before a European colonizer. By reducing her art to a brief and erotic performance, the sequence reinscribes racialized hierarchies of difference that Baker and Dunham's writings sought to contest. However, within this demeaning framework Baker both mocks her representation and evidences the African diasporic artistry that underpinned her work. She announces her arrival by placing her thumbs on either side of her temple and flapping her hands at her would-be-colonizer in a popular variant of "thumbing the nose," a gesture intended to signify disrespect. She slides gawkily across the stage, landing in a forward split, before rising to her feet and gyrating her pelvis. Her phallic-shaped skirt and male stage audience signal the sexual innuendo implicit in such an action. Yet as Dunham's writings have shown, hip-centered movement was central to Black Atlantic dance practices and frequently had spiritual significations. Baker also complicates erotic readings of her performance through an anarchic execution of such a gesture, which includes varying the speed and rotation of her movements while at the same time spinning in a circle, and which ends with the star flashing her bottom at the colonizer.

After these early cinematic experiences, Baker secured a starring role in *La Sirène des tropiques* (Siren of the Tropics) (1927), a film designed especially for her. She also featured in *Le Pompier des Folies-Bergère* (The Fireman of the Folies-Bergère) (1928), a single-reel advertisement for *Un vent de folie* (A Gust of Madness) (1927), her second show at Paris's most famous music hall. *Pompier*'s threadbare narrative, which centers on the erotic hallucinations of a drunken fireman, serves to promote the venue's naked feminine displays. Baker is the only woman who keeps her bra on in this cinematic peep show, in which actresses are filmed first with clothes and then without and firemen transform into naked women. The measure of modesty and physical agency that Baker enjoys in an otherwise sexually explicit film should not discount her sensual appeal, but it shows how she retained her individuality in opposition to the music hall's display of passive femininity, a creative contrast that would recur throughout her cinema career.[5] While the film's naked women mostly perform coordinated movements, Baker delivers an improvisatory dance that combines miming and comical facial expressions with a brief Shimmy and fast-paced Charleston. Baker's allusion to a rich history of Black artistry complicates tendencies to read the dancer as an embodiment of European primitivist fantasies. Equally, the location of her performance—inside a Paris Metro tunnel and before a gigantic advertisement for the new medium of radio—situates her at the vanguard of interwar French culture.

These sequences show how French cinema distorted Baker's talents but still provided limited space for independent artistry. As would equally be the case with Dunham's screen performances, Baker's silent films are a visual legacy of a corporeal dialogue rooted in African diasporic dance and serve as vital correctives to the racist misperceptions of interwar European reviewers. This chapter examines Baker's two feature-length silent films, *Revue* and *Sirène*. I show how their staging of Baker's dancing body plays into early-twentieth-century colonial and primitivist fantasies but simultaneously allows the star to showcase a self-referential performance style whose origins lay in Black vaudeville. These two films provide vital insights into the psychological, intellectual, and cross-cultural underpinnings of a public identity that engaged pragmatically with primitivism—as Baker's memoirs have elucidated—and whose effects appealed to Black as well as white audiences. I also juxtapose Baker's work with the regimented routines of white chorus girls and trace her film stardom's impact on contemporary African American audiences. What is particularly significant about Baker's performances in these films is that they occur in silent cinematic contexts. As this chapter delineates, silent films' reliance on physical expression and dance in particular provides Baker with space in which to cultivate a witty, highly individual performative persona. As we will also see with Baker's sound films and Dunham's cinematic roles, the narratives privilege white femininity but they also enable Baker to construct a self-image rooted in African diasporic artistry. As with Dunham's work, the coexistence of competing significations in Baker's films underscores the fundamental ambiguity of her performances, which allow for readings of both subjugation and contestation.

Baker was the first Black actress to enjoy a leading role in a major motion picture when she appeared in *Sirène* and her early films are rare moving documents of her dance style.[6] However, her silent performances have garnered little attention. Perhaps because she appeared only in French productions, Baker's pioneering achievements on celluloid continue to be overlooked in African American cinema histories. *Hallelujah!* (1929) performer Nina Mae McKinney is frequently cited as the first Black actress to star in a mainstream motion picture, but she did not appear onscreen until nearly two years after *Sirène* was released.[7] No critical space has been afforded to *Revue*, while in-depth studies of *Sirène*, a production that was screened widely in African American cinemas, are limited to Phil Powrie's comparison of Baker and the film's male lead's acting styles and Ylva Habel's article-length investigation of its impact on Swedish—and therefore European—audiences.[8] Terri Francis has sought to call attention to the significance of Baker's artistry onscreen.[9] However, a detailed analysis of her filmed dance scenes has yet to be undertaken. Thus, almost no consideration has been given to the visual significances of performances that shed vital light on Baker's artistry and early-twentieth-century Black dance more generally, her pioneering place in African American screen history, and her engagement with an interwar European imaginary. This section of my study seeks to redress these critical imbalances, showing how Baker's silent film performances intervened in contemporary racial ideologies, and how African American audiences in particular responded to *Sirène*.

Sirene's marginal place in film history speaks to a wider gap in our understanding of early screen authorship. Substantial work has been done to recover performers' authorial contributions to silent cinema. However, most of this work has centered on Hollywood productions and little attention has been given to dance as a form of silent screen authorship.[10] Yet silent cinema and social dance both entered the cultural mainstream in the first decades of the twentieth century and shared a concern with the body in movement, with early filmmakers turning frequently to dance for its expressive qualities. This chapter makes the case that Baker's dance performances in *Revue* and *Sirène* were in fact key sites of cinematic authorship. In these sequences, the camera defers to her artistry to the extent that she is able to transfer her stage persona to the screen and trouble the films' demeaning narratives. Given that the Black Atlantic origins of early-twentieth-century dance trends were obscured, and Black women were afforded few opportunities on the silent screen, the scenes are additionally significant for granting meaningful cinematic space to a Black woman dancer.

Revue is a feature-length production shot in Pathécolor, an early color process, and set in the 1920s Paris music hall. Much of the film is a visual document of *Un vent de folie*. It is thought to be Baker's second screen role after *La Folie du jour*, which film journal *Cinéa-ciné pour tous* praised for showcasing her "plastic play," correctly speculating that she would soon star in a major feature.[11] Apart from the banana dance fragments described above, little remains of *Folie*. However, *Revue* was made by the same director and production team and expands its vision, adopting the same color and long-shot framing techniques to emphasize the music hall's elaborate tableaux. The film bridges the gap between Baker's stage career and her later cinematic representations via its theatrical framing style and limited camera positions and provides a vital starting point for conceptualizing her public persona when she first arrived in Paris. The stage version of *Un vent* was notable for its cinematic experimentations: it incorporated an oversized projection of Baker dancing the Black Bottom as she performed the same routine on stage with the apparent purpose of satisfying voyeuristic fantasies of her dancing body.

Revue is also a cinematic showcase of performances at the Grand Palais des Champs-Elysées, the Moulin Rouge, and the Folies-Bergère, three of Paris's grandest music halls, during *les années folles* (the crazy years) of the 1920s. Alan Lareau calls it an "unmatched document of the art of the revue" on the eve of its eclipse by cinema.[12] The Art Deco stage sets and costumes designed by Erté and George Barbier create a lavish theatrical display, and the color footage showcases the extravagant visual spectacles for which the Folies-Bergère was renowned. Mae G. Henderson identifies the music hall as a site in which early-twentieth-century Parisians "typically confronted the Other in performance" to underscore links between pseudo-ethnographic fascination and popular entertainment, and many of the tableaux mimic non-European cultures.[13] They include an Arabian Harem, a South American "Les Cafés" sequence featuring pale-skinned women dancers but which purports to represent all the "cafés" of the world, and an Egyptian temple. The production therefore visualizes themes of exoticism and colonialism that Black artists such as Baker and Dunham were forced to negotiate and shows how heavily Baker's early French stage and screen career was implicated in such tropes.

Baker is not *Revue*'s lead but merely a prominent stage performer. The chief focus is Gabrielle Dérisau (Hélène Hallier), an out-of-work seamstress who finds fame on the Parisian stage and becomes "Gaby Derys" in a cinematic tribute to early-twentieth-century music hall star Gaby Deslys. However, the plot is fleeting, serving mainly to link the music hall sequences, and the second half of the film is devoted to documenting *Un vent*. Baker's two performances, "Plantation avec Joséphine Baker et The Thompson Jazz Orchestra" (Plantation with Josephine Baker and the Thompson Jazz Orchestra) and "La Même en 1927" (The Same Setting in 1927), are among the only tangible records of her early dance career. They offer a close approximation of the persona that she adopted at this point and provide vital insights into her dance style. In these short sequences, traces of African American vernacular dance practices, including Pecking, the Itch, the Shimmy, and the Charleston, which are themselves traceable to Caribbean and even African dance forms, can be unearthed. *Revue* also establishes thematic and stylistic trends pivotal to Baker's subsequent screen roles. It sets the structural groundwork for the poverty to success narratives that are central to Baker's memoirs and her later films, *Sirène*, *Zouzou*, and *Princesse Tam-Tam*. The musical scenes also feature showgirls and chorus lines. Formation dancing by pale-skinned chorines frequently preceded Baker's onscreen dance scenes, establishing her body in kinetic contrast, and this film implies that such a trope originated in her early Parisian shows. As we will see, Dunham's dancing body would also be subsumed by or set in contrast to white femininity on screen, which underscores the race-centered cinematic exclusions that Black women have historically been forced to endure on both sides of the Atlantic.

The first six Folies-Bergère tableaux pay homage to the Christian calendar and take place beneath a giant clock. Baker is introduced in the next scene, "Plantation avec Josephine Baker," at which point these temporal signifiers disappear. The disappearance of a clearly defined sociohistorical context upon Baker's arrival plays into conceptions of Black cultures as timeless and thus precivilized. By invoking such beliefs about nonwhite societies, the sequence can be read as an appeal to fascinations with racial Otherness and bears striking similarities to ethnographic film recordings, which were popular with European and U.S. audiences in the early twentieth century. Fatimah Tobing Rony links Baker's screen work to ethnographic cinema and therefore to early actuality films, which as Alison Griffiths has shown were concerned less with scientific rigor than with satiating voyeuristic fascinations with non-European cultures and which represented "a way of using the cinematic medium to express ideas about racial and cultural difference."[14] Read in this way, Baker's films can be seen as cultural articulations of early-twentieth-century anthropological observer-subject hierarchies that Dunham's fieldwork technique of physical participation sought to break down. As Griffiths asserts, in early ethnographic films, "the culture under view was segmented, externalized, short-lived, and commodified to maximize legibility and difference and turn a good profit."[15]

Baker's short *Revue* scenes in particular are evocative of films that were structured to reduce human societies to visually thrilling, nonthreatening entertainment and whose effect was to reinforce perceived racial differences. In the Plantation tableau, a full moon and dense undergrowth create the effect of nighttime revelry concealed from white eyes. A world of enslavement and subjugation is consequently reimagined as a scene of physical abandon, an insinuation that is heightened by Baker's seemingly unstructured dance performance. A group of African American musicians, the Thompson Jazz Orchestra comprises a banjo player, drummer, trombonist, trumpeter, and saxophonist. Emerging from the undergrowth and hearing their music, Baker begins a sequence of fluid and athletic dance movements, many of which are identifiable as African American vernacular styles such as tap and the Shimmy. In this way, what is communicated is a spontaneous, pleasure-seeking dance performance, with the audience appearing to have gained privileged access to the "primitive" in its natural state.

Baker's movements were frequently described in zoomorphic terms. Early-twentieth-century music halls such as the Moulin Rouge and the Folies-Bergère took thematic inspiration from venues such as the *Jardin zoologique d'acclimatation*, which exhibited colonial subjects in cages and alongside wild animals. Baker was dehumanized in literature and art partly through descriptions of her as the embodiment of heightened sexuality but also via allusions to her an exotic beast. In his review of *La Revue Nègre* for *Candide*, Pierre de Régnier likened Baker to both a "boxing kangaroo" and a "giraffe," while dance critic André Levinson called attention to her "simian suppleness."[16] Sieglinde Lemke observes that, "The image of Baker as an exotic animal was so prevalent that Paul Colin captured it in one of the paintings in his series *Le Tumulte Noir*."[17] She maintains that, "The fact that Baker is caged [in Colin's painting], and thus inaccessible, increases her allure even as it makes her into something like a wild beast."[18] In this scene, Baker bows her long bare legs and thrusts out her bottom as she scurries playfully onto the stage. Approaching the musicians, she bobs her head in imitation of the pecking motions of a chicken. At the end of the performance, having performed on all fours, she raises herself on stiff legs. Baker's use of the animalism trope played into notions of the primitive self, licensing abandon for European audiences as a perceived remedy against social fears engendered by rapid industrial change.

However, although Baker's work was depicted as primitive, a reading that she played up in her memoirs by constructing her onstage behavior as spontaneous, it in fact built on and mimicked African American vaudeville performances for its own self-assertive purposes, as the Plantation footage demonstrates. In much the same way that Dunham transposed dance movements that she witnessed in the Caribbean to the concert stage, Baker underscored the artistry of African diasporic dance forms by presenting them on the stage and screen. Although such movements were esoteric to European audiences, Baker's manner of adapting them in the Plantation scene reveals a self-reflexive creativity that calls attention to its own artifice and resists readings of impulsivity. Baker's movements refute easy interpretation because they are so experimental. Her performance reconfigures the shapes and spaces of the dancing body. Although it is rooted in African American styles including the Charleston, Baker's dance is disjointed and has no clear choreographic pattern. She dances on the spot, on all fours, and while sat on the floor, as seen in figure 2. The physical parameters of expression are broken down into anarchic mannerisms. Baker's slippery performance challenges racist imaginaries by defamiliarizing European perceptions of Black identities. In so doing, she asserts artistic autonomy within the film's demeaning framework.

Baker is at one stage birdlike and at another appears feline, positioning her animalism as self-conscious artifice and refuting readings of the scene as an "authentic" re-creation of Black life. Baker's allusion to animalism may even be read as an intellectual comment on the African American dances that had recently been popularized by white performers such as Vernon and Irene Castle. Analyzing the Black vernacular performance styles that had crossed over into prewar white, middle-class society, Marshall and Jean Stearns concluded that animal dances were particularly prominent.[19] Animal themes have been traced to African and Caribbean dance practices. In regard to Baker's pecking gesture, it has been noted that Pecking has a rich history,

FIGURE 2. Baker dancing on the floor in *La Revue des revues* (Star Films Edition, 1927).

having "found to be similar to a Yanvallou [*sic*] dance in Trinidad and a Dahomean dance in West Africa."[20] Dunham performed the dance-prayer Yanvalou during her *lavé-tête* and it became a core Dunham Technique training exercise, which illustrates how both women's careers made visible a diasporic history of Black dance. In a still of the Plantation tableau from the original *Un vent* program, Baker is shown with her upper arms drawn to her torso and with bent wrists pointing away from her body.[21] This dance move has striking similarities to the Crow Dance, a Bahamian practice that Zora Neale Hurston researched in Florida and staged and performed in her folk revue *The Great Day* (1932). As Anthea Kraut acknowledges, "Requiring both its lead and supporting performers to simulate a bird and other animals, the Crow Dance exemplified mimicry, one of the primary 'Characteristics of Negro Expression' as Hurston defined them."[22] Baker's adoption of such a movement demonstrates that her Folies-Bergère performances were rooted in Black Atlantic expressive practices despite European perceptions of them as erotic dances.

Baker's idiosyncratic performance with its roots in a rich history of Black Atlantic artistry therefore creates disjuncture with the demeaning cultural framework in which she is situated, challenging exoticizing readings of her art and highlighting her authorial independence from such a performance context. The sequence is a cinematic record of Baker's choreography and by extension movement patterns developed in response to slavery, many of which were related to the cultural practices that Dunham witnessed in the Caribbean, in which dance was frequently imbued with spiritual significance and served as a psychologically vital act of self-affirmation. It serves as cinematic evidence that Baker's dance stagings were informed not by primitivist conceptions of Black identities but instead built on a slavery-derived tradition of Black artistry in which gestural creativity functioned as a necessary means of negotiating crude and occlusive social environments.

As discussed in chapter one, interwar colonial and primitivist ideologies informed Baker's Parisian image. In *La Revue Nègre*, she danced nearly naked alongside the equally scantily dressed Martiniquan dancer Joe Alex in what was read by critic André Levinson as a "*pas de deux* of the savages."[23] Baker's persona was modeled on the sensual native girl Fatou-Gaye, the popular literary fantasy of nineteenth-century French author Pierre Loti. Her performance as a "Fatou-Gaye" type was a reference to the *doudou*, a female Caribbean character of French colonial literature whose unrequited love for her male colonizer constructed the region as hyperfeminine and dependent on imperial authority. As well as satiating fantasies of a sensual female Other, it positioned Caribbean subjects as racially and socially inferior—the *doudou* is rejected by her would-be lover—and masked imperialist abuses by reassuring France of the benevolence of its territorial expansions, for, according to this trope, the colonized is in love with her colonizer. As Brent Hayes Edwards asserts, "Providing the mythical foundation for any number of poems, sentimental novels, and travel narratives, the figure of the *doudou* came to serve as a reservoir of immediately recognizable tropes to inscribe the 'wonderful islands' and to propel readerly desire."[24] Edwards contends that Baker projected a homogenous image of sensual non-European womanhood that played into colonial myths such as *doudouisme*.[25] Such a reading links her to a wide range of pseudo-ethnographic iconography in photographs and advertisements, which, as summarized by Brett A. Berliner, "ripped the *nègre* out of the stream of history and naturalized various fictions of him to stabilize cultural categories that World War I and modernity had undermined."[26]

However, Edwards's claim that Baker was the "locus of a metonymic operation" in which her "writhing limbs and 'sculptural' gestures" became "interchangeable objects of colonial desire" does not correctly account for the ways in which she crafted a dance style rooted in African American vaudeville to intervene in these fictions, as her idiosyncratic Plantation performance evidences.[27] Although she became a living signifier for a range of colonial identities on stage, her persona did not adhere straightforwardly to such constructions, as can be seen by the initially positive responses of Black Americans and African and Caribbean immigrants in Paris to her career. African American newspapers followed her contributions to Parisian style with interest. For example, the *Chicago Defender* noted that shops were using models of Baker to display their latest outfits and that her portrait was featured in the 1928 Paris Salon.[28] Although he acknowledges contrasts between Baker's Parisian reception and the harsh realities experienced by ordinary Black French people, Tyler Stovall maintains that, "Baker's triumphal Parisian debut with the *Revue nègre* in 1925 cemented the idea of France as a land open to Black [American] talent."[29] Baker's fake marriage to her manager Giuseppe "Pepito" Abatino, who impersonated an Italian count to fool the world into thinking that a Black woman from St. Louis had married into European aristocracy, and the five-figure contract that she secured for performing in Budapest, drew particular attention.[30] Baker's actions, both real and perceived, influenced antiimperialists' language and newspapers such as *La Dépêche Africaine* (*The African Dispatch*) celebrated her achievements. Although she shows that Caribbean women would eventually become critical of Baker's emphasis on bodily display in the 1930s, Jennifer Anne Boittin asserts that, "For some colonial men and women, Baker was a symbol of all that Black culture could hope to accomplish for France."[31]

A possible explanation for such responses can be found in the Black dance practices that Baker adopted, and which are recorded on celluloid in her Plantation performance. Martiniquan writer Jane Nardal read the star's onstage exploration of contemporary dance styles as having "shaken up" if ultimately reinvigorated interest in *doudou*-derived narratives.[32] Nardal suggested that, although "she is still clothed in feathers or banana leaves . . . she brings the latest Broadway products (the Charleston, jazz, etc.) to the Parisians."[33] Baker's performances were framed by pseudo-ethnographic costumes and settings that featured ostrich feathers, banana skirts, and live animals, but the dances that she executed were rooted in Black Atlantic creative practices and an African American vaudeville tradition of improvisation. As Baker's memoirs have shown, the improvisational aesthetic of Black vaudeville, which would become a key feature of jazz and tap dance, allowed practitioners to counter puritanical mores and celebrate physical expression, thereby encouraging Black as well as white audiences to recognize Baker's performances as sites of self-affirmation. Baker's reception points to more ambiguous contemporary understandings of her artistry than are often acknowledged: as well as appearing to embody the primitive, she was perceived as part of an "Americanization" of French culture epitomized by the nation's increasing global dominance in cinema, art, and architecture and as articulated by jazz. As Matthew F. Jordan observes, "When they denounced the presence of jazz in France, cultural traditionalists often echoed standard discursive riffs about the dangers of Americanization."[34]

Baker's emphasis on African American-derived dance forms disrupted colonialist tendencies to view Black cultures as ahistorical. She foregrounded jazz styles, which contemporary European audiences acknowledged as cultural responses to rapid industrialization and social change. White Parisians did not necessarily perceive in Baker's work two oppositional cultural forms: primitivism and modernism. As Jody Blake shows, for many contemporary cultural critics, "the *tables rases* of the Dark Continent and of the New World were mutually reinforcing," and there was "no contradiction" between what was perceived as "animal vitality and technological power."[35] Blake affirms that a "cult of America" came to replace Africa in the European consciousness during the 1910s, as its "urban 'jungles' and mechanical 'beasts' appeared to represent a veritable modern barbarism."[36] Yet although both readings situated Baker's work as a threat to French "civilization" and cultural purity, they also acknowledged it as an intrinsically modern artistic expression that was part of an international cultural exchange and which spoke to contemporaneous social concerns.

Baker challenged constraining production frameworks and claimed agency over her screen performances by referencing and reworking Black dance forms. The dancer was given no credit for her dancing in *Un vent.* In the show's program, Madame Komarova was listed as the sole choreographer. However, Baker's work differs in style from the ritualistic movements of "Le Temple Egyptien" (The Egyptian Temple), Komarova's only performance in *Revue* and which immediately follows "La Même en 1927." Komarova's work onscreen bears similarities to Denishawn principles of modern dance, which combined Orientalist fantasies with a system of movement based on the heavy stylizations of the Delsarte system of expression, a performance method that used strong gestures to communicate emotions. Such distinction between practices designates Baker as the author of her own work, and her performance incorporates a great deal of visual humor, including Baker's trademark eye-crossing and riffing on other dance movements. The comedy of Baker's act underscores the idiosyncratic nature of her performances. *Un vent*'s chief difference from *Folie*, apart from its inclusion of film footage, was that its director Louis Lemarchand omitted what he deemed vulgar out-and-out comedy in favor of the Folies-Bergère's most famous spectacle: tableaux of seminude show- and chorus girls. Yet Baker's performance in this scene subtly incorporates physical comedy. Near the end of the dance number, she performs a version of the Itch, a seemingly involuntary comic display in which the hands pass rapidly over the body in a shuddering rhythm as if to catch a source of irritation.

The humor of Baker's performances has garnered surprisingly little attention. In a rare acknowledgment of the comedic nature of Baker's work, Samir Dayal writes, "Especially in her early years, Baker was noticed 'not because of her dancing . . . but because of her irreverent and comic antics on stage.'"[37] However, such a statement creates an illusory separation between Baker's dance and comedy performances. As her memoirs show, her stage technique was based on a comedic approach to dance, which allowed her to retain artistic autonomy within the regimented chorus line. In a review of Broadway show *The Chocolate Dandies* (1924–1925), the first production in which Baker enjoyed a starring and solo role and her final show before leaving for Paris, the *New York Amsterdam News* praised Baker as a "comedienne."[38] The Harlem-based newspaper applauded the performer's "cleverness" and "exceedingly droll" imitation of a Charleston dance number, likening her to the celebrated eccentric dancers Charlotte Greenwood and Pâquerette.[39] The article also pointed up Baker's unusual feat of achieving individual expression within the chorus line, which, it noted, normally only allowed dancing girls to display "personal beauty and grace of movement."[40]

As *Revue* demonstrates, this humorous behavior, which Baker adapted from earlier African American stage traditions, was the basis of her Parisian performance style. The sequence shows Baker dancing on her knees, referencing an earlier action by Manolo Titos in the tableau "Les Golfeurs" (The Golfers), which also features women formation dancers the "Albany Girls." In celebration of modern leisure society, the dancers in this scene are dressed for the outdoors and swing golf clubs. Golf became a popular sport of the emerging middle classes on both sides of the Atlantic during *les années folles* and Titos wears plus fours, a sweater vest, and a tie in a Windsor knot to emphasize his status as a man of leisure. Baker's allusion to the scene asserts her technical superiority as a dancer. She mimics with ease a feat that previously seemed shocking in its dexterity. Her action challenges notions of mindless spontaneity by revealing the visual wit of her performances. Baker ruptures through parody the bourgeois social order depicted in the earlier scene, rendering it absurd. By claiming the male dancer's movements, she also upsets gender roles and affirms her authorship in opposition to the female dancers' regimented display. Baker's willingness to shift gender roles points up disjuncture between her erotic reputation and her onstage performance style. As Baker's memoirs have shown, the dancer professed disregard for her body before arriving in Paris and developed a comedic stage presence to offset a physical identity that producers deemed "too dark" and "ugly" for a chorus girl. As the Plantation sequence evidences, Baker retained these idiosyncratic mannerisms in Paris. Although such performances were structured within a framework of exotic Black womanhood, *Revue* suggests that comedy rather than sexuality was the central feature of her art and that the "primitive" act that French critics supposedly witnessed was really rooted in her work on the African American vaudeville circuit.

Three Spanish-themed sequences and a tango by Hallier follow the Plantation sequence. The film then moves to "Une hostellerie sous Louis XIII" (A Country Inn in the Reign of King Louis XIII) filled with noblemen and ladies. Russian-born dancer Elizaveta "Lila" Nikolska, wearing a "gypsy" skirt and rags and dark makeup, performs a series of rapid spins to physically disrupt the scene's formal ostentatiousness. The setting then jumps forward three centuries to "La Même en 1927" (The Same Setting in 1927), where Baker's dancing body takes over and echoes that of Nikolska. Baker performs before a high-society Parisian café audience and white musicians playing classical instruments join her. Her claiming of a space occupied by a European elite once again breaks down the traditional social order and hints at Paris's transformation into a cosmopolitan city. The sequence links her both to fantasies of a physically liberated bohemian past and to contemporary U.S. urban culture, which exemplifies the concurrent discourses of primitivism and modernism surrounding her image. An "American Bar" can even be seen in the background. Baker is once again the muse of a white artist, yet on this occasion she dictates the terms of her embodiment via a shared creative performance. Her rapid dance movements convey her physical dynamism. Throughout the scene, she gyrates her whole body, including hips, neck, and shoulders, and positions herself at awkward angles. Foreshadowing Dunham's hip-centered method, which she perceived to be a central component of Caribbean dance cultures, Baker emphasizes her pelvis throughout the scene, creating a suggestive conversation with the violinist, as shown in figure 3. On two occasions, she performs the Mess Around, placing her hands on her hips and rotating her bottom flirtatiously in the

FIGURE 3. Baker engaging in flirtatious physical dialogue with a violinist in *La Revue des revues*.

direction of the musicians. Her actions become increasingly anarchic; her dance picks up speed midway through the scene and she engages in a rapid tapping and handclapping session with the musician. Baker's flirtatious dialogue plays into erotic fantasies while simultaneously locating her within a Black Atlantic performance tradition. It provides a striking contrast to the visual segregation that Dunham encountered in Hollywood, which avoided references to interracial relationships on screen.

Baker begins her performance with rapid taps in high heels before gyrating her pelvis in circular movements. Rotating her body downward, she slaps the floor before clapping her hands and smacking her bottom, treating her body as a percussive instrument. Her movements recall Patting Juba, a nineteenth-century African American dance in which body parts would be slapped to create a rhythmic display. Patting Juba was developed as a direct response to U.S. slavery, in which drums were banned to prevent slave revolts. As with the Caribbean dance rituals that Dunham described in *Journey to Accompong* and *Island Possessed*, Baker's performance recalls a tradition of physical self-expression within dehumanizing confines. Baker shakes each leg in the air, a movement that can be read as a variant of the Pigeon Wing, a dance in turn descended from the Ring Shout, a religious ritual performed by enslaved men and women in the United States and the Caribbean. The Ring Shout involved the whole body and incorporated flat-footed shuffles, tapping, clapping, and arm waving. It would reach a secular audience via minstrel shows and is believed to have influenced a wide range of other dances, including the Cakewalk, the Big Apple, and the Charleston.

In their history of jazz dance, Marshall and Jean Stearns identify the Ring Shout as "Perhaps the most clear-cut survival of African dance in the United States."[41] Despite its origins, it developed a particular social meaning under slavery as its movement pattern offered a means of subverting Protestant bans on secular dancing, which was defined as crossing the feet while moving. The dance speaks to a history in which enslaved men and women developed improvisational techniques to signify on and contest physical conventions that policed their movements and to create acts of corporeal expression on their own terms. Baker's performance is therefore important for visualizing onscreen a history of African diasporic artistic expression, as elucidated by Dunham in her anthropological memoirs, in which dance functioned as self-affirmation. In turn, Baker built on this tradition to devise her own challenge to bodily behaviors and social structures.

As well as articulating a history of Black Atlantic dance, Baker's individualistic performance can be read as defiance of the physical restrictions of female chorus lines. Her gestural creativity presents a striking contrast to the subsequent sequence, a synchronized performance by British-based chorus line forerunners the Tiller Girls. In *Josephine*, Baker recalled that Noble Sissle initially rejected her from all-Black Broadway musical *Shuffle Along* (1921) because he wanted his chorus girls to "look like the Tillers," meaning a physically standardized—and implicitly white—version of womanhood.[42] Peter Jelavich considers the Tiller Girls as embodiments of a deindividualization of performance that was itself symptomatic of the dehumanization of the worker in the modern era. He contends that the Tiller Girls and their synchronized kickline subsumed individuality: "the kickline sacrificed bodily wholeness in favor of a dismembered succession of bodily parts . . . they revealed—or perhaps disguised?—an underlying sense of economic and military order that demanded the dissolution of all personality and the dismemberment of the person."[43] Chorus lines created a sanitized and socially unthreatening illusion of womanhood that robbed women of sexual and artistic individuality. As Baker's unruly dialogue with a violinist in *Revue* attests, her art countered such a myth by physically freeing the woman dancer. Her performance places her at odds with the Tiller Girls in ways that highlight fundamental differences in their styles, with Baker appearing to represent abandon and by extension reasserting readings of Black cultures as uncivilized, and the Tiller Girls symbolizing European refinement. But it also presents Baker as an independent woman who challenges the unthreatening passivity that such feminine displays epitomized.

Baker and the chorus girls' contrasting styles should be understood as divergent responses to an earlier history of female performance that found expression in the burlesque genre, which was closely related to the vaudeville tradition from which artists such as Baker emerged. U.S. burlesque developed partly from minstrelsy: burlesque scenes were added to the end of minstrel shows in the 1850s and it initially copied its predecessor's structure when it developed into a separate genre. But burlesque became codified as a feminine practice through the transatlantic careers of European artists such as Lydia Thompson and acts such as *The Black Crook* (1866), whose assertive sexuality challenged the United States' puritanical attitudes to the body. Burlesque brought a deeply disruptive feminine presence to the stage, "a new sense of female sexuality and public presence" as described by Jayna Brown, and which, even as it made woman's sexuality spectacular, upset gender and social roles by constructing a body whose unruliness was "a horribly pretty parody of masculinity" according to Robert C. Allen.[44] It also troubled racial identities as women with both African and European ancestry participated in the genre. Performing nonwhite nationalities interchangeably, such women pointed up the ambiguities of racial identities even as they played into imperialist fantasies, much like Baker's Parisian acts would do in the 1920s. However, as seen in *Revue* and as the discussion of the Ziegfeld Girl in the next chapter will exemplify, such identity displays would soon be overtaken by the racially homogenizing and physically restraining chorus line.

In *Voyages*, Baker asserted, "I do not like all those artists who survive on a single repeated tic. The artist who has only one face, one gesture, a single expression: it is a machine."[45] Baker's statement situates her performances against an early-twentieth-century music hall culture in which women performers were deprived of agency and molded into synchronized dancing bodies. Although her early Parisian performances were structured within a primitivist framework, her scenes in *Revue* show that she deliberately cultivated an improvisational and witty dance style rooted in a history of Black Atlantic and burlesque performance that allowed her to challenge rigid social structures and assert her authorship.

Yet Baker was not always allowed to exercise such creative freedom onscreen. In her summation of *Sirène*, her first starring film role, she concluded that, "If I had to go today, for what I shot, before a cinematography court, I would, no doubt, be found guilty, but also, more importantly, and primarily: irresponsible."[46] Baker felt that the film's directors had sacrificed artistry for financial profit and provided her with no guidance on how to behave onscreen.[47] The film demeaned Baker by playing on issues of race for comic effect and by isolating her character from mainstream French society. She also denounced the "implausibility" and "deception" of a production set in the Caribbean but filmed in the French forest of Fontainebleau.[48] However, *Sirène* is historically significant as the first major motion picture to feature a Black woman as its star. It heralded Baker's first international tour by helping to promote her public persona outside of France, and it generated excitement among African American audiences when it screened in the United States. The film is a thinly veiled homage to Baker's stardom and artistry that conflates the performer with her role, affording her substantial autonomy, at least in her dance scenes. These silent cinematic environments provide Baker with space to articulate an unruly dance style rooted in African diasporic artistry. Most markedly of all, it provides the most complete cinematic record of her trademark dance style, the Charleston. As in *Revue*, Baker's performance scenes in *Sirène* are important documents of her work that articulate the cross-cultural complexities and social unruliness of her artistry and which also privilege Baker as the film's star.

Baker accepted French film roles in the 1920s to enhance her fame but also because she believed that such work would enable her to appear onscreen without participating in Hollywood's racial codes. As we will see, Dunham also turned to European film in her determination to resist Hollywood racist paradigms that severely limited her U.S. screen career. Biographer Lynn Haney asserts that Baker turned down opportunities to act in Hollywood prior to *Sirène*, fearing racial typecasting.[49] Baker's participation in the film implies that she believed that French cinema was not structured according to such codes and that she would be able to individualize her role. According to Sauvage, Pepito and Baker made frequent script suggestions to make the film appear more autobiographical, and producers were compelled to implement some of their ideas, perhaps the first time in history that an African American woman exercised behind-the-scenes authorship over a mainstream film.[50] However, Baker's influence over *Sirène* was ultimately extremely limited. She could not read the script, which she claimed was never translated from French and put together "as and when we were shooting."[51] When she saw the finished film she concluded that it belittled her character's intelligence and hence her artistry. Instead of glamorizing Baker, the production emphasized her physical expressions, crudely, in her opinion, and presented her as an uninhibited child of nature. Humiliated by the experience, she recalled that, "The finished film brought tears to my eyes. Was that ugly, silly person me?"[52] She declared the movie a "total waste of time."[53]

Baker expressed particular frustration with a production that conflated Caribbean dance cultures with her idiosyncratic style. She remembered being instructed that, "It's time for your belly dance," and noted cynically that, "naturally Papitou danced exactly like Mademoiselle Baker of the Folies."[54] Baker's comments underscore the filmmakers' misperceptions of Baker's art and non-European cultures more broadly. In an interview during production, one of the film's directors described the male lead as a "young African settler" even though the film was set in the Caribbean.[55] He also conflated Baker with her exotic role by suggesting that, "it is Josephine Baker who personifies the native girl and it is her triumph that we film today."[56] Yet Baker ultimately was persuaded to perform her *danse sauvage* because Abatino advised her that it would be "one of the reasons people will come to see the film."[57] Such a statement indicates that the film relied on Baker's self-reflexive artistry as one of its chief selling points. My reading of *Sirène* does not intend to overlook its crude representation of Baker. However, I will demonstrate that the production affords her some creative freedom and represents a platform by which interwar African American audiences could celebrate her dancing talents and stardom. Baker remains locked in the film's derogatory framework, but in the dance scenes she transgresses it. As we will see throughout the rest of this study, dance on film represents a self-reflexive critique and can function autonomously within a film's plot, allowing artists such as Baker to shape a production's aesthetics and complicate its identity configurations.

Sirène was directed by *Folie* and *Revue* producer Mario Nalpas and actor-director Henri Étiévant, with future Surrealist filmmaker Luis Buñuel working for a short time as their assistant. The film moves between the fictional Caribbean island of Monte Puebla and Paris and is concerned with Sévéro (George Melchior), a lecherous marquis who has designs on his goddaughter Denise (Regina Thomas). He attempts to dispose of her lover André (Pierre Batcheff) by sending him on an expedition to Monte Puebla, where he is fated to be murdered by one of Sévéro's employees. Baker plays Papitou, a half-European, half-"native" islander who rescues and falls in love with André and follows him back to Paris. In an echo of Baker's rise to stardom, Papitou soon finds fame on the city's music hall stage. But she cares only for André and finally finds him, only to discover that he loves Denise. When André is forced into a duel with Sévéro for the honor of Denise, Papitou hides in a tree and shoots the marquis. Papitou then sacrifices her own happiness so that André and Denise can be together and returns to her stage career.

Papitou's status as a racial Other is exemplified in an extended sequence in which she travels from the Caribbean to Paris, and which reduces Baker to a comic spectacle. In this segment, heavy-handed visual codes emphasize that Papitou has no place in French society and her clumsy attempt to pass as a "lady" to secure passage on the ship renders her a fool. She has no concept of money and attempts to pay her fare with a "fetish"; when this fails, an intertitle states that she resorts to a "war cry" in frustration. She is alternately blackened by coal dust and whitened with flour in her efforts to evade capture as a stowaway en route to Paris (see figure 4). As Baker recalled in *Voyages*, "I saw all colors and I was seen in all colors in this film."[58] Conversely, the production betrays an erotic interest in Baker's body by featuring her in two naked bathing scenes. *Sirène* thus betrays an intense ambivalence to Baker, constructing her in equal measures as a childlike and grotesque figure while satisfying voyeuristic fascinations with her alternately naked and dancing body.

Papitou's mixed heritage alludes to Baker's own complex ancestry, of which the star made no secret. As noted in chapter one, although Baker

FIGURE 4. Baker covered in flour in *La Sirène des tropiques* (Etablissements Louis Aubert, 1927).

never identified her father, she claimed that he was white. *Les Mémoires de Joséphine Baker*, whose publication coincided with *Sirène*'s release, suggested that he was "Spanish."[59] However, Papitou's unrequited love for a Frenchman evokes the *doudou* myth of colonial literature, and her European ancestry plays into another imperialist literary trope, the Antillaise, a biracial female character that articulated fears of racial contamination. The figure of the Antillaise, like her U.S. literary cousin the "tragic mulatta," was doomed to isolated misery because of her ethnic "oddness" and was considered sexually dangerous.[60] According to Berliner, "The Antillaise . . . was a highly eroticized figure in the French imagination. She was popularly considered a mulâtresse, dangerously ambiguous racially and defined by the sexual crossings of racial boundaries. . . . The Antillaise was civilized enough to be considered beautiful and desirable but also primitive enough to be feared, especially for seducing white men and rendering the color line ambiguous."[61] Papitou therefore can be read as a character who threatens physically to contaminate French society and who must be kept separate for a happy narrative resolution to be achieved. Such a reading plays into pseudo-scientific conceptions of racial purity that Baker's memoirs sought to undermine. All of Baker's starring films ultimately reinforce racial difference. In *Zouzou*, Baker's character's love for a white man also goes unrequited and in *Princesse Tam-Tam* her attempt to participate in Paris's *beau monde* is thwarted. Yet Baker's films also subtly complicate readings of her characters as racial Others because they allow her to showcase her aesthetic practice. As in *Revue*, her dance performances celebrate her artistry and in so doing unsettle the film's racial narrative.

Sirène is largely absent from studies of Black cinema, but it serves powerfully to illustrate the prescribed nature of Black cinematic roles on both sides of the Atlantic in the 1920s. Writing in the 1970s, film historian Thomas Cripps dismissed the production for its racism, citing the Associated Negro Press's conclusion that it "renders the Negro ignoble."[62] But his disparaging description of Baker as "short on talent" was misplaced and his claim that the film "burned the fingers of everyone who touched it" simplified audience reactions in both Europe and the United States.[63] *Sirène* was a critical and commercial success in France and Baker's performance received particular praise. *Cinéa-ciné pour tous* described it as a "high-class" film and *Le Figaro* called Baker's physically expressive performance "a real revelation . . . vivacious, touching, and so amusing that the audience was shaken by uncontrollable laughter."[64] Bennetta Jules-Rosette argues that Baker's overstated mannerisms in the film may seem crude to modern cinemagoers but in fact adhered to contemporary expectations of silent performance, and that, "To be melodramatic in silent film was a positive attribute, for it was through exaggeration that emotions could be conveyed visually."[65] The film's impact on Black audiences and critics will be discussed in more detail later, but it is worth noting here that it was greeted enthusiastically when screened in African American cinemas under the English title *Siren of the Tropics* in 1929. Together with *Harlem is Heaven* (1932), which starred tap dancer Bill "Bojangles" Robinson in his first film role, it was one of the two highest grossing independent Black movies of the pre-World War II era.[66]

In her first dance in the film, Baker performs alongside her *La Revue Nègre* partner Joe Alex at a Caribbean village social gathering. They are accompanied by a group of Black musicians and dance in a circle as André looks on. This scene is based on Baker's opening night performance in Paris, her *danse sauvage*. Baker and Alex's performance is constructed explicitly for a white colonial gaze, reinforcing observer-subject hierarchies that Baker and Dunham both sought to challenge in their writings. In particular, the scene evokes ethnographic cinema's display of non-European societies for voyeuristic consumption. The scene also appears to exemplify what Laura Mulvey termed the "to-be-looked-at-ness" status of women in cinema, which implied that the traditional role of women in cinema was to be "simultaneously looked at and displayed" and thus to be passive objects for the consumption of male voyeurs.[67] For Mulvey, women on film have traditionally been "bearer[s] of meaning, not maker[s] of meaning."[68] However, as Phil Powrie argues, Batcheff, who was of Estonian and Russian descent, was also positioned as an ethnic Other on film as his roles reinforced a "'Slavic' image whose key characteristics are renunciation, effacement and 'reduced efficiency.'"[69] It is André's passivity rather than Baker's that pervades the film. Papitou rescues André from certain death in the Caribbean and shoots his opponent before he can prove his marksmanship in the film's climatic duel. Powrie suggests that Baker's animated performance style enables her to take control of the gaze in a way that Batcheff cannot and that the latter is the film's "fetishized pin-up."[70] Baker, on the other hand, is still constructed as a racial Other, but her acting style enables her to "shift across multiple boundaries so as to play into fetishization while at the same time interrogating it."[71] Powrie's reading points to Baker's use of corporeal expression to circumvent straightforward consumptions of her screen identity, but he overlooks her dance scenes, which are the silent film's most autonomous—and thus potentially unruly—sites of expression. These cinematic moments enable Baker to articulate an identity that is not beholden to the narrative and which instead is centered on African diasporic dance.

Baker and Alex's village dance is presented as unrehearsed, reinforcing primitivist fantasies of an uninhibited Black essence. Baker wears a short dress and Alex an open shirt. Part of Baker's early appeal rested on the incorporation of dance with nudity, an aesthetic decision made by *La Revue Nègre* director Jacques Charles because he wanted Baker, an American, and Alex, from Martinique, to look "like true Africans."[72] In their cinematic reunion, Alex performs playful pelvic movements that Baker then mimics, actions that could be read as titillating. Alex shakes his rear end in direct imitation of Baker's banana dance, a gesture that conjures up the colonialist tropes of her iconic stage image. Moreover, Baker and Alex dance alongside each other: theirs is a challenge dance, not a partner dance, and their intimacy is broken by the inclusion of a third dancer at the end of the scene.

But the pair's movements are all witty allusions to Black vaudeville traditions, which suggests that the eroticism and exoticism of Baker's performances do not wholly explain her appeal. Matthew F. Jordan draws on contemporary critical responses to *La Revue Nègre* to demonstrate that many critics did not read Baker and Alex as "true Africans" as Charles intended but instead "questioned the sincerity or authenticity of the music and dance and conveyed an intense ambivalence about the show."[73] He quotes *Comœdia*'s opening night review of *La Revue Nègre*, which declared that, "The true newness of this show is, for us, in the continuity itself of its effects, the rhythm and grooving [*rainant*] of the ensemble and the *personal valor* of several of the artists, overall of the star, Josephine Baker."[74] Similarly, dance critic André Levinson maintained that Baker's artistry "transcended the character" of what he termed "negro dance," which he dismissed as "formless and purely instinctive motor energy."[75] Surrealist Michel Leiris compared *La Revue Nègre* unfavorably to the U.S. revue, *Blackbirds of 1929*, which he held to be a more "authentic" representation of Black culture.[76] Jordan therefore insists that, "It was the *quality of the performance*, not merely its exoticism, that made the show a success."[77] He concludes that, "even as the troupe conformed their otherness to the fantasies swirling in the French imagination, the avant-garde modernness of their art and the *ambiguousness* of the cultural response they provoked served to deconstruct notions of fixed racial characteristics and led critics to reevaluate the extent to which jazz, or any culture product for that matter, could be considered a pure expression of race."[78] These critical responses to Baker's early performances point up interpretations of her work that are too frequently obscured: she was not read straightforwardly as a figuration of the primitive, and her charismatic, parodic, and technically accomplished stage presence was equally significant to her perceived sensuality. They pinpoint the fundamental ambiguity of Baker's art, showing that she projected a vision of Black female artistry that generated competing, and even contradictory, interpretations.

Baker and Alex's scene visualizes an important disjuncture between Baker's early dance performances and pseudo-ethnographic fantasies because, like *Revue*, it reveals that such work was both technically complex and a satirical engagement with African American vaudeville traditions. As analysis of Dunham's filmed dance performances will also illuminate, it shows how such scenes functioned as platforms for, and served as cinematic documents of, a rich history of African diasporic artistry. The *danse sauvage* was superficially a European construct grounded in primitivist imagery and was devised at the last minute to promote Baker as the show's star over singer Maud de Forrest. But African American dancer Louis Douglas oversaw the choreography, rooting the dance performances in Black vaudeville. Equally, in *Sirène*, Baker and Alex perform a call-and-response routine that features a series of African American- and Caribbean-originated movements, including the Shimmy, the Charleston, the Mess Around, the Jig Walk, and the Camel Walk, and Baker repeats gestures from "La Même en 1927," even wearing a similar costume in this scene. As in *Revue*, Baker incorporates African American dance patterns and creatively reworks them. Anthea Kraut refers to this scene as proof of the improvisatory nature of Baker's performances, which elucidates her authorship. Kraut asserts that, "In the moment of performance, she unfailingly articulated an individual style even as she drew on communally generated dance steps and aesthetic codes."[79] Although Baker and Alex were situated within an eroticizing framework, the sequence illustrates that they personalized their performances by riffing on Black vernacular dance forms.

Baker and Alex's idiosyncratic employment of Black Atlantic dance practices allows them to satirize the absurdity of their pseudo-Caribbean surroundings. By shaking his bottom and flailing his arms in a manner that could be read as a cheeky exaggeration of Baker's iconic banana dance, Alex upends gender roles and reduces her apparent display of female desire to farce. Baker and Alex call further attention to the ridiculousness of their roles—and by extension the film's narrative—by adopting physical language that is both unruly and teasingly disrespectful. They humorously mimic and mock one another's movements, with Baker in particular barely disguising her mirth at their display. Alex taunts Baker throughout and at one stage raises his right leg in what could be read as an implied sexual gesture. Baker responds by quickly pushing his leg to the ground, revealing prudishness that is at odds with her sexual image. Baker and Alex's refusal to take their performance seriously points up their authorship over the scene and serves as a self-reflexive critique of the film narrative's fantasies of Black lives.

Baker's next major dance sequence occurs at the Place de la Concorde in Paris, where a character played by Abatino spots her teaching children how to Charleston. He secures for her a starring role on the Parisian stage, where she is introduced as "The latest thing in modern civilization." Papitou's arrival on stage is preceded by theatrical footage of chorus girls, including acts from the Grand Palais des Champs-Elysées section of *Revue*. Among the repeated sequences are the high-kicking synchronized dancers of the Palais Ensembles, "One Night in Mexico," and "Les Golfeurs," which Baker parodied in her Plantation sequence in *Revue*. Camera shots of the audience stress its boredom and structure these sequences in negative contrast to Papitou's dance, suggesting that her work represents a glimpse of an exciting new world. Papitou is shown first briefly performing Baker's Plantation scene. She next executes a tap-based Charleston. An article in *Cinéa-ciné pour tous* recorded the filming of the Charleston. It describes Baker as "docile," noting that, "the black star listens attentively to her director's instructions," which implies that she had little control over the scene.[80] The piece hints at Baker's frustration with what appears to have been a physically limiting performance. It observes that she "does not feel at ease in her dress with its long train," and that, "She unfailingly stops after a few steps and having called her dresser, orders him to cut the cloth that discomforts her."[81] Baker was literally confined by the film frame in this sequence, her movements delineated by chalk marks, which underscores the restrictions of her role.[82] Baker alludes to this incident in *Voyages*. She recalls that she eventually ripped off the bottom of her dress on her own, so frustrated was she not only with her "loose" and "too long" outfit, but also at having to perform before "monstrous projectors" in a theater "packed with volunteer spectators and 'critics.'"[83]

Yet within this constraining framework, Baker's Charleston is energetic and virtuosic. While remaining fixed on one spot, she executes at tremendous speed a series of tap steps, kicks, and the Bee's Knees, an iconic Charleston movement in which a dancer's hands cross and uncross over their knees as they join together and spread out (see figure 5). By performing a variety of different movements rather than a structured routine, Baker demonstrates

FIGURE 5. Baker executing the Bees Knees in *La Sirène des tropiques*.

mastery over difficult steps and thus control over her performance in a routine that draws on her stage material. Her exceptional physical skill and improvisational approach make her the dictator of the movements that she executes, while the fact that she performs work from her own routine connects her cinematic persona with her stage image. Shots of the audience and the blurring of Papitou's physical location and performance style with those of Baker rupture the theatrical illusion and remind the viewers that they are watching the star in action.

The Charleston had a transformative effect on popular culture. Skirts became shorter as women sought to execute the dance. It encouraged emulation, breaking down participant-observer binaries that theatrical dance displays had traditionally helped to uphold. The practice contained no steps that were deemed feminine; consequently, traditional gender conventions were subverted, as men became leading practitioners of a popular American dance step for the first time. The routine also challenged social and artistic boundaries. Tap dancers devised a tap Charleston, uniting ballroom and tap and disrupting artistic hierarchies. As Cynthia R. Millman has acknowledged, "the Charleston marked the most pervasive involvement to date of all the socioeconomic classes, from tycoons and socialites to domestics and laborers, in the same social dance behavior."[84]

Baker's contribution to the Charleston has been overlooked despite her central role in its success, which points to a wider elision of Black artistry. Baker did not introduce the Charleston to Europe, but she did popularize the dance and became widely associated with it.[85] A revaluation of Baker's association with the Charleston helps to recover Black artists' key influence on early-twentieth-century transatlantic dance cultures. Widely understood as a product of the "Jazz Age," Euro-American choreographers and dancers, most notably Ned Wayburn and Bee Jackson, are frequently cited as key practitioners of the dance, and white artists such as Bessie Love and Joan Crawford performed it in Hollywood. In *The Art of Stage Dancing* (1925), Wayburn claimed to have conceived and arranged the Charleston in both its ballroom and exhibition variations.[86] But Charleston-like movements have been traced to much older practices in the Caribbean and parts of Africa. Dunham's anthropological mentor Melville Herskovits professed to have found it in West Africa and Dunham herself recognized it in the Haitian dance *La Martinique*.[87] The routine has also been linked to the Jay-Bird, an African American dance. Zora Neale Hurston emphasized the Charleston's African American origins, speculating that it dated as far back as the 1890s and was "danced up and down the Atlantic seaboard from North Carolina to Key West, Florida."[88] Marshall and Jean Stearns insisted that a Charleston movement called the Bee's Knees was derived from Patting Juba, signaling that at least some of the dance's steps were developed as interpretive responses to slavery.[89] The sequence therefore provides further visual testimony of the ways in which, like Dunham, Baker played a key role in bringing a rich history of Black dance to the attention of transatlantic audiences. At a time when Hollywood associated the Charleston with white womanhood, Baker's starring role in French cinema asserted to European filmgoers the dance's Black Atlantic origins.

Evidence suggests that some form of the Charleston appeared in *Shuffle Along* and that it first gained popularity in another all-Black Broadway show, *Runnin' Wild* (1923), with *Shuffle Along* performer Elida Webb teaching the dance to both Baker and Jackson. Baker's success with the dance consequently points to the wider significance of *Shuffle Along*, which also adapted the Black Bottom for the Broadway stage, in shaping early-twentieth-century dance cultures on both sides of the Atlantic. Baker first performed the Charleston in *The Chocolate Dandies*. In "That Charleston Dance," Baker parodied the new craze, an act that, as Sally Banes observes, "engraved it on posterity's imagination."[90] When Baker arrived in Europe, her appearance underwent significant modification to cater to European notions of Black performances. But her films show that she was able to retain her parodic Charleston performance and this scene in particular demonstrates that her dance work in Europe was rooted in a style that she had already helped to popularize in the United States. As in *The Chocolate Dandies*, in *Sirène* she calls attention to the absurdity of a craze that has become the pinnacle of fashion by satirizing the dance and taking its steps to an energetic extreme. As with her witty reference to "Les Golfeurs" in *Revue*, her act of showmanship can be read as a self-reflexive critique of the caprices of its European practitioners, for whom the dance represented the height of stylishness. As in the Golfers scene, Baker uses physical expression to speak back to her audience and comment on her status as a bourgeois European fantasy.

If Baker's work both shaped and parodied European dance culture, then it also had a psychological impact on African American audiences. Almost two years after its European release, *Sirène* (anglicized as *Siren of the Tropics*) became the focus of a publicity machine that sought to market Baker to African American cultural consumers. The premiere was a major cultural occasion in Harlem attended by New York City Mayor Jimmy Walker. The *New York Amsterdam News* recorded the moment as the first visit by a major city official to a Harlem cinema.[91] Presiding over the occasion was a Provisional Company from the 369th Infantry Regiment (Harlem Hellfighters) band, which had played such an important role in introducing jazz to Europe. Also featured was tap dancer Bill "Bojangles" Robinson, whose presence in musical revue *Blackbirds of 1928* led to him becoming the first African American dance headliner on Broadway and who would shortly follow Baker onto celluloid. Jewish Black-cast theater producer and distributor Jack Goldberg made possible the film's international circulation. He became a notable producer of independent Black films during the 1930s and was responsible for the early Robinson vehicle *Harlem Is Heaven*. *Siren* gave Black American cinemagoers a glimpse of the stardom that Baker had achieved in Europe. The critical response to the film was mixed, but its commercial success reveals African American audiences' optimism toward cinema at this time. For a fleeting period at least, Baker was a U.S. movie star.

Siren received its Harlem premiere just one month after *Hallelujah!*, Hollywood's first successful Black-cast film. *Hallelujah!* was devised to capitalize on the commercial possibilities that Black musical talent was perceived to offer at the advent of sound cinema. However, producers' interest in Black performers was limited and based on racist notions that African Americans had superior singing and dancing abilities to people of European descent.[92] Nevertheless, the groundbreaking employment of Black casts in films such as *Hallelujah* and *Hearts in Dixie* (1929) helped to shift Black critics' attention away from independently produced "race films" to Hollywood as a site where Black performers might finally begin to enjoy meaningful screen roles. But the apparently humanizing potential of sound-era Hollywood proved to be a false dawn, as the only major Black star to enjoy notable success at this stage was Stepin Fetchit, a figure renowned for his lazy and servile persona. The repercussions of such unfulfilled expectations on Baker and Dunham's efforts to achieve Hollywood stardom in the 1930s and 1940s will be discussed later, but it is worth noting here that such limited and demeaning roles continued to endure throughout the studio era.

Black audiences anticipated that *Siren* could build on *Hallelujah!*'s achievements. The *New York Amsterdam News* reported that, "Harlem and Broadway are awaiting this new entrant endeavoring to gain a foothold for her race and sell in 'talkiedom.'"[93] Michel Fabre asserts that, for African American cultural consumers, Baker's stardom "symbolically signaled a recognition of racial equality by European cultural institutions, and thus they heralded the desirability and/or imminence of comparable moves in the United States."[94] The psychological significance of Baker's achievements is illustrated by the excitement with which African American cultural consumers in New York greeted the film. Much was made of the fact that it was the first mainstream picture with a Black woman lead and feature-length to boot.[95] However, Goldberg exaggerated its cultural significance. Critics were misled into describing it as a million-dollar picture and the "most elaborate production made during the past year by any European film company" and also into suggesting that it had broken previous Parisian box-office records.[96] Goldberg also falsely promised that *Siren* would be shown in all the large theaters throughout the United States and Canada and that Baker would be awarded a U.S. movie contract if the film garnered enough ticket sales.[97] In reality, *Siren* was screened only in Black cinemas. Such a publicity campaign eventually caused some critics to reject the event as anticlimactic.[98]

Reviews of the film ranged from celebratory to vitriolic. The *Baltimore Afro-American* headlined with "Jo Baker Film Shows Equality of Races" and applauded the "many brilliant dancing scenes in color" and what it deemed the sight of a "Negro woman held tightly in the loving arms of a white man on terms of absolute social equality, with the colored actress playing the leading role and thoroughly dominating both scenes and story."[99] The *Pittsburgh Courier* praised Baker's acting and charm, celebrating her as an "'it' girl" and a "tribal flapper" to underscore her significance in breaking down racial barriers and achieving status as a glamorous Black woman.[100] Like the *Afro-American*, it concluded that, "Romance is depicted, stripped of any barrier as to race."[101] Conversely, the *New York Amsterdam News*'s reviewer insisted that Baker's role would "make any self-respecting Negro feel ashamed."[102] Similarly, Charles Magill of the *Chicago Defender* asserted that the "amateurish" production would have no appeal outside of Race Theaters and "failed to find anything to rave about."[103] He acknowledged that, "Josephine dances well" and that her acting is "good in spots," but he criticized the plot and her depiction as a "sort of wild elfin"; he noted her character's unnecessary nudity; and he described the steamship scene in which she was both whitened with flour and blackened by coal dust as a "foolish and grotesque affair."[104]

More frequently, critics were measured in their praise but applauded Baker's dancing and stardom, indicating a willingness to celebrate her artistry as a small victory over the subjugating plot. Another report in the *Afro-American* acknowledged that the film was "something new, but its temperature is quite a number of degrees below perfection."[105] It stated that, "The love making that is done, is done by Miss Baker, and that, to us, was very weak and almost servile."[106] However, it separated her dance performance from the narrative, concluding that, with such scenes taken into account, "(*and that's why the picture was made*, we guess) . . . you will find . . . that you've not spent such a bad evening."[107] Similarly, the *Philadelphia Tribune* acknowledged its "conventional" plot but nevertheless suggested that it had "touches of splendid originality" when it reviewed the film in Paris prior to its U.S. release.[108] Noting that it had attracted Parisian crowds for the past month, the article praised Baker's performance in particular, affirming that she was "splendid throughout with her frolicsome and original ways."[109] In the reviewer's opinion, Baker attained a measure of individuality in opposition to the film's demeaning narrative. Anticipating that the production would enjoy a long Parisian run, the *Tribune* also observed that, "Several of the leading illustrated journals have recently carried her picture on their covers, speaking highly in praise of her film."[110] For these critics at least, Baker's performance was a small victory that served as evidence of her high cultural status in France.

Ordinary viewers' interpretations of Baker's performance are more difficult to determine, as there are few records of their reactions to the film. However, *Siren*'s commercial success suggests that African American audiences generally responded positively to Baker's first starring role. In separate articles, the *Pittsburgh Courier* remarked that the picture had broken records in Harlem, packed Baltimore houses, and played to sell-out audiences in Pittsburgh's Elmore Theatre.[111] The *Amsterdam News* reported that the event's premiere at the Lafayette Theater on Seventh Avenue in Harlem had inspired hundreds of cinemagoers to queue from thirty to forty-five minutes to see the film.[112] The article does not comment on the picture itself, but it emphasizes the applause that it generated, concluding that "it was a huge success," and credits Goldberg for bringing the production to the United States.[113] Such a response indicates that Baker's cultural visibility held psychological significance for many African American viewers, who privileged her dancing and stardom over her servile role. *Siren*'s reception thus uncovers the expectation with which Black filmgoers greeted the first mainstream film to star a Black woman and suggests that its transatlantic screening formed part of a briefly optimistic moment in which African American audiences dared to hope that mainstream cinema was finally starting to create space for Black talent. Critical responses also reveal that the film was deemed concurrently to be a triumph and a degradation of Black artistry, which shows that attitudes to Baker on both sides of the Atlantic were complex and frequently ambivalent.

Sirène is historically significant as the first mainstream film to star a Black actress and for the excitement that it generated when it was screened to interwar African American audiences. Yet although Baker's silent films afford her freedom from Hollywood's minstrelsy-derived characterizations of Black performers, they still conceive of her as a racial Other and play up her perceived difference. *Revue* and *Sirène* are important cinematic documents of Baker's early performances that show how she was constrained by production frameworks that borrowed from colonial literature and betrayed fundamental ambivalence to her sexuality. However, Baker's dance practice enabled her to intervene self-reflexively in these restrictive cinematic environments, and her performances onscreen reveal an experimental technique drawn from Black Atlantic performance traditions that parodies racial, social, and gender codes and wittily calls attention to its constructed status, thereby challenging illusions of racial "authenticity." The complex dialectic of themes, imagery, and performance in the two films facilitate manifold interpretations. But they also reveal that Baker's dance style was rooted in a rich history of Black Atlantic dance practices and female burlesque and thus not a straightforward reconstruction of primitivist myths of Black performance.

After *Sirène*, Baker took a hiatus from cinema, choosing instead to embark on a world tour (as described in *Voyages et aventures de Joséphine Baker*), to perfect her French, and to develop a singing technique that drew on Parisian music hall traditions. She also learned how to dance *en pointe*. After criticizing *Sirène* in *Voyages*, she began to omit it from her life story and there is no reference to the production in either *Une vie de toutes les couleurs* or *Josephine*. By the early 1930s, Baker had reinvented herself as a glamorous *chanteuse* and international star and when she returned to cinema in the middle of the decade she had new hopes for her representation onscreen.

CHAPTER FOUR

Cinematic Stardom

Baker and the 1930s French Musical Film

Early on in her first sound film, *Zouzou*, Baker's character spots her shadow projected against a stage backdrop and decides to dance. Baker's body, amplified and cast in black against a white background, is turned into an oversized, one-dimensional spectacle, a dehumanized icon for voyeuristic consumption. Her performance is positioned as spontaneous, reinforcing readings of innate Black creativity and obscuring the labor behind her art. But as in the sequence in *Voyages* in which she wears out a too-fast orchestra that tries to dictate her performance, Baker uses gesture self-reflexively to manipulate the scene's framework. She responds to her projection by dancing, fracturing the contours of her image with an unruly, humorous display. She molds the shadow's shape, and hence its significations, by imposing her performative identity on the screen. Baker's playfulness within this space underscores the idiosyncrasy of her dance practice and the scene becomes a cinematic platform for her stage artistry. The sequence epitomizes the conflicting representation of Baker in her two starring sound films, *Zouzou* (1934) and *Princesse Tam-Tam* (1935). The narratives ultimately reinforce her image as an exotic Other, yet the productions were constructed to promote her as an international film star. As in *Revue* and *Sirène*, they therefore grant Baker some control over her dance scenes, enabling her to articulate a self-referential screen image that intervenes in and disrupts racial binaries.

Like her silent films, Baker's sound-era work highlights competing attitudes to the performer and her place in French culture. This chapter examines *Zouzou* and *Princesse Tam-Tam* as cinematically ambivalent in their portrayal of Baker as both a "primitive" performer and a glamorous *chanteuse*. The productions play up pseudo-ethnographic fantasies of Black subjects while their narratives subjugate Baker's characters. And yet their ambitious musical numbers associate her with Eurocentric notions of beauty in an attempt to establish her as a film star. In so doing, they provide Baker with a level of screen authorship not possible in mainstream U.S. cinema. Consequently, Baker should be recognized as the chief author of her musical numbers as she uses these scenes to create a multifaceted and self-referential screen image, negating simplistic readings of a performative Black womanhood. As evidenced by Baker's reception in the Broadway show, *Ziegfeld Follies of 1936*, which will be discussed alongside the films, the attention to Baker's artistry and beauty in these sequences offers a compelling contrast to interwar U.S. racial codes. By extension, they highlight interwar European cinema's cultural significance in affording midcentury Black artists meaningful screen roles and even stardom to an extent not possible in the United States.

In the 1930s, Baker cultivated a seemingly Europeanized stage persona. She developed a *chanson* singing method, an intimate, confessional style indebted to the Parisian music hall. She also learned to dance *en pointe* and played the title role in a revival of French composer Jacques Offenbach's *opéra comique La Créole* (1934). Her image diversification was part of a wider trend as music hall icons sought to survive in a rapidly changing entertainment industry. However, the outpouring of xenophobia that Baker encountered during her first international tour, as recalled in *Voyages*, also precipitated her transformation. In an interview on returning to France in 1929, she stated that in her opinion it was the only country in which a person could live in peace from racism. She began to identify more explicitly with the nation, declaring, "But I am French. I'm a Black Frenchwoman."[1] Baker's reinvention caused European critics to read her concurrently as a symbol of innate Black performance and as a highly trained artiste, an ambivalent attitude that Dunham would in turn encounter in the 1940s. For example, Gilbert Bernard described Baker as a "born dancer" but also acknowledged that she had "worked flat out, learned French and singing, so that today she is reaping the results of hard work and the laurels of success."[2]

Previous scholarship on *Zouzou* and *Princesse Tam-Tam* has centered on the films' narratives to position them as either symptoms or satires of French colonial mindsets.[3] With rare exceptions such as Felicia McCarren's discussion on the expressive potential of cinematic versus photographic representations, Saër Maty Bâ and Kate E. Taylor-Jones's call for a reading of Baker's films that focuses on her dancing body, and Edwin C. Hill Jr.'s consideration of her singing, such analyses have foregrounded production frameworks over Baker's performances.[4] Yet *Zouzou* and *Princesse Tam-Tam* shed vital light on Baker's stage image as well as the level of creative autonomy that she enjoyed during the 1930s. Although they were not her only sound-era roles—she also appeared as a cabaret performer in *Fausse alerte* (premiere 1940; official release 1945)—they were designed specifically for her and provided substantial platforms for her art.[5] In this regard, they show how significant was the European screen in affording Black artists with a level of celebrity and creative freedom unattainable in mainstream U.S. cinema. Through close study of Baker's artistry, I show that these films are in fact tonally ambivalent. They are enmeshed in narratives of racial difference but complicate such narratives in their efforts to establish Baker as a credible screen star. I compare these films with Baker's experiences in the Broadway production, *Ziegfeld Follies of 1936*, both to show that her sound-era roles were failed launching pads to a Hollywood career and to evidence the contrasting treatment of Black women in 1930s U.S. and French cinema. I also demonstrate that Baker brought significant individuality to her performance scenes to resist the films' racially subjugating narratives and assert her authorship.

Shortly before starting work on *Zouzou* and *Princesse Tam-Tam*, Baker declared her wish to perform in "a great film, beautiful and true."[6] The star wanted to deviate from what she perceived to be misrepresentations of her artistry in *Revue* and *Sirène* by producing films that more accurately reflected both her public and personal identities.[7] French cinema appeared to offer a liberating alternative to the limiting roles assigned to Black performers in classical Hollywood; as chapter six shows, such a perception would also underpin Dunham's European career. Scott Balcerzak examines *Zouzou* as evidence of an important distinction between the 1930s French and Hollywood film industries: unlike the centralized studio system, French cinema was comprised of small production companies, which "allowed performers such as Baker to create personal showcases in a less exploited atmosphere."[8] In particular, films did not have to adhere to a specific aesthetic or creative practice and there were no racially proscribed moral codes.

Such cinematic independence afforded Baker's Italian lover-manager Giuseppe "Pepito" Abatino tremendous authorial control, and he wrote the scenarios and was "artistic director" of both films. Baker and Abatino also probably helped to finance them, and their friend Arys Nissotti produced them. The films' production, marketing, and timing suggest that they were devised as ambitious attempts to turn Baker into an international cinema star, a reading corroborated by a draft script note likely authored by Pepito, and which was sent to Baker for her approval. The note stated that, "For a star with Miss Josephine Baker's unique qualities, what is important is not to have a complicated, artful plot, but rather a scenario that gives scope to the star's talents."[9] Pepito's choice of words locates Baker within an early history of French film stardom. Interwar French cinema was not a centralized industry with a well-defined "star system" as in Hollywood. However, Jonathan Driskell shows how leading French screen actors during this period chose their own film roles and used marketing strategies to create consistent star personas.[10] In *Josephine*, Baker underscored *Zouzou*'s promotional purpose by affirming that, "Pepito had created *Zouzou* especially for me," and screenwriter Carlo Rim visited the performer with the intention of capturing her "essence" on screen.[11] The films were accompanied by aggressive publicity campaigns as they incorporated narratives and visual spectacles designed to showcase Baker's public image, all of which are identifiable as key elements in the construction of a film star.[12] Dresses modeled on Zouzou's outfits and bananas labeled with the message "Josephine Baker is Zouzou" went on sale, and a *Zouzou* newsletter offering instruction on love and fashion was circulated internationally. A poster competition for *Princesse Tam-Tam* was launched and an exhibition of entries was held on the Champs-Élysées a month before the film's release.[13]

Unlike *Sirène*, *Zouzou* and *Princesse Tam-Tam* were not distributed formally in the United States.[14] Yet they still should be seen as optimistic attempts to circumvent Hollywood racial typecasting by establishing a cinematic star identity for Baker that they hoped to export to the land of her birth. As chapter six will demonstrate, Dunham's European screen career was driven by a similar goal. In a retrospective on Baker in British film magazine *Sight and Sound*, Robin Buss argued that *Princesse Tam-Tam* "clearly set out to rival Hollywood musicals" and contemporary critics identified stylistic parallels.[15] *Zouzou* was described as "the only music-hall film, made in France, that bears comparison with American productions" and *Princesse Tam-Tam* was praised as "a superior showpiece to Hollywood film ballets."[16] Before filming *Princesse Tam-Tam*, Abatino secured for Baker a leading role in the *Ziegfeld Follies*, an annual revue series that was widely recognized as a stepping-stone to Hollywood, and he packed a print of *Zouzou* in his suitcase when he traveled in New York to negotiate the deal. Abatino tried unsuccessfully to secure a film contract for Baker during her *Follies* run. Roles discussed included a starring part alongside Paul Robeson and the lead in a film of *Porgy and Bess*, which opened on Broadway the month that Baker arrived in New York.

Zouzou and *Princesse Tam-Tam* provided Baker with central roles in mainstream films and liberated her from the racist exclusions that drove Dunham eventually to abandon Hollywood, as discussed in chapter five. However, the productions parody but ultimately do not subvert French social structures. *Zouzou* and *Princesse Tam-Tam* are enmeshed in narratives of racial difference and recall the *doudou* trope that underpinned Baker's representations in *Revue* and *Sirène*. Although Baker directed Rim not to depict her dancing nude in *Zouzou*, she appears to have enjoyed little control over the films' plots and claimed that the "sly" Abatino coerced her into accepting *Zouzou*'s unhappy ending, in which a white man rejects her character's love.[17] Tyler Stovall argues that Baker presented a cinematic vision of womanly independence that ultimately had to be subdued and which prevented her characters from achieving the status of romantic lead. He acknowledges that, "in Baker's films this very assertiveness generally boomeranged. . . . Baker as the New Woman loses out to the woman who represents tradition and modesty, the woman who allows the man to be pursuer instead of pursued."[18] However, if we move beyond a narrative-centered analysis of the films, we find that they nevertheless provide Baker with a cinematic platform for performances that complicate contemporary colonial and gender ideologies. Baker is also able to exercise some authorship over her performances by hamming up her acting style with gestures borrowed from her theater work. Baker's musical performances blur her stage image with her character, rupturing the theatrical illusion by calling attention to the performative nature of her role and encouraging audience identification even as they locate her as a racial Other. Baker also draws on European performance techniques in these scenes to construct herself as a glamorous Frenchwoman and refute exotic readings. Together, these scenes serve as key moments of Black female self-authorship on the 1930s commercial screen.

In the first film, Baker plays Zouzou, a young Martinique-born woman who is raised in a French circus as the "sister" of a fair-haired, pale-skinned boy named Jean (Jean Gabin). In the opening sequence, Zouzou and Jean, played at this stage by child actors, are introduced as "siblings" in one of the circus' exhibits. The scene makes a spectacle of their physical difference, and by implication Zouzou's Otherness, and she is labeled as "strange" by a group of boys who sneak backstage to view her. As Jules-Rosette asserts, interracial mixing is immediately positioned as "freakish," an "outlandish carnivalesque curiosity."[19] After the show, Zouzou is caught backstage whitening her face with makeup. As an adult (played by Baker), she is chided as a "cannibal" after biting a stagehand that tries to stop her fleeing following her impromptu shadow dance. The film also features footage of a Black woman at a Manila port dancing topless in a grass skirt, a reminder of Baker's early music-hall image. However, these moments are rare, and the film otherwise presents a striking contrast with classical Hollywood due to its general lack of visual and verbal references to race and integration of Zouzou into a French family and workplace.

Yet racial difference is a key thematic device. As Eileen Julien observes, racial identity has no visible influence on Zouzou's dancing talents or on her status in society; instead, it functions as a "silent specter" that prevents her from achieving happiness.[20] The adult Zouzou is no longer a circus spectacle. However, she is deeply in love with her adopted brother, whose emotional disinterest and occupation as a soldier evoke the unsympathetic colonizer of *doudou* narratives. Zouzou almost sacrifices a burgeoning stage career to rescue Jean when he is falsely accused of murder. However, he loves a French woman (played by Yvette Lebon), whose whiteness is encapsulated by her name, "Claire," which translates into English as "clear" or "light." In a scenario that parallels *Sirène* and therefore the *doudou*'s fate, the film ends with Zouzou failing to achieve acceptance into mainstream French society through the love of a white man. Like Papitou, she returns unhappily to the social isolation of the stage.

Zouzou was greeted with critical and commercial acclaim in France. The film's premiere at the Moulin Rouge movie theater in Paris took place before a packed house and *L'Humanité* applauded Baker as a "comédienne" who "drives the whole film, communicating to all the fire that is in her."[21] But the production provoked ambivalent feelings in its star. Recalling *L'Humanité*'s praise in her 1949 memoir, she remarked, "Who could ask for more?"[22] "In this film, the dancer in bananas avoided bananas," she affirmed, implying that the production had allowed her to reinvent herself onscreen as a glamorous *chanteuse*.[23] However, she also hinted at frustration with her prescribed role, in which she was told that, "You are made for comedy. . . . You cannot play a 'lady'!"[24] In response, she resolved to perform "without composition" and "confuse everything," suggesting that she adopted a performance strategy at odds with the narrative's intentions to deny a comfortable viewing and assert her authorial independence.[25] That Baker personalized her role is apparent in the overstated performance style that she adopts throughout the film. As we will see, it is particularly perceptible in her musical numbers.

Baker's conflicted attitude to her role is indicative of a production framework that superficially at least was rooted in the pseudo-ethnographic imagination of her earlier films. *Zouzou* director Marc Allégret was a respected commercial filmmaker. His first motion picture had been the ethnographic documentary *Voyage au Congo* (1927), a companion piece to his uncle André Gide's tract of the same name, which recorded the two men's ten-month journey to French Equatorial Africa. Allégret and Gide began their trip in 1925, the year that Baker arrived in Europe, and their adventure was fueled initially by primitivist fantasies of exotic sensuality. Gide hoped to discover a society not yet "deformed by clothes, civilization, laws, the usual morality," and he dedicated his memoir to *Heart of Darkness* author Joseph Conrad, who had died the previous year.[26] Gide critiqued the poor running of the colonial administration and its concessionary companies' mistreatment of African workers. However, he continued to support France's *mission civilisatrice*.

Allégret's film ignored the colonial system altogether and Jeffrey Geiger claims that he was fixated instead on capturing a European fantasy of sensual Black bodies, listing *Zouzou* as an inheritor of *Voyage au Congo*'s voyeuristic vision.[27] Yet *Zouzou* in fact visually downplays notions of racial difference; unlike *Sirène* and *Voyage au Congo*, whose camera lingers on frequently unclothed Black bodies, it does not reduce Baker to a state of undress, and it aestheticizes her during her performance scenes. Geiger insists that *Zouzou* "immortalized the *danse sauvage* and portrayed her, in the film's closing scenes, as a feathered bird in a golden cage."[28] In fact, the *danse sauvage* is not among the diverse range of performance styles that Baker showcases in the film. Geider's reading risks simplifying Baker's artistry and the filmmakers' intentions; close analysis of *Zouzou* reveals that it does not straightforwardly reinforce exotic fantasies but instead allows Baker a certain artistic autonomy and positions her as a glamorous star.

Zouzou is first introduced to the stage halfway through the film. Jean has quit the navy and become an electrician in a Parisian theater; Zouzou is employed in a nearby launderette. Balcerzak points out the autobiographical undercurrents of Zouzou's role as Baker's mother was a laundress, while Elizabeth Ezra reads it as part of Zouzou's failed attempt to become a "*blanchisseuse*, one who whitens" and thus to assimilate into French society.[29] Such conflicting connotations, whether or not deliberate, situate the film both as a meaningful tribute to Baker and as a cultural engagement with interwar French racial ideologies. While delivering costumes to the theater, Zouzou tries on a leotard, hoping to impress Jean. Her adopted brother is unmoved by her tight-fitting outfit but invites her to stand in front of the stage spotlight before secretly raising the curtain and revealing her performance to the theater managers. The oversized double cast against the stage backdrop recalls *Un vent de folie*'s cinematic projection of Baker performing the Black Bottom. It accentuates the contours of her body, linking it to a nineteenth-century photographic history in which Black women's bodies were distorted and reduced, in the words of Deborah Willis and Carla Williams, to either a "sexualized mythology or a neutered anomaly."[30] Kelley Conway refers to Baker's shadow as an "extreme, potentially dehumanizing abstraction of a Black woman," and Julien affirms that, "Here Zouzou becomes an icon of Baker as a spectacular, myth-sized exotic Black body."[31]

In two eighteenth-century examples of the silhouette's racial history, Gwendolyn DuBois Shaw refers to the profile of an enslaved woman named Flora—created apparently to help identify her if she ever tried to run away—and the work of Swiss physiognomist Johann Kaspar Lavater, who used its imprint to "prove" his theory that a person's head shape determined her or his character, anticipating the racist thinking of physical anthropology.[32] However, Shaw also shows how Black visual artists such as the formerly enslaved Moses Williams and contemporary practitioner Kara Walker have used the silhouette's margins to signify on—and talk back to—racial iconography.[33] Daphne A. Brooks refers specifically to Baker's shadow performance in an essay comparing Baker and Walker's "disobedien[t] . . . pickaninny figurations."[34] Thus, Baker's dance in the spotlight allows her to intervene self-reflexively in racist iconography to point up her artistry and to challenge simplistic readings of her image. The scene's apparent lack of structure—Baker simply acts out a series of African American dance styles—enables her to defy the role of passive spectacle and achieve physical autonomy.

Stylistically, Zouzou's performance does not mark a comprehensive break from Baker's earlier film roles and she celebrated the fact that, "I show that I can still dance in *revue tableaux* that have a rather sensational character."[35] Her statement reveals a desire to be physically expressive and her routine recalls the unruly gestural strategies that she employed in *Revue* and *Sirène*. She forces an engagement with the creativity rather than the sexuality of her performance. Zouzou begins by playing with the shadow, wiggling her index fingers, one of Baker's trademark stage gestures. Her action is much like the wagging finger that was a feature of Jump Jim Crow, an early-nineteenth-century dance that helped to popularize blackface minstrelsy. The sequence therefore recalls a cultural-historical framework in which artistic traditions with ritual significances were crudely reappropriated, their meanings obscured, and their practitioners degraded. But her performance in turn shows how Black artists such as Baker improvised on and reinterpreted racist iconography to create new significations. Brooks suggests that such an action directs the audience's gaze away from Baker's body: "Here the hands of the shadow puppeteer shift our attention away from the overdetermined, sexualized body parts of Baker and black womanhood and toward the virtuosic hands that make both recognizable and nonsensical shapes that transmogrify and transfigure in the space of the shadow."[36] But while Brooks foregrounds Baker's hand actions, I contend that she also uses bodily gesture to rupture colonialist configurations of Black womanhood and assert her authorship.

Jean instructs Zouzou to stand still: her dance before the spotlight is an act of disobedience. Her performance is a re-creation of Baker's stage image, which affords her some freedom from the plot's boundaries. As in *Revue*, she claims authorship by executing a series of apparently random movements borrowed from her vaudeville career, including tap, the Bees Knees, and Pecking, and she raises her shoulders in imitation of a Camel Walk, a popular ragtime dance (see figure 6). She does drop on all fours, encouraging

FIGURE 6. Baker Pecking in front of her shadow in *Zouzou* (Corona Films, 1934).

readings of her work as animalistic. She also crouches, mimicking the position of a soldier firing a gun, which, Ezra contends, "invokes the *tirailleur sénégalais*, the *zouave* (*native colonial soldier*) in which the name Zouzou originates," a figure generally represented in the post–World War I French cultural imagination as a *grand enfant*, or big child.[37] But Baker's adoption of this movement is sexually transgressive and parodic. She places her forefinger on her head and twirls as if she were a spinning top, literally shaking up the performance framework. This movement, a trademark act of her early Parisian career, was probably borrowed from Rolf de Maré, manager of the Théâtre des Champs-Élysées, who oversaw *La Revue Nègre* and performed the gesture on Baker in the run-up to the show that launched her to European fame. Baker's borrowing of such an action both acknowledges and signifies on—or talks back to—her status as a commodified spectacle.

The theater producers witness Zouzou's spotlight dance and hire her as the venue's main attraction when its star, "Miss Barbara," elopes with her Brazilian lover. In her first stage role, Zouzou plays a caged bird pining for her lost homeland of Haiti. Her feathered costume recalls the revealing outfit that Baker wore in *La Revue Nègre*, which consisted of ostrich feathers and beads, and which *New Yorker* correspondent Janet Flanner would later remember as a single "pink flamingo feather between her limbs."[38] Baker's performance therefore appears to play into exotic fantasies of Black sensuality. Zouzou reflects despondently on her exile, singing, "Far from your shores, the most beautiful cage, isn't that a prison? Yes! My desire, my cry of love: Haiti. It is to return to you one day."

Haiti, the first independent Black republic, was a former French slave colony. As Dunham's *Island Possessed* experiences have shown, in 1934 the island was at the end of a nineteen-year U.S. occupation. Scholars have argued that French colonialism, threatened from without, was already in "severe decline" by the interwar years and Ezra reads the scene as evidence of nostalgia for its dying empire.[39] Baker's gestural strategies are reined in as the cage physically restricts Zouzou. Unlike Jean, a sailor who can voyage to France's overseas territories, she is literally imprisoned as a site of exotic fascination, her body and voice serving to idealize a former French territory. Evoking the figure of the *doudou*, her passive status can be read as a justification for colonial intervention. Zouzou's Martiniquan origins are conflated with Haiti, marking Caribbean national identities as interchangeable in the French imagination. When she finally leaps from her cage at the end of the scene, she lands in the arms of white men; thus, she is unable to escape their control and by implication her exoticized status. However, earlier in the film Zouzou releases caged birds and this concern with freedom allows for a simultaneous reading of the scene as an allegory for her frustrated attempts to surmount France's antiassimilation policies and therefore as a critique of the nation's mistreatment of its colonial subjects. The guiding principle of colonial rule in the 1930s was to deny overseas subjects full citizenship on the basis that they were supposedly racially too different for French social inclusion. At the film's end, Zouzou is again shown in her cage, underscoring the tragedy of her inability to break free from such exclusions and achieve romantic happiness with a white man. As noted in chapter one, Baker expressed a desire in *Josephine* to fly away like a bird from the trappings of her role, which invites readings of Zouzou's plight as an autobiographical comment on the star's own victimization by a society that dehumanizes and isolates her as an exotic commodity.

The scene also departs from crude misrepresentations of Black subjects and locates Baker within a European beauty ideal. Unlike the fetishizing "anthropological imagination" of Haiti that Millery Polyné identifies as a key aspect of interwar U.S. culture, *Zouzou* presents the nation as an idyllic land.[40] Such contrasting depictions underscore the arbitrariness of U.S. and European racial imaginaries. Baker's glamorous image also marks a notable divergence from the minstrelsy-derived distortions of Black performers in interwar Hollywood. Baker is aestheticized onscreen via soft-focus camera shots, a key technique for constructing a star image. Her character's leap into the arms of white men also communicates her desirability. Such close contact with her male partners also allows Baker to commit metaphorical miscegenation, a flagrant breach of a classical Hollywood censorship rule, written down in the United States Motion Picture Production Code of 1930, or Hays Code. The Code was Hollywood's regulatory body between 1930 and 1967 and it articulated a single concern with "race" in films: that "miscegenation (sex relationship between the white and Black races)," must not be depicted.[41] Consequently, Baker attains a cinematic status not possible in the United States during this period, as her catastrophic appearance in the *Ziegfeld Follies of 1936* two years after *Zouzou* demonstrates.

Baker's "Haiti" persona bears striking similarities to the image that she presented in her *Follies* performance and thus highlights contrasting transatlantic attitudes to her artistry and the inevitable failure of her Hollywood venture. In both "Haiti" and the *Follies* production, Baker broke a U.S. racial taboo by performing with white men. She also challenged artistic hierarchies by adopting a glamorous role normally reserved for white women. As with Baker's performances, the annual *Follies* series emerged from late-nineteenth-century burlesque and vaudeville and, also like Baker, it obscured its lowbrow origins and pandered to the middle-classes by drawing on the perceived glamour of the Parisian music hall. Robert C. Allen asserts that Florenz Ziegfeld's shows succeeded with bourgeois audiences because "he managed to package feminine stage sexuality in such a way that his audiences connected the *Follies* not with the working-class sexuality of burlesque but with the cosmopolitan worldliness of Paris."[42] The Polish-French singer Anna Held, Ziegfeld's common-law wife and first female star, persuaded him to copy the formula of the Folies-Bergère, which would later become the site of Baker's banana dance. The result was a series of annual spectacles that combined ribald entertainment with feminine displays. Initially located on the Roof Garden of the *Jardin de Paris* in a deliberate evocation of Parisian cosmopolitanism, the show's only initial difference from its forebear was that it included minstrelsy and vaudeville routines. In fact, it quietly appropriated the work of Harlem shows such as the *Darktown Follies* (1913) for white cultural consumers.

The *Follies*' most iconic feature was its Ziegfeld Girls, a chorus girl troupe whose unambiguous whiteness and identical appearance and movements reinforced an extremely elegant yet standardized vision of womanhood. The Ziegfeld Girl was a direct descendant of the Tiller Girl, who appeared in *Revue*'s Folies-Bergère scenes.[43] However, she was even more regimented than her predecessor. Folies-Bergère producer Paul Derval claimed to select chorus- and showgirls by personality, and Baker quoted him as asserting that, "I offer something for every taste."[44] By contrast, Ziegfeld described his Girls as "strictly American," by which he meant Anglo-American, and they performed synchronized dance routines in which women were grouped by size, with the tallest and slimmest girls coming to represent Ziegfeld's ideal of womanhood.[45] Baker would later describe the Ziegfeld Girl's hyperfeminine and unambiguously European illusion of North American womanhood as seeming to be "factory made."[46]

Baker was the only Black woman ever to star alongside the Ziegfeld Girls. Two Black men, blackface comedian Bert Williams and tap dancer John W. Bubbles, had appeared in the *Follies* in 1910 and 1931, respectively, and acrobatic tap duo the Nicholas Brothers featured in the same show as Baker. But these figures performed comedic and acrobatic routines that were kept separate from the Ziegfeld Girls' displays. Baker's three scenes, which included a stylized Conga, a ballet, and a vocal sequence in which she played an Indian princess at the Parisian races and danced with white men, were choreographed by George Balanchine, staged by Vincente Minnelli, and based on *Follies* director John Murray Anderson's statement that, "You are from Paris. It's stupid to let you sing Harlem songs."[47] Baker therefore became the first—and only—Black performer to emulate the glamor of the Ziegfeld Girl, and she would later maintain that her "glittering show was faithful to Ziegfeld's 'glorification of the American girl.'"[48]

However, critics condemned Baker's performance, using derogatory terms that suggested she had stepped outside of her perceived racial role. The *New York Times*' Brooks Atkinson revealed the upset that Baker caused by proclaiming that, "When the two Nicholas Brothers follow her with some excellent Harlem hoofing . . . they restore your faith in dusky revelry."[49] The implication was clear: Black performers were boisterous entertainers, not artistes, and should stick to tap dance. *Time*'s anonymous reviewer used undisguised racism to refer to Baker as a "St. Louis washer-woman's daughter who stepped out of a Negro burlesque show," and declared that, "In sex appeal to jaded Europeans of the jazz-loving type, a Negro wench always has a head start."[50] Criticism focused mainly on the quality of Baker's voice and Atkinson described her singing as "only a squeak in the dark."[51] *Follies* songwriter Vernon Duke noted the "smallness" of Baker's vocal projection, yet he praised her as an "exquisite" singer who was able to master a technically difficult part.[52] Baker had the strength to perform the lead in Offenbach's *La Créole* to acclaim and had "an unusual range and the purest sound" in the words of *Fausse alerte* writer Michel Duran.[53] In her final performance number, "5 A. M.," she delivered a two-octave vocalization so challenging that it was removed from a 1999 concert revival and subsequent CD recording of the production because the singer did not have sufficient vocal range to master it.[54]

French critics' positive response to *Zouzou* exemplifies the contrasting transatlantic attitudes to her image. Although the nation's embrace of Baker was rooted in ideologies of exotic Otherness, such a framework nevertheless provided her with a creatively liberating artistic environment. In *Zouzou*'s "Haiti" sequence, she shows off an impressive range and masters technically difficult techniques such as trills and high register notes. Her performance concludes with a long cadenza, an ornamental solo section that allows her to break from the orchestra's tempo. Her style contrasts with low-register blues singing and formed part of a deliberate attempt to counter racially coded performance styles to which Black artists were expected to adhere in the United States, as the reaction to Baker's *Follies* appearance demonstrates. As Richard Dyer observes, Paul Robeson's tonally pure delivery method was so successful at least in part because it was held to represent an authentic performance of Black folk singing, appearing to "exemplify Albert C. Barnes's view of the essence of the spiritual—'natural, naive, untutored, spontaneous.'"[55] Black performers who did not fit such a model struggled to achieve success. Singer Lena Horne, one of the first Black women to secure a long-term Hollywood contract and who fought against maid and "jungle" roles, recalled being turned down for work by nightclub managers because she did not fit their idea of "what a Negro entertainer should be like" and because "she [didn't] sing the blues."[56] She also remembered being criticized for being "tepid and treacly" in *Stormy Weather* because she did not convey the "rich earthiness of Ada Brown or Bill Robinson."[57] Baker purposely rooted herself in European singing traditions and took lessons with Madame Paravicini, the coach of French music hall star Yvonne Printemps, who was known for her delicate singing style. When Baker arrived in the United States for her *Follies* show, she rebuked comparisons with Ethel Waters, then the only Black woman star on Broadway, by declaring that, "Any artist must develop a technique of his own, and I have tried to avoid singing 'colored mammy, back to Alabammy' songs. Not all Negroes have to jump around as though they were monkeys or African savages. Besides, I sing soprano, and that would hardly adapt itself to the traditional blues and other Beale Street ballads."[58] Her statement shows that she deliberately adopted European performance techniques to circumvent racist representations. As Phyllis Rose affirms, "What she meant by her snide remarks about Ethel Waters was that she was glad she hadn't had to make a career of being black. She was not the person called in when the white theater needed a maid or a mammy or a novelty act. She could simply sing, a 'soprano,' not a black singer."[59] Baker's assertion overlooked Waters's own appropriation of white theatrical singing styles, yet her determination to avoid racially coded performances indicates her desire, as expressed in her memoirs, to complicate racist myths and identify with a Euro-centric womanly ideal. While such a stance was ultimately ambivalent considering her intervention in French colonial ideologies, it allowed her to critique U.S. racial intolerance and point up the greater artistic freedom that she enjoyed as a Black woman in Paris. It shows that she was able to achieve a much greater flexibility of roles and situate racial identities as fluid and ultimately ambiguous by emphasizing her femininity even as she played into exotic constructions.

In *Zouzou*, Baker positions herself as a French artist even as she sings of Haiti. Her emotional expressivity links her work to the French *chanson* tradition whose songs rely more on successful storytelling than on dynamic power, cultivating intimacy and empathy with the audience in a confessional style that blurs the distinction between the singer and their performance. In turn, it allows Baker to destabilize racial boundaries. In his study of the *chanson*, Simon Frith observes that, "the *chanteuses* also took a part *within* their narratives . . . the singers were taken to live the same lives as their characters, with the same melodramas, the same oppressions, the same romance, the same sadness."[60] Baker's appropriation of this musical style encourages audience identification and enables her to resist readings of exotic Otherness. As Jules-Rosette has noted, in contrast to the heavy Eastern European accent of Miss Barbara, the singer she replaces, "Baker's vocal performances emerge as ideal."[61] As in *Sirène*, which situates Pierre Batcheff as a passive male lead, it is the Eastern European character who functions as the Other and who serves as a foil to promote Baker's star image.

Zouzou's next performance, "C'est lui" ("He's the One"), associates Baker even more explicitly with European artistry. In a visual contrast to the "Haiti" scene, Zouzou emerges onto an elaborate stage set of Paris surrounded by white men in suits. Baker wears a fur-lined gown, tiara, and rhinestone earrings. The namelessness of "lui" (him) imbues the song with universality, allowing male viewers to fantasize that Baker is singing about them. In a challenge to the male gaze, the admirers do most of the dancing, engaging in synchronized swaying as Baker sings. The final verse of "C'est lui" at first glance appears to return Zouzou to unassimilated Otherness and to foreshadow her rejection by Jean: she is visually isolated from her male dance partners and sings wistfully on the bridge. The "lui" of the song's title is unattainable: "he gives happiness to others," but as for her love, "he does not get it." However, the scene simultaneously allows Baker to position herself as French. She sings about a "man in Paris" before an elaborate replica of the city at night. The scene ends with her singing alone on a stage imitation of the city's Pont Alexandre III, as shown in figure 7. The bridge's Art Nouveau–style architecture is a reminder of Baker's status as a contemporary Parisian cultural figurehead. Her performance takes place across from the fashionable Avenue des Champs-Élysées, which recalls her *La Revue Nègre* performance at the Théâtre des Champs-Élysées and her "primitive" past, but also situates her at the heart of modern Paris. The sequence is a celebration of Parisian culture and Baker's place within it. The "C'est lui" scene therefore functions in opposition to the film's narrative, as it allows Zouzou—and, by extension, Baker—to emphasize her Frenchness. It underscores the film's ambiguous representation of Baker, which sought to play into exotic fantasies but also to establish her as a credible screen star.

FIGURE 7. Baker singing "C'est lui" on the Pont Alexandre III in *Zouzou*.

As in *Revue* and *Sirène*, Baker's performances are juxtaposed with chorus girl routines. In sequences that both precede and follow the "Haiti" scene, pale-skinned women perform synchronized movements against a gigantic stage set. *Zouzou*'s credited choreographer was Floyd Du Pont, "producer des danses" of *La Joie de Paris* (1932–33), Baker's second show at the Casino de Paris. However, Baker's self-referential style in the shadow dance and Du Pont's reputation as the Casino's "spécialiste des grands spectacles" suggest that he was responsible simply for the elaborate chorine sequences and that Baker choreographed her own work. The chorines' uniformity recalls the Tiller Girls' coordinated movements in *Revue* and their light complexions reinforce the Ziegfeld Girl's idealized myth of womanhood, which was based on normative constructions of whiteness. At the beginning of the sequence, women emerge from a giant bed, which immediately situates them as passive participants in an erotic fantasy.

Zouzou uses an overhead camera to record the chorines, a stylistic trope borrowed from Busby Berkeley, who immortalized the Ziegfeld Girl type on film. In productions such as *Footlight Parade* (1933) and *The Gang's All Here*

(1943), Berkeley used ambitious tracking shots to further subjugate chorines as his film camera held ultimate visual control over immense dance sequences that reduced women to seemingly identical bodies. Zouzou's solo performance by contrast affords her individuality while simultaneously underscoring her apparent separateness from European womanhood. But although Zouzou is physically distanced from the dancers, the film does attempt to link her aesthetically to them. The chorines serve as introductions to Zouzou's performance and *Le Matin* reported that the girls "help to enhance the dancing and eccentric talents of Zouzou."[62] Their lack of individuality emphasizes Baker's stardom. At the end of their scene, their outstretched arms reach up to Zouzou as a curtain rises to reveal the performer in her birdcage. Therefore, although *Zouzou* structurally reinforces separation, the musical scenes disturb racial boundaries by situating Baker as the central focus in a world of European glamour.

The film's ambiguous positioning of Baker as both a racial Other and its key box-office draw is encapsulated in its final scenes, after Zouzou discovers that Jean loves Claire. Zouzou walks alone past posters promoting her show. The advertisements evoke Paul Colin's sketches of Baker for *La Revue Nègre* and can be read simultaneously as a reference to her exotic image and to her star status. Zouzou has become the rejected racial Other of *doudou* and "tragic mulatta" narratives, and the final sequence underscores her exclusion by showing her alone in her birdcage. But the poster scene can be read paradoxically as an effort to situate Baker as a popular heroine in the poetic realist tradition of 1930s French cinema, a movement that reflected a growing concern with social issues on screen. It is worth noting that, although Baker reacted ambivalently to the film, she did consider it an honest portrayal of working-class life, describing her characterization as a "simple, credible role which perfectly fit my idea of the cinema: to make you believe what you saw."[63]

Rémi Fournier Lanzoni defines poetic realism as a film genre concerned with a working-class individual whose life is depicted as a "series of lost illusions, love deceptions, and existential disenchantment."[64] The scene's adoption of poetic realist tropes unsettles colonialist readings by encouraging audiences to associate Zouzou's plight with wider class concerns and therefore to identify with her. Close-up shots of Baker's face force the viewer to acknowledge her character's anguish. Zouzou is positioned as a tragic figure, a performance that plays into *doudou* and related "tragic mulatta" narratives by ultimately confirming her lack of racial belonging, but the scene's framing of Baker enables her to inject emotional depth into her role in a stark contrast with classical Hollywood, which consigned Black performers to comedic and musical routines. Such cinematic humanization fits into Colleen Kennedy-Karpat's observation that, while Zouzou does not ultimately win Jean, "The successfully matched interracial couple of [*La Dame de*] *Malacca*, a film by the same director and released only three years after *Zouzou*, suggests that Zouzou's love for a white man goes unrequited not because of inescapable social pressure, but rather because of Baker's star image."[65] As discussed early in this chapter, Abatino initially formulated the film as a platform for Baker's talents. Although the narrative fails to imagine a future for Zouzou in French society, the production's broader concern is to position Baker at the forefront of French cinema by constructing her as a plausible screen icon.

If *Zouzou* is a cinematic *doudou* narrative about racial Otherness, *Princesse Tam-Tam*, Baker's second sound film and her final leading role, is a tongue-in-cheek exploration of racial difference. Baker had just finished performing in *La Créole* when she appeared in the production, which she claimed that Abatino conceived as part of a relentless drive to reinvent her public persona. In *Josephine*, she states, "When my engagement at the Marigny ended, Pepito decided it was time for me to make a film again. Not another story of backstage life or a dramatic comedy like *Zouzou*, but *something new*."[66] Such a statement acknowledges Abatino's control over the narrative. It also suggests that he devised *Princesse Tam-Tam* in thematic opposition to *Zouzou* to display Baker's versatility as both an actress and musical performer and therefore to establish her credibility as a screen icon. Consequently, key aspects of the two films, including much of their plots and Baker's performances, operate in counterpoint: while *Zouzou* is concerned with working-class Parisian culture and the music hall, *Princesse Tam-Tam* engages directly with colonial contact and represents a social critique of Paris's upper classes. However, Baker's character in both scripts is at best ambivalent as she fails ultimately to attain inclusion in French society.

Princesse Tam-Tam is a Pygmalion-style social experimentation narrative in which Baker plays Alouina, a Bedouin shepherdess and beggar from Tunisia who becomes the target of Max de Mirecourt (Albert Préjean), an upper-class French novelist seeking to regain the attention of his wife Lucie (Germaine Aussey), who has run off with a maharajah. In a prolonged sequence that is later revealed to be the European writer's dream, and which provides an excuse for two extended performance numbers featuring Baker, Max persuades Alouina to play the part of a North African princess so that he can introduce her to French high society and provoke Lucie's jealousy.

Alouina initially succeeds in the role but is unmasked when she performs an impromptu Conga at a high society ball. Max turns his dream into a novel while in reality Alouina never leaves home, and the final scene shows her living contentedly in Tunisia with her husband and new baby in Max's former villa, which is now overrun with animals. Max titles his book "Civilization" and gives a copy to Alouina. Symbolically, it remains unread and is soon eaten by her donkey. The two cultures are therefore constructed as binary opposites, with Alouina's world signifying as an unsophisticated but spiritually pure alternative to the sterility of European "civilization." But as in *Zouzou*, the film complicates visually such a reading by aestheticizing Baker and providing a platform for her artistry.

Like *Sirène* and *Zouzou*, which re-create cinematically Baker's "discovery" on the Parisian stage, the film acts as a fantastical biography of its star. Like the silent short featuring Baker, Sauvage, and Colin discussed at the beginning of this study, Max's experiment and appropriation of Alouina's life for his novel is a cinematic visualization of European writers' and producers' intervention in Baker's public identity. Alouina's donkey destroys Max's "Civilization" story, but the film narrative itself is a white male fantasy that shows how cultural producers distorted Baker's persona to fit their primitivist imaginings. *Princesse Tam-Tam*'s story-within-a-story framing also evokes the memoirs that Baker coauthored with Marcel Sauvage. It draws attention to the ways in which her image was externally mediated, recalling with no apparent irony her 1927 memoir which, as we have seen, was a commodified, exotic vision of the performer concocted by Sauvage and Colin.

However, the film's effort to construct Baker as a star does provide her with some autonomy within this framework. Olivia Lahs-Gonzales observes, "Although she was frequently cast as the exotic in Pygmalion-like transformation myths on stage, Baker also undermined these recurring themes by presenting herself inside these characters as a sleek art deco *moderne* with a smooth sculptured body and close-cropped hairstyle," an observation that can also be applied to her screen work.[67] Alouina's transformation into a member of Parisian high society provides Baker with an opportunity to model expensive ball gowns and references her own reinvention as a glamorous music hall star. Caricature-style images of Alouina intended to symbolize her conversion appear to be old drawings of Baker, as they feature her iconic lacquered hairstyle, and the painting of Alouina that the maharajah keeps in his home is an actual portrait of Baker.[68] As in her previous films, *Princesse Tam-Tam* also provides Baker with a measure of self-authorship by allowing her to realize her idiosyncratic performance style on screen.

Although Baker mentioned *Princesse Tam-Tam* briefly in *Josephine*, she overlooked it in her 1949 memoir. As discussed in chapter one, deeply troubled with her representation in *Sirène*, Baker omitted it from *Une vie*; instead, she anticipated *Princesse Tam-Tam* as her "second" film.[69] Her sporadic literary acknowledgment of *Princesse Tam-Tam* suggests that she was similarly disturbed by the production's depiction of her and wished, at various stages of her life, for it to be forgotten. Unlike *Zouzou*, the film plays overtly on race for comic effect. Max refers to his secretary and coauthor Coton (Robert Arnoux) as "my slave."[70] Alouina's depiction as a Bedouin woman is crude. In her first appearance in the film, she is shown hiding among cacti and then running through the desert with a sheep on her back, emphasizing her closeness to nature. Later in the film, she chases a monkey up a tree. Tunisia was a French colonial territory between 1883 and 1956, and while *Sirène* relied on a French forest to stand in for the Caribbean, *Princesse Tam-Tam* was shot on location with the permission of colonial authorities. Raynaud claims that the film "participates in the French colonial venture, offering idyllic visions of Roman ruins (Dougga) with aloe plants in the foreground, aristocrats going on a tour with a local guide and picnicking in the open air, and the local color of the market scenes."[71] T. Denean Sharpley-Whiting connects the primitivist persona constructed for Baker in *Princesse Tam-Tam* with a wider cinematic endeavor to extol French colonialism. She contends that, "In dire need of civilizing, the Baker cinematic Venus became a synecdoche for the colonies' savage and sensual state, a Frenchman's paradise ripe for continued conquest. Simply put, Baker/Aouina personifies an unruly Africa."[72]

But Sharpley-Whiting misreads the film's antiassimilationist stance, which critiques the excesses of French high society and shows that Alouina is content with her humble existence. It suggests that, instead of dominating overseas territories, they should be left alone, and it is Lucie and Max's society that requires "civilizing." Lucie is depicted as egocentric and self-indulgent, and when Alouina asks why she must pretend to be a princess Max tells her vainly that he wants to get even with his wife and the "disgusting snobs" of Paris's *beau monde*. Short sequences bleed into one another to position Parisian attitudes and lifestyles in negative contrast to Alouina's world. In one scene, Lucie and a friend talk flippantly about money; in the next, Alouina is depicted begging. Lucie and her friends imagine and describe Alouina as a "savage" and "cannibal" who must have arrived in Paris naked. Their criticisms of her facial features evoke pseudoscientific racist theories that equated character with physical attributes, with Lucie remarking on her nose and a friend declaring, "She's google-eyed, and that mouth." The group's criticisms are undercut by the following scene, in which Max declares a glamorously attired Alouina to be "charming." However, the film retains throughout a myopic approach to non-European cultures even as it deplores upper-class French decadence. Baker's role as a Bedouin woman is a convenient conflation of non-European cultures, and in a telling example of the film's cultural insensitivities, French actors in blackface play the maharajah and Alouina's eventual husband Tahar. By also suggesting that cultures should remain separate, the film plays into a post–World War I shift in colonial policy from a *mission civilisatrice* to a fear that granting citizenship rights to colonial subjects would threaten the French "race."

But the creative freedom that the film allows Baker as the film's star provides a visual counter-reading that helps in part to undermine its narrative of racial separation. *Princesse Tam-Tam*'s half-British, half-French director Edmond T. Gréville had worked with both "exotic" performers and former Ziegfeld Girls as assistant director on the British production *Piccadilly* (1929), starring Chinese American actress Anna May Wong and Shimmy popularizer Gilda Gray, and *Prix de Beauté* (1930), featuring the Hollywood star and style icon Louise Brooks. Gray and Brooks both started out as Ziegfeld Girls and Gray introduced the Shimmy to the Follies in 1922, sparking a nationwide craze. She claimed falsely to have invented the dance, whose origins Marshall and Jean Stearns traced to Nigeria.[73] But Gréville is most likely to have been chosen to work on *Princesse Tam-Tam* because of his growing reputation as an experimental director. The film uses a variety of techniques, including image juxtapositions and sudden camera angle changes, both to communicate the film's racial narrative in figurative terms and to create an ethereal, dreamlike world. *Le Petit Parisien* accused Gréville of being so obsessed by "technical acrobatics" that it had become "a kind of mania" and left the film with "many instances of unnecessary audacity."[74] But Gréville's evocative style merely sought to imitate the visual ornamentations of Hollywood musicals, and other critics comprehended the purpose of such "audacity": to promote Baker's star image. *L'Ouest-Éclair* concluded that the film was nothing but "an excuse to present the exotic star to us and especially to make her heard."[75] Gilbert Bernard wrote that, "the film was built for [Baker] in order to emphasize the extent of her talent, and to present her to us as alternately playful, wild, romantic and choreographic."[76] Such a framework complicates the narrative's construction of Alouina as an exotic Other and shows that the film is concerned simultaneously with establishing her as a credible Hollywood star.

Alouina's first performance takes place in the ancient Roman city of Dougga in northern Tunisia. In a scene that evokes Papitou's Charleston lesson on the Place de la Concorde in *Sirène*, Alouina dances and performs a handstand for a group of children, which reduces Baker's artistry to play. The location acknowledges the vast Roman and Islamic empires of which the North African nation was once a part, but the film employs such a backdrop to distance Alouina from such societies, even if to critique their excesses. Kathryn Kalinak suggests that Alouina's performance before the ruins places her "like a priestess in harmony with the mysteries of some pagan cult, intimately connected to ancient civilization."[77] But Kalinak's reading of Alouina as at one with her surroundings conflates the scene's complex dialectic between "ancient" and "modern" societies and obscures its satirical intentions. Tellingly, Alouina is shown dancing on the ruins of a fallen *Latin* civilization. Reading her performance alongside Max and Lucie's misbehavior implies that, while corruption and overindulgence will cause such societies to fall, the innocence of the primitive will endure.

However, references to Baker's early stage performances show that she was able to exercise some control over this scene, which allows her to interrogate her role and establish her screen image at least partly on her own terms. Alouina begins by performing Pecking, an African American vaudeville movement seen previously in *Revue* and *Zouzou*. She also anticipates the Conga sequence at the end of the film by executing movements from the routine. By performing modern Black dance practices, she reduces the scene's depiction of "primitive" societies to farce. As in *Zouzou*, Du Pont is listed as *Princesse Tam-Tam*'s choreographer, but Baker's performance again contrasts with his revue spectaculars and borrows heavily from her repertoire, meaning that she can credibly be judged as the dance's author.

Baker's next musical number is a solo vocal performance that anticipates Alouina's imagined journey to Europe and takes place during a boat ride with Tahar (white actor Georges Péclet), the "native" Tunisian that she will eventually marry. In "Le Chemin de bonheur" ("The Way of Happiness"), Alouina sings that "the ocean is the road to happiness" and fantasizes about sailing to Europe. Her wistfulness is intercut with Max's discovery that his wife is enjoying a scandalous relationship with a maharajah to show that Alouina's imaginings are misplaced and that she will not be happy in the petty world of Parisian high society. Although the scene creates a sense of cultural simplicity that is at odds with the discords of French "civilization," it allows Alouina to project emotional contemplation and longing, creating a sense of intimacy between Baker and the audience. Like the "Haiti" and

"C'est lui" sequences in *Zouzou*, it also permits her to assert her authorship by showing off her soprano technique, and her performance prompted a critic to exclaim, "She sings . . . in such an attractive manner!"[78]

Soft focus close-ups aestheticize Baker to accentuate her star image (see figure 8). Jules-Rosette has argued that such shots underscore Baker's "erotic appeal" and that the scene "retains the naïve simplicity of the primal vixen" even as it anticipates Alouina's glamorous transformation.[79] Jules-Rosette bases her reading on Sharpley-Whiting's argument that, "the camera's soft-filtered long takes of a youthful Baker with pencil-thin eyebrows, heavily made-up doe eyes, and long, false eyelashes, and a smiling or childishly pouting mouth," draw attention to her "exotic" appeal.[80] But such a look is Hollywood-inspired, and the scene's focus on Baker's face, together with her complex vocal performance, which like "Haiti" makes use of a high register and sustained notes, foregrounds her feminine beauty. Hollywood developed glamour lighting in the 1910s and 1920s based upon a study of European portraiture to create a dazzling, respectable vision of white womanhood, a "visual vocabulary for the presentation of the star," as Richard Dyer

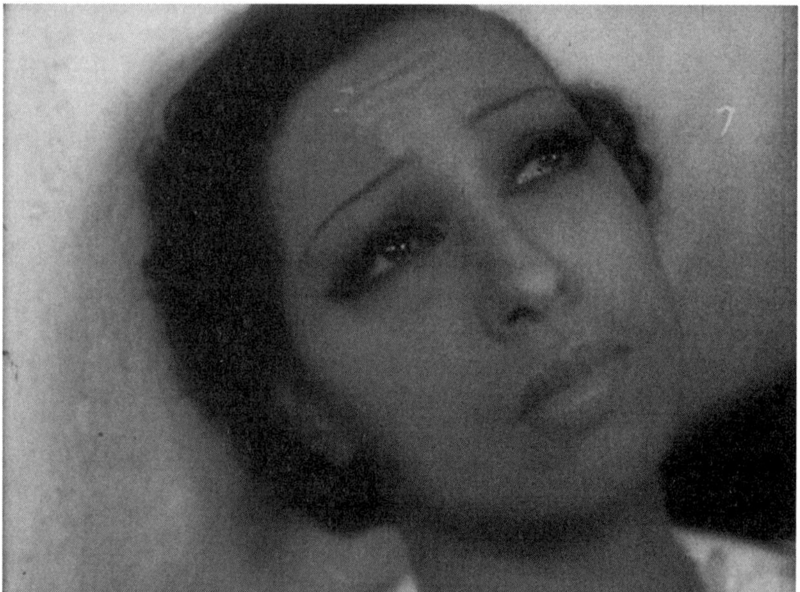

FIGURE 8. Soft-focus close-up of a wistful Baker in *Princesse Tam-Tam* (Di Ci Mo, 1935).

summarizes.[81] Such a technique was intended to suggest sexual and racial purity and was rooted in a Christian rhetoric of saintly femininity.[82] The racially occlusive, and sometimes purposefully racist, effects of such lighting are apparent in *The Birth of a Nation* (1915), which pioneered the technique to position its white star Lillian Gish in visual and moral contrast to its Black characters, most of whom were played by white performers in blackface.[83] By aestheticizing Baker in the same way as Hollywood's white female stars, the scene upends such racist visual codes and connects the artist with this womanly ideal. The sequence's purpose is not to reinforce Baker's eroticism and exoticism, but rather to locate her within Hollywood constructions of female beauty.

Alouina's transformation into a "princess" provides an excuse for another performance. Homesick and uncomfortable with the restrictions of Paris's *beau monde*, she runs off with Tahar to a sailors' bar in a sequence that operates in thematic contrast to "Le Chemin de bonheur" because it stresses her unhappiness in Paris. In "Sous le ciel d'Afrique" (Under the Skies of Africa), Alouina sings wistfully of her homeland and "its magic call" while the bar's African and European patrons nod their heads in sympathy. Baker again adopts a soprano singing style, and soft-focus upper-body shots position her performance as ideal.

The scene's tone does shift suddenly: the music's tempo increases and Alouina launches into a dance. Her routine is constructed as a spontaneous and playful break from Parisian upper-class life and ends with rapidly edited close-ups of her face to convey its psychological effect on her. But it is also technically accomplished and based on Baker's dance style. Fundamentally, it is a showcase for Baker the artist and star. Beginning with Shimmylike shoulder movements that she repeats in the Conga at the end of the film, she performs brushing steps with her right foot, an action that recalls the Sand Dance of African American vaudeville. Her swinging arms, backward glide, and sideways kicks reference the Charleston, and she also executes a brief tap step. In the midst of the dance, she stops at the bar and raises a glass to her mouth without using her hands, an action that underscores her athletic virtuosity. It can be read as proof of Alouina's uninhibitedness, but it also enables her to assert her belonging in the bar's cosmopolitan working-class community. Her action prompts a white sailor to join her dance; a potentially erotic reading of the scene is negated by the fact that they perform synchronized steps toe-to-toe as Tahar looks on. The scene allows her to transgress national boundaries, positioning her as a comrade of the international working class rather than a spectacle for its visual pleasure. As Raynaud asserts, "Analysts of the racial and colonial imaginary of France in the 1920s and 1930s often fail to note that the film also portrays 'the people.' . . . This inclusion should be stressed as an element that complicates a mere reading of 'the French' as all embodying the same degree of colonial arrogance and racist bigotry."[84] By situating Baker's character within such a community, the scene encourages audience identification and substitutes racial difference for class difference, allowing the film to be read, not as a colonial fantasy, but as a critique of French upper-class society and as a cinematic vision of international egalitarianism.

Baker's final dance sequence marks the point of Alouina's unmasking. One of Lucie's friends (played by Viviane Romance) witnessed the fake princess' performance while herself "slumming" in the bar and plies her with alcohol so that she repeats the act at the maharajah's high society ball. The ball section opens with a series of feminine displays. In this ambitious sequence, which represents the ball's official entertainment and is intended to signify highbrow artistry, a range of camera tricks are used to create a dreamlike vision of European womanhood. The scene begins with fireworks and opens onto a magnificent three-tiered spiral stage. A turbaned man places a spinning glitter ball on a dance floor and its shining surface fills the screen and is overlaid with a series of revolving spirals, creating a hypnotic cinematic effect. In a disregard for perspective, an array of pale-skinned chorines in polka-dot costumes emerges from the ball onto the stage. Like *Zouzou*, the sequence can be read as an attempt to re-create the spectacle of the Parisian music hall and Berkeley's Hollywood musicals. As with the Ziegfeld and Berkeley productions, women are constructed merely as props in a dizzying visual spectacle: the man in a turban blows them over, moves them around on a giant chessboard, and perches one on a spinning plate. The man's presence plays up miscegenation fantasies and can be read as an allusion to Lucie's relationship with the maharajah. The dancers are so passive that most of them initially remain stationary and are moved around on a revolving floor; others merely twirl. They do briefly perform basic steps, but the camera is more interested in the patterns formed by their bodies than in their artistry. Two particularly artful overhead shots show the dancers forming shapes with their collective bodies to create a kaleidoscopic effect.

The scene is broken by a shot of a Black man banging a drum and Alouina jumps onto the stage and launches into a lively Conga that shatters her princess persona. She throws away her heels and removes her gown to reveal a lamé version of the peasant dress she wore earlier in the film. Alouina literally strips to bare her "true" self, and according to Baker the original intention was for the dress to be more suggestive—"a filmy Black creation"—but Nissotti objected, believing that the outfit made her look "*almost* naked" and might prevent the film from being shown in the provinces and abroad.[85] The scene plays into notions of primitive abandon and operates in visual and thematic juxtaposition to the previous sequence. In contrast to the chorine's ordered routine, Alouina's dance is physically expressive. Quick close-up cuts of Baker's face are interspersed with shots of the drummer and hands holding wooden instruments to construct her performance as anarchic (see figure 9). As Sharpley-Whiting has observed, the Black drummer is not a member of the ball but has been "intercut in these sequences for racial affect."[86] The instruments function as expressions of Alouina's psyche, accentuating readings of her performance as atavistic. The film's depiction of African-style hand-drumming would have been considered daring to 1930s European audiences, having been introduced to the stage just a few years before *Princesse Tam-Tam* was released.[87] Anne Anlin Cheng argues that this fragmented cinematic effect occludes readings of "fetishistic voyeurism" because it is "surprisingly nonspecific and non-singular": the audience

FIGURE 9. A close-up shot of Baker dancing the Conga in *Princesse Tam-Tam*.

is presented with "entangled and writhing hands, arms, legs, and feet that belong to everyone and to no one."[88]

However, these disjointed body parts all belong to non-European characters. In this regard, the fractured sequence speaks to ethnographic entertainment as articulated in early cinema and the music hall, which was interested less in geographical specificity than in voyeuristic display and which tended to homogenize complex non-European societies as "precivilized" racial Others. Kalinak suggests that the rapid camera shots are in fact "techniques of objectification and containment," and that Baker is "rigidly inscribed by the camera."[89] Although the scene is a physically liberating contrast to the refined femininity of the chorines, Alouina remains locked in a frenzied racial fantasy of the camera's making. If we read the scene as an attempt to transfer Baker's music hall image to the screen, then we must once again acknowledge the role of pseudo-ethnographic display in Baker's public image and its prominence in music hall and early cinema more broadly.

But as in her silent films, Baker retains her vaudeville dance style, which drew on and parodied modern African diasporic forms of artistry to disrupt racial ideologies. If Baker's artistry as well as the film's satirical intentions, class concerns, and attempts to transform her into an international cinema star are considered, a reading is possible that counters the scene's pseudo-ethnographic vision and recognizes Baker as artist and star. As described earlier, the bar sequence establishes Alouina's performative persona not as erotic but as an expression of international egalitarianism, which was a chief concern of Baker's memoirs and the focus of her post–World War I career. Alouina's Conga can be interpreted in such a spirit. Lucie's friend believes that Alouina's performative break from Parisian decorum will destroy her reputation. Instead, the chorines welcome her, and the audience literally embraces her work, with male admirers rushing onto the stage to carry her in their arms in a physical collapse of cultural and racial barriers. The chorines function as a warm-up to Alouina's act and they continue to dance during it. The women operate merely as foils to accentuate Baker's stardom. In this regard, the scene plays into the narrative's primitivist rejection of European artifice in favor of an "authentic" African past. But it also grants Baker control over her representation, allowing her to rupture gender and race conventions. The scene is a further demonstration that Baker was able to retain some agency within the film narrative's confines. As in her silent films, her dance is self-choreographed; in contrast to the synchronized routine, it breaks with, rather than reinforces, the sultan's Svengali-like control over the chorines and enables Alouina to maintain independence. As in *Sirène* and *Zouzou*, Baker creates a visual contrast to regimented dance performances that deprived women of individuality.

Baker's routine is also intended to popularize African diasporic art forms. Her highly self-referential and improvisational dance incorporates popular styles from the 1920s and 1930s onto the screen. She performs a Mess Around, as seen previously in *Revue*, by placing her hands on her hips and gyrating her bottom. Yet much of the act, which includes Shimmylike shoulder movements and high kicks, is an improvised interpretation of the Conga, an extremely popular dance in mid-1930s Paris. In *Josephine*, Baker claimed that what she most enjoyed about the film was "the chance it gave me to introduce the Conga to France."[90] In fact, the dance arrived in Europe when white Cuban expatriate Eliseo Grenet adapted Afro-Cuban Carnival music for the French ballroom, simplifying its rhythms for European audiences. In 1936, the year that Baker performed the dance in the *Ziegfeld Follies*, he brought his creation to New York, precipitating a worldwide craze. Grenet wrote the music for *Princesse Tam-Tam*, suggesting that the scene was devised purposely to capitalize on the dance's popularity. Grenet's Conga speaks to a history of cultural appropriation of African-derived artistry. In the United States, the Conga would soon become associated with white Cuban bandleader Desi Arnaz. However, Baker's performance to its rhythms and her assertion in her autobiography that she introduced it to France reclaims it as a Black art form. At least one film reviewer assumed that the Conga was Baker's creation. *Le Matin* affirmed that *Princesse Tam-Tam* would give audiences "the pleasure to see Josephine create a new dance known as the Conga, whose entirely new rhythm will seduce Terpsichore fans."[91] The scene therefore acknowledges the Conga as Black artistic practice and positions Baker—a Black woman—at the vanguard of 1930s dance culture. It is also semiautobiographical, referencing her "discovery" at *La Revue Nègre*, and can be read as an attempt to replicate her Charleston's transformative effect on Parisian culture ten years earlier.

At the end of *Princesse Tam-Tam*, Alouina's Pygmalion-like transformation is revealed to have been Max's fantasy. As in *Zouzou*, the racialized social order that Alouina has threatened to unravel is restored. Both film narratives play up Baker's status as an "exotic" novelty and socially exclude her characters. However, critical fixation on the film plots overlooks their principal purpose, which was to establish Baker as a plausible cinema star and to export this persona to the United States. Consequently, the films draw on visual conventions associated with star imagery that were denied to African American artists in Hollywood, and their performance scenes serve as platforms for Baker's stage persona. These self-referential sequences allow her to exercise authorial control over her screen image and to present an unruly and cross-cultural fantasy of womanhood even as the films' narratives reinforce readings of racial difference.

Baker's sound films demonstrate that she cultivated a glamorous image in the 1930s that tapped into Eurocentric notions of beauty. Her failure to transfer this image to the United States underscores the strength of its racialized cultural hierarchies and, in turn, the contrasts between European fascinations with exotic Otherness and mainstream U.S. society's denials of Black women's beauty. High production value films such as *Zouzou* and *Princesse Tam-Tam*, which were designed deliberately to promote a Black woman's aesthetic appeal, could be made in interwar Europe, but not in Hollywood. Yet Baker's performance in the *Ziegfeld Follies* should not be deemed wholly without significance. She was the first American-born woman to work with Balanchine, and as noted previously, there is evidence to suggest that she influenced his concept of the feminine ideal and that the jazz dance influences that Brenda Dixon Gottschild identifies in his work can be traced back to Baker.[92] Although the Russian-born choreographer's attempts to incorporate Black dancers into his productions largely stalled due to U.S. racial sensibilities, he did work with the Nicholas Brothers in *Babes in Arms* (1937) and devised, funded, and directed the all-Black Broadway production *Cabin in the Sky* just four years after the *Follies* show. *Cabin in the Sky*'s screen adaptation was one of only six Black-cast Hollywood feature films made between 1929 and 1954 and one of only two from the 1940s. The other was *Stormy Weather*, a subject of the next chapter. *Cabin in the Sky* included the daringly sensual Sweet Georgia Brown, a Black woman described in the original script as "voluptuous, good-looking," and "full of sex appeal."[93] Dunham originated the role of Brown on stage and claimed that Balanchine chose her personally to star in, stage, and help choreograph the production.[94] Her performance led to work in Hollywood, and it is to this aspect of her career that this study now turns.

CHAPTER FIVE

Cinematic Segregation

Dunham in World War II Hollywood

In Black-cast musical *Stormy Weather* (1943), protagonist Selina Rogers (Lena Horne) performs in a fantasy stage spectacular. Clad in a bra, skirt of animal pelts, elaborate jewelry, and an ostrich-plume headdress, she sings of being "so very diga diga doo by nature" while women dancers in animal-print leotards sit cross-legged around her and topless male drummers, including tap-dancer Bill "Bojangles" Robinson, perch in a tree above her. The dancers wiggle their bodies and slap their knees in time to fast-paced, jazzy music. Adapted from *Blackbirds of 1928*, the number pays tribute to Broadway shows such as *Shuffle Along* (1921), which afforded Black artists such as Baker entry into the U.S. theatrical mainstream. It references specifically Robinson, *Stormy Weather*'s male lead, whose work in *Blackbirds* made him a household name. However, the scene pays equal homage to the exotic and erotic cultural frameworks in which such performers were forced to work, signaling the endurance of such homogenizing and hypersexual depictions of nonwhite identities in midcentury U.S. culture. When Selina departs, the scene becomes increasingly anarchic: the music grows faster and louder and the women's movements gain momentum as they engage in a stylized stomping routine that coincides with the arrival of a tribal warrior and his female conquest. Like the *danse sauvage* that Baker performed on her opening night in Paris, in which she was introduced as the seemingly dead prey of her partner Joe Alex, the scene becomes a sinister mating ritual.[1] A mask of war paint and feathers obscures the warrior's identity and he drags his unwilling partner into the midst of the performers and throws her to the floor before chasing her around the stage. Once his "prize" has been caught, the warrior and the women perch on all fours like animals and jump up and down with exaggerated excitement.

Selina returns to the stage later in the film to sing the title song. In a striking parallel with the earlier sequence, her performance is again merged with an imagined and sexually charged "exotic" world, in which gyrating Black bodies—this time those of Dunham and her company—interact physically. Dunham's troupe employs sexual themes and gestures, a similarity between the two scenes that allows for primitivist readings of its performance. Described by the *New York Times* as "a short, blistering jungle dance," the sexuality of the sequence visualizes a distorted cultural history that depicted Black bodies as physically uninhibited and which exercised a powerful influence on Baker's European career.[2] But like Baker's performances, which combined primitivist iconography with African diasporic forms of dance and European artistry, Dunham's scene reconfigures such constructions. It combines ballet with dance techniques that Dunham witnessed in the Caribbean while also alluding to the fashion adornments and performance venues of World War II African American youth culture. In the sequence, the physical expresses the psychological and sexuality is used to lay claim to notions of high art. Dunham's emphasis on artistic experimentation and dignified movements challenges crude misrepresentations of Black performers and creates an aesthetic vision of African diasporic dance cultures that stakes a claim for their significance as key sites of modernist expression.

This chapter examines Dunham's interventions in World War II–era U.S. cinema. Dunham's film roles serve as valuable visual records of her stage image and creative goals, as well as the challenges that she faced as a Black choreographer in Hollywood and midcentury U.S. culture more generally. I investigate the ambiguities resulting from Dunham's attempts to resist screen stereotypes and create an image of dancing bodies rooted in her anthropological research within a constraining and frequently exploitative production framework. Focusing on three of Dunham's Hollywood films—the dance short, *Carnival of Rhythm* (1941); the propaganda revue, *Star Spangled Rhythm* (1942); and the Black-cast musical, *Stormy Weather*—the chapter recovers Dunham's groundbreaking contribution as a Black woman choreographer to midcentury U.S. cinema. I show how Dunham's performances represented a negotiation of studio-era racial codes but also how she mediated such codes and was able, to some extent, to assert her authorship by presenting a vision of Black dancing womanhood in Hollywood that was pioneering its open engagement with sensuality, cultural diversity, and choreographic allusions to ballet. I establish that Dunham was the first Black choreographer to gain onscreen credit for her work in Hollywood and evidence a separation between cinematic narratives and Dunham's performances similar to Baker's films. As with Baker, I also trace the ways in which contemporary Black audiences received her work.

Dunham has yet to receive her due as a pioneering Black woman choreographer in Hollywood. The only published studies of her work on *Carnival of Rhythm* are brief analyses by Joanna Dee Das and Daphne Lamothe, and criticism of her performance in *Star Spangled Rhythm* is currently limited to Thomas Cripps's assertion that it gave the dancer and her costar a "rollicking spoof of zoot suit style in all its calculated outrageousness."[3] Dunham's contribution to *Stormy Weather* has received critical attention, but not through the lens of midcentury film history.[4] Nevertheless, her dance formations enjoyed significant mainstream success at a time when Black performers in the United States were generally consigned to segregated musical numbers, as Baker found to her cost when she appeared in the *Ziegfeld Follies*. Like Baker, Dunham's work was indebted to early-twentieth-century African American vaudeville, although her engagement with the genre was less direct. As *A Touch of Innocence* reveals, Dunham visited vaudeville houses as a child but her formative schooling was in ballet and modern dance.[5] She combined this training with her Caribbean experiences to develop a cross-cultural choreographic technique that complicated Hollywood's prescriptive tap- and vaudeville-based depictions of Black dancers. As former Dunham company member Tommy Gomez recalled of *Stormy Weather*, "the country had never seen ballet movements by a Black company in a film before."[6]

The intention of this chapter is not to overlook the representational issues at the heart of Dunham's performances but to highlight the ways in which, like Baker, her exploration within a field of spectacle, voyeurism, and racialized artistic hierarchies reveals a creative play within these very distortions that defies straightforward interpretations. The cinematic restrictions that Dunham and her company endured as Black artists suggest that Baker's attempt via the *Ziegfeld Follies* to transfer her European film stardom to Hollywood could only have ended in failure. They serve as visual testimony of the frustrations that would cause Dunham to abandon Hollywood after World War II. Yet they also show how, like Baker, Dunham worked within such limitations to present an artistically and aesthetically appreciative vision of Black femininity onscreen. In *Carnival of Rhythm* and *Stormy Weather* in particular, Dunham's artistry had a determining influence on the films' aesthetics. Such sequences are valuable cinematic records of her creative practice and African diasporic dance traditions more broadly as well as revealing accounts of her fight for recognition as a Black woman artist in midcentury U.S. culture.

Superficially, Dunham appears to have enjoyed little influence as a Black woman working in midcentury Hollywood, and certain members of the Black press criticized her for a film career that they felt played into the racist imagination of a Euro-American production framework. As Julia L. Foulkes observes, "The critic Don Deleighbur worried that Dunham had let Hollywood and commercial success inspire a taste for 'the glitter and glamour of the extravaganza and mimicry.' The worry masked a concern that Dunham had fallen sway to white ideals of entertainment, copying their idea of dance for African Americans—with its emphasis on sexual provocation—and losing the racial originality she had possessed earlier."[7] Dunham had limited space to realize her artistry in such an environment, which could either distance her performances from film plots or remove her altogether. Her choreography was omitted from the 1943 film version of *Cabin in the Sky*, and her performances in *Star Spangled Rhythm* and *Stormy Weather* were restricted to one-off dance routines.[8] *Stormy Weather* star Lena Horne, who at this time was the only Black performer on a long-term Hollywood contract, endured similar treatment, which underscores the radicalism of Baker's French cinematic stardom. However, tendencies to overlook Dunham's screen roles for their subjugated status obscures the ways in which, as in Baker's films, such scenes defer to her authorship and in so doing showcase a pioneering cross-cultural choreographic method that challenged homogenizing representations of Black women.

Carnival of Rhythm, an eighteen-minute Technicolor short devoted to Dunham and her company, shows how she blended her anthropological training with dance to intervene in classical Hollywood racial codes. The film's investment in rhythm and sensuality reinscribes fantasies of Black performers as "exotic" spectacles. However, it also sheds light on Dunham's wider project to enact a cultural legitimization of historically dispossessed Black Atlantic dance practices by incorporating them onto the U.S. stage and screen. It is a rare acknowledgment of African American behind-the-scenes authorship in classical Hollywood that also visualizes the cultural and global diversity of African diasporic forms of artistry. Its stylish performance numbers and innovative use of color, conveyed largely by outfits created by Dunham's costume designer and future husband John Pratt, also ensure that it should be recognized as an early art film that is groundbreaking in its expressionistic style and aesthetic treatment of Black Brazilian performance cultures.

Carnival of Rhythm was released through Warner Brothers' short subjects division, the Vitaphone Corporation, and employs traditional song and dance forms from Dunham's repertoire to depict a day in the life of a Brazilian rope-weaving community. The film was shot in Technicolor and director Jean Negulesco was renowned for his innovative cinematography and use of rich color.[9] He would later make the Marilyn Monroe film *How to Marry a Millionaire* (1953), one of the first productions to use the CinemaScope photographic process, and was also responsible for an extremely rare and surprisingly sympathetic, if largely white-centric, cinematic dramatization of the Haitian Revolution, *Lydia Bailey* (1952). Negulesco employs experimental camera shots to create an artistically appreciative vision of an Afro-Brazilian rope-weaving community and the film is notable as one of Hollywood's first engagements with modern dance. Writing eight years after its release, critic Margaret Lloyd deemed it "The most satisfactory color dance film to date."[10] Asserting that, "modern dance is still the exception in the commercial picture," Lloyd interpreted *Carnival of Rhythm*'s stylized use of color and camera angles to be an unusually effective cinematic engagement with modern dance practices.[11] Joanna Dee Das asserts that its inclusion in the "first all-dance film festival" at New York's Fifth Avenue Playhouse in June 1942 made it "part of the vanguard of dance on screen."[12]

Yet the film is even more unusual for the authorial control and acknowledgment that it grants to a Black choreographer in 1940s Hollywood. As the originator of the film's dance and musical material, Dunham exercised an exceptional level of influence over the production for, as Roy Thomas observed, "This short film is the single Hollywood production in which a professional film editor and choreographer determined jointly what the final film would look like."[13] Equally significantly, *Carnival of Rhythm* opens with a credit sequence that attributes the "origination of production and choreography" to Dunham at a time when Black dancers were rarely acknowledged for their artistry. The term *choreographer* was new to the United States at this time, "dance director" being the preferred term.[14] However, *Carnival of Rhythm* still marked the first onscreen acknowledgment of Black dance authorship. As the previous two chapters have shown, Baker was not credited onscreen for dancing that owed everything to her Black vaudeville-derived stage style. Dunham's achievement was such that it was not until former

Dunham dancer and *Carnival of Rhythm* lead, Archie Savage, worked on the Biblical epic *The Last Days of Sodom and Gomorrah* (1962) that a Black artist received onscreen credit as a choreographer of a major Hollywood production.[15] Such belated recognition speaks to studio-era Hollywood's reliance on uncredited Black artistry. Dancing and singing star Marie Bryant, a former teacher at the Katherine Dunham School of Dance in New York, became a freelance instructor to leading Hollywood stars in the late 1940s and early 1950s. Her students included Betty Grable, Lucille Ball, and Cyd Charisse, as well as Paulette Goddard who, like Dunham, appeared in *Star Spangled Rhythm*. However, Bryant was credited for her "dance direction" on just one film, *The Lady Says No* (1951). As Robert Jackson observes, "Bryant's contributions to white-cast musicals were systematically obscured to audiences."[16]

Carnival of Rhythm is divided into four musical sequences that together create a complex vision of everyday indigenous and Afro-Brazilian lives. A brief introduction depicts Dunham dancing before the camera as a voiceover states, "Dunham, who has traveled the world over studying the rhythm from every land, paints . . . a portrait of life itself, set to music." In this way, the film acknowledges the choreographer as a scholarly authority on and visual interpreter of international dance practices. However, a production framework that foregrounds the perceived exoticism of Dunham's material works against her cinematic exploration of Black Brazilian cultures. In an essay published around the time of *Carnival of Rhythm*, Dunham asserted that ritual dance forms and Broadway musicals were linked by their "similarity in function."[17] She suggested that dance's social purpose, especially its role in strengthening community identity, was effectively always the same, regardless of geographical or cultural location.[18] But Hollywood filmmakers did not share Dunham's vision and, similarly to Baker's experiences on the French screen, frequently exploited her art's perceived sensuality, creating a tension between her intentions and cinematic representations of her work. In the words of Lamothe, "Hollywood convention undercut Dunham's efforts to bind form and function in her choreography, often reducing it to its most base and simplistic uses where rhythmic isolations were linked to sexual impulses."[19] However, close study of Dunham's performance scenes reveals that her artistry is legible even within these distortions.

Carnival of Rhythm's opening scene is darkly lit, and a barelegged Dunham spins and performs Shimmylike shoulder movements to a fast-paced beat set by a group of drummers who sit behind her. The shadowy background and rhythmic intensity of the scene create a mood of sensuality and abandon, as shown in figure 10. The film's voiceover indulges in romanticized inventions of Latin American cultures. The narrative opens with the line, "rhythms from Latin America, rhythms ancient as the beat of voodoo drums, modern as the flash of bolero," conflating South American and Haitian performance practices and contrasting the supposedly "modern" Spanish-derived bolero with the apparent timelessness of Black cultural forms. As in Baker's films, in which non-European identities were employed interchangeably, the opening scene creates a homogenizing portrait of African diasporic communities.

The film then cuts to a marketplace, in which a vivid blue background is used to evoke a bright morning as workers sing the popular march, "Cidade Maravilhosa" (Marvelous City), a song composed for the 1935 Rio de Janeiro Carnival that later became the city's anthem. The scene is a tribute to Brazilian working-class cultures but is exaggerated and idealistic. Dunham balances a basket of fruit on her head and sings as she strides across a set populated by colorful fruit and tropical birds. She becomes a source of fascination for the villagers, who congregate around her and then march in single file behind her. The fruit functions as a metaphor for sex, with Dunham throwing fruit from her basket to suggest her availability. The film constructs Dunham as a

FIGURE 10. *Carnival of Rhythm*'s (Warner Bros., 1941) shadowy opening sequence.

voluptuous Brazilian woman, which appealed to contemporary U.S. fantasies of Latin American exoticism. Hollywood representations of "Latina" bodies fulfilled audience fascinations while strengthening perceived cultural binaries between North and South America and providing a cinematic justification for U.S. imperialism. As Myra Mendible notes, "the Latina body offered a tempting alter/native: an exotic object of imperial and sexual desire."[20]

Dunham's personal secretary Jeanelle Stovall described *Carnival of Rhythm* as the result of Hollywood's perceived "need" for a Brazil-set film.[21] World War II U.S. economic and foreign policy concerns led to increased Hollywood interest in Latin America. The film formed part of a cultural attempt to sell President Franklin D. Roosevelt's Good Neighbor Policy of friendly relations with Latin American countries, which aimed to protect vital trading markets and prevent the United States' neighbors from forming alliances with Nazi Germany. Hollywood was also becoming increasingly reliant on Latin American cinemagoers to offset audience losses in Axis territories. Like other Hollywood films from this period, *Carnival of Rhythm* aimed to create an idealistic, nonthreatening vision of South America. But the image that Hollywood constructed was rooted in geographical ignorance and condescending conceptions of exotic sensuality that were widely removed from human realities.[22]

However, *Carnival of Rhythm* remains significant for the ways in which Dunham navigates these clichés to present a visually evocative and, in many respects, transformative depiction of Black cultures. Dunham developed the film's music and choreography and her correspondence with one of its producers reveals creative demands that led to script modifications and a voiceover less crude than originally intended. An early draft included the phrases, "our little Bahiana girl plays with love like a child with a bright green and red ball," and "poor little Bahiana girl! Hear her sing against the gathering shadow, her song of sorrow," which Dunham dismissed as "extremely unsophisticated and precious."[23] She offered to rewrite parts of the narrative and appears to have enjoyed some success in persuading producers to remove particularly condescending phrases and include "more native flavor rather than tourist flavor in the commentary."[24] At the very least, she prevented the filmmakers from infantilizing her presentation of mature sexual encounters in a Brazilian village. Pratt was also granted creative control over the costumes. In her letter to Sobelman, Dunham requested that her partner's artistic vision be adhered to and declared, "I would prefer to have the general tone of the thing remain within the general tone of our work heretofore."[25] Sobelman responded that Pratt would be given "entire responsibility for costuming the motion picture in a way successful in Technicolor": Pratt would design the costumes, but the producers would oversee his color choices.[26]

Such instructions draw attention to the negotiations and representational conflicts of Dunham's Hollywood work. They echo Baker's frustrations with and ultimate disavowal of many of her films and hint at the impossibility of a Black dancer achieving fame in classical Hollywood on her own terms. The costumes' bold colors play into flamboyant myths of Latina womanhood popularized by Carmen Miranda, the Portuguese-born Brazilian singer whose increasingly caricaturized persona functioned as a metaphor for South American abundance and who became a cultural figurehead for the Good Neighbor Policy. But at the same time, the stylishness of Dunham's outfits imbues her character with glamour and beauty rarely attributed to Black women, and Afro-Brazilian women in particular, in studio-era Hollywood.

These tensions are particularly apparent in the film's first major dance-based number, in which Dunham performs a solo entitled *Batucada*. The Batucada is a traditional Samba with an African-influenced percussive rhythm. The scene is a cinematic document of one of Dunham's most popular dances, which was also known as *Bahiana* and which remained in her repertoire throughout her thirty-year performance career. She is dressed as a woman from Bahia, an Afro-Brazilian community that was the uncredited visual source for the pale-skinned Miranda's star image.[27] Dunham's character is willingly ensnared in a rope held by Archie Savage's fisherman. She then slowly spins while performing rhythmic pelvic movements, actions that cause the rope to tighten around her waist. Dunham's flirtatious behavior entices the men around her, and she wears stylizations of traditional dress with jewelry to celebrate the beauty of Bahiana women.

Dunham incorporated Brazilian composer Don Alfonso's song "Batucada" into her repertoire before *Carnival of Rhythm* was made, which reveals her creative influence over the film's music as well as its choreography. The song became so closely associated with her company that she recorded and released it through British record label Decca during her postwar European tour. The record's sleeve-note emphasizes the African origins of the song, stating that, "The title, Batucada, indicates that the singer represents a member of the Batuque people, an African tribe transplanted in Brazil," while also noting that its narrative "is that of a woman calling attention to the charm of her jewelry, costume, and person."[28] Anthropologist Harold Courlander recorded the Batucada's sacred significance, describing its devotees as a "guild of the dispossessed for whom Batucada means spiritual fulfilment"; Dunham's promotion of it demonstrates her concern to recover African diasporic dance and celebrate its practitioners.[29] "Samba" was used as a synonym in the late nineteenth century for Afro-Brazilian dances and parties held by enslaved men and women. Bahian migrants brought the elements that would make up the modern Samba to Rio in the late nineteenth century, and it was codified as a distinct genre in the households of elderly Bahian matriarchs, known respectfully as *tias* (aunts). The practice was initially socially despised and suppressed. It eventually entered into and was appropriated by middle-class society through the impersonal conduits of records and the radio. Such measures led this initially derided art form to be reconceived as a symbol of Brazil national identity in the 1930s.

Bahiana women were therefore excluded from their own artistic legacy, an elision that Hollywood and, to a slightly lesser extent, the Brazilian film industry reinforced. Despite Miranda's commercial success, Black performers rarely appeared in Latin American Hollywood musicals and were generally consigned to minor and background roles in Brazilian cinema.[30] Their absence from Hollywood was such that, of the Rio-set musicals made in the United States between 1933 and 1953, only the pre–Hays Code-era production *Flying down to Rio* (1933), which did include the African American singer Etta Moten and light-skinned Black dancers dressed as Bahiana women, featured them.[31] On the contrary, Miranda was widely perceived to represent a vision of Latin American womanhood deemed racially unambiguous. For example, Atlanta film censor Zella Richardson thanked MGM for what she considered to be the all-white cast of Miranda feature *The Gang's All Here* (1943).[32] In the words of Priscilla Peña Ovalle, Miranda "personified a difference that was ultimately divorced from Blackness."[33] Equally, Robert Stam refers to Black artistry in Brazilian cinema as a "veiled presence" that marked its practitioners' "*absence* from the screen."[34] Dunham's experience while making *Carnival of Rhythm* emblematizes Black people's systematic exclusion from midcentury Hollywood. Warner Brothers producers tried to halt work on the film when they found out that the cast was African American, and the choreographer and her troupe had to fight to claim the right to play Brazilians.[35] The producers contended that people with dark skin did not have the right to represent the nation's folk culture despite the substantial numbers of Brazilians with African ancestry. Dunham mounted a counterchallenge to this treatment by inviting Brazilian diplomats to view the performances, and their positive responses ultimately rescued the production.[36] However, Hollywood censors demanded that the film's original title, *La Bahiana*, be changed as it signaled too clearly that Black dancers were performing as Brazilians.[37]

The *Batucada* scene serves as a corrective to Bahiana women's cultural elision as it represents a dignified vision of Black Brazilian womanhood and Black womanhood more generally. Dancers Archie Savage and Talley Beatty take turns to dance with Dunham, as seen in figure 11, and the scene ruptures midcentury U.S. race and gender conventions. Considering Dunham's dignified staging of human relationships in her ballet *Rites de Passage*, which was first staged in 1941, the year that *Carnival of Rhythm* was released, John O. Perpener asserts that, "Among white producers, it was considered taboo to portray a Black man and woman in a meaningful intimate relationship . . . productions that showed Black performers intimately involved were acceptable as long as the image created could be interpreted as crude and animalistic."[38] Dunham and Pratt contest this derogatory framework using costuming and carefully devised choreography. They construct a vision of Afro-Brazilian working men and women's lives in which they are depicted using their bodies in a manner that is not crude but instead is delicate and refined, and which presents them as equal partners. In this way, Dunham and Pratt stage a noteworthy challenge to classical Hollywood racial codes.

FIGURE 11. Katherine Dunham and Talley Beatty dancing as Archie Savage looks on in *Carnival of Rhythm*.

By presenting a vision of Brazilian nationhood centered firmly on its Black population, such work also contests Brazilian cinema's foregrounding of white performers. Dunham's decision to open the film with "Cidade Maravilhosa," an anthem for Rio de Janeiro that was originally commercialized by Carmen Miranda's younger sister Aurora, can be taken as proof that she sought deliberately to redress such narratives.

However, the filmmakers imposed a more sexual reading on the scene by causing Dunham and Savage's playful interaction to give way to her interpretation of a Maracatu, a fast-paced, more intimate Brazilian dance.[39] In this sequence, Savage and Beatty are both bare-chested and Dunham is barefoot. Beatty executes angular movements to a rapid drumbeat while Savage performs equally rapid Shimmylike shoulder isolations and Dunham lifts her skirt, seemingly inviting her partner to perform Vacunao, an erotic pelvic gesture in Latin dance. The scene satisfies audience expectations of "hot" Latin rhythms. In vain, Dunham expressed frustration at such a shift in tone, declaring, "Since the Maracatu is an established Indian rhythm, it would hardly seem likely that I would, as a Bahiana, change character enough to do an Indian dance."[40] Dunham's letter reveals the extent to which her film performances were caught in a conflict between her artistic intentions and distorting production frameworks. She sought to stage social interactions and cultural rituals in Caribbean and South American folk communities, but her work was frequently marketed and read as erotic entertainment in the United States.

However, Sobelman did acknowledge that the film's purpose was to portray "four vital moods in a woman's life," and the performance numbers together create a tonal complexity that challenges straightforward readings of promiscuity and allows Dunham to present a rich human portrait of an African diasporic community.[41] After the Maracatu, Dunham and Savage's characters are forcedly parted, triggering a slow-paced mourning sequence entitled "Tristessa" in allusion to *tristeza*, the Portuguese word for sadness. Dunham, attired in an elaborate Black costume, reclines despondently on a bridge and gazes down at her watery reflection while singing a *fado*, or Portuguese lament, for her departed lover. The other women in her community, similarly bereft of their men, lean on tables and fan themselves equally sorrowfully. Close-up camera shots and dark colors, which incorporate purple shadows to suggest dusk, signify complex emotions. Dunham described this sequence as "really the song of a woman, and quite full of the sorrow of experience and maturity" in an explicit negation of the infantilizing representations of Brazilian womanhood that producers sought originally to convey.[42] The final sequence, a late-night dance number, builds on this heightened emotional intensity. Fishermen returning from work sing the slave lament, "Adeus Terras" (Goodbye Homeland), which acknowledges the community's African ancestry. Savage's character is among the men and the narrative imagines the "mighty days in his own far off land, the wonder of old Africa." The sequence's emphasis on the African origins of Brazilian working-class cultures helps to reinforce an illusory concept of cultural purity, disregarding the Black Atlantic's place as a key site of modernity. But it also calls attention to enslaved communities' human endurances and evidences Dunham's wider objective to visualize African diasporic experiences on the stage and screen. The male workers perform a slow-paced march that conveys their physical prowess, presenting a commanding and dignified vision of Black Brazilian masculinity.

The scene also allows Dunham to stage her Caribbean anthropological observations onscreen by performing a trancelike ritual. The women respond to the men with propulsive and hypnotic gestures based on Yanvalou, an ecstatic movement dedicated to the serpentine loa Damballa in which the torso undulates like a snake. It is therefore possible to interpret this sequence as a re-creation of Dunham's immersion in Haitian Vodou, as recounted in *Island Possessed*. Four years after recording *Carnival of Rhythm*, Dunham premiered *Shango*, a staged translation of a Vodou rite that drew on her research in Haiti and Trinidad, which became one of her most famous productions. The sequence thus functions as a key text that shows her scientific observations transformed onto a commercial platform. But the sequence's staging undercuts the ritual's psychological significance by situating the movements as sexually suggestive, and close-up, rapid camera shots reinforce readings of Dunham's dance as unrestrained. The sequence's editing bears striking similarities to Baker's visually fragmented Conga sequence in *Princesse Tam-Tam*, serving as further evidence of the ways in which Black women's artistry was distorted on screen to play up primitivist fantasies. Dunham is shown falling to the ground, moving hypnotically, and arching her body to an increasingly fast-paced rhythm, thus playing into popular fears of "possession," and of "voodoo" cultures. The narrative eroticizes Dunham and her dancers still further, describing the rhythm that draws the men as "untamed and violent, savage as the night from which it comes."

Carnival of Rhythm was caught in a conflict between Hollywood racial codes and a World War II–fueled cinematic interest in Latin America. Within this framework, Dunham managed to assert her authorship and create an aesthetically appealing international vision of Black womanhood based on her anthropological observations of the everyday lives and dance practices of interwar Caribbean communities. The finished film plays into exotic fantasies of South American lives but still is significant as a rare classical-era Hollywood depiction of Black Brazilian cultures. *Star Spangled Rhythm*, the next film to feature Dunham, implicated her more directly in Hollywood's war concerns by including her in a recruitment drive. The production exemplifies the ways in which war-era Hollywood employed the "specialty number" to maintain racial segregation while at the same time appropriating Black artistry for propaganda purposes. But Dunham's performance also represents a complex engagement with Hollywood's race and gender roles and, like Baker's work in *Sirène*, appears to have had a positive psychological impact on war-era Black audiences. Her scene alludes to the fashions of African American youth culture and acknowledges the "street" as a site of creativity. It also links cinematically the art of Dunham and George Balanchine, who worked on the film with his second wife, Norwegian-German ballerina Vera Zorina. The film's inclusion of choreography by both Balanchine and Dunham illustrates the porous nature of perceived "high" and "low" cultures. Yet such linkages are nevertheless contained within a racially segregated film framework that speaks to the contrasting social status of Black and white women dancers in World War II–era Hollywood. Consequently, Dunham's work simultaneously enters into and critiques derogatory cultural depictions of Black women.

In 1942, Hollywood's interest in Dunham's art reached its peak. She participated in two all-star box office hits.[43] Universal's *Pardon My Sarong* was an Abbott and Costello vehicle, and Paramount's *Star Spangled Rhythm* was a war propaganda film filled with leading actors and artists, including Bob Hope and Balanchine, who both worked with Baker on the *Ziegfeld Follies*. As noted previously, Balanchine collaborated with Dunham on *Cabin in the Sky*, and there is evidence to suggest that she helped to choreograph its dance sequences. Hollywood's interest in Dunham shows that it recognized the commercial potential of her art. Equally, her limited onscreen roles underscore the extent to which World War II–era Hollywood sidelined Black performers. Both films exploit Dunham's choreography and yet marginalize their author. In *Pardon My Sarong*, Dunham and her dancers are omitted altogether as white women perform her work. *Star Spangled Rhythm* features Dunham, but in a racially segregated role.

Star Spangled Rhythm has received almost no scholarly attention, yet its structure and narrative are key examples of World War II Hollywood propaganda. The film is set within the grounds of Paramount Pictures and centers on "Pop," a security guard who has led his sailor son to believe that he runs the studio and who maintains his charade when his son takes his comrades on a studio tour. The plot serves as a pretext for a troop show featuring some of Paramount's most bankable actors. Claiming to have "the biggest all-star cast ever assembled in one picture," the film's famous faces include Paulette Goddard and Veronica Lake.[44] Dunham appears in a single four-minute musical sequence in which she jitterbugs alongside Eddie Anderson to "Sharp as a Tack" by white musicians Harold Arlen and Johnny Mercer. Anderson was famous for playing "Rochester," the valet on the radio show, *The Jack Benny Program*, and starred in the film version of *Cabin in the Sky*. In contrast to *Ziegfeld Follies of 1936*, Baker's failed challenge to musical theater segregation, *Cabin in the Sky* maintained the racial status quo and proved a boon to Dunham's career. *Star Spangled Rhythm*'s partnering of Dunham and Anderson and employment of Balanchine elsewhere in the film positions it as a cinematic effort to capitalize on *Cabin in the Sky*'s critical and commercial acclaim.

The scene begins on a stage street. Anderson plays "Jackson," a style-conscious African American who arrives on a motorbike sidecar chauffeured by pioneering Black football star Woody Strode. Strode worked frequently with director John Ford in later years and was nominated for a Golden Globe for his work in Stanley Kubrick's *Spartacus* (1960), but his appearance here is silent and uncredited. Jackson pauses on the street to show off his zoot suit, an elaborate costume that consists of a chain and pleated seam, with a belt fastening at the back of the jacket. His costume attracts the attention of passersby before being overshadowed by the even more elaborate attire of Dunham's unnamed protagonist, who wears a silk dress with tassels and a feathered headdress. Dunham's glamorous appearance and flirtatious manner seduce Jackson, and they perform a jive until another man's military uniform distracts Dunham. Upon realizing the superior allure of army attire, Jackson trades suits to enlist and regain his dance partner. The scene ends with the pair performing a variant of popular shuffling step dance Truckin' as they move offstage together.

The sequence exemplifies war-era Hollywood's manipulation of the musical revue as propaganda. Military endeavor is constructed as rewarding, a sign of communal pride, and a means of attracting the opposite sex. Jennifer R. Jenkins argues that the troop show was an important setting for Hollywood musicals because its revue structure enabled a wide variety of performers to participate in the war effort. Quoting Rick Altman's formulation that musical numbers function "not so much [as] a spectacle as an exercise in solidarity," she stresses that, "these formerly self-serving production values appear as the collective fulfillment of a duty, namely keeping up the boys' morale and demonstrating the potential success of team-work, often thematized by the mounting of a 'show.'"[45] Overtones of warfare permeate *Star Spangled Rhythm*'s musical numbers. Betty Hutton sings "I'm Doing It for Defense," part of Zorina's dance scene is set in an army barracks, and a Rosie the Riveter–influenced song-and-dance sequence features showgirls in an airplane factory. But the "jive" scene is the film's most explicit engagement with army recruitment because it depicts an enlistment. Moreover, the sequence had a specific propaganda role: to increase African American participation in the war effort. An article in Black newspaper the *Baltimore Afro-American* entitled "Rochester and Katherine Dunham Head Colored in Paramount Film" underscores the scene's purpose. It features a propaganda poster that the pair made while they were rehearsing, which reads, "delivering a message of 'zipping your lip' to keep the enemy from learning military secrets."[46]

Dunham and Anderson's scene in *Star Spangled Rhythm* was impelled by a war-fueled sense of urgency in Hollywood that African Americans be fairly depicted. The U.S. Government's Office of War Information (OWI) sensed that negative racial representations were affecting African Americans' allegiance to the nation and compromising the United States' attempt to depict itself as a beacon of democracy overseas. Black entertainers were promoted onscreen to foster social hegemony and national pride, and Dunham and Anderson's scene should be read as part of this propaganda outburst. Anderson was even one of the performers the OWI's racial adviser Milton Starr suggested for such a purpose.[47] As Clayton R. Koppes and Gregory D. Black observe, however, "there were clear limits to how far the Bureau of Motion Pictures would go on this issue. . . . The propagandists hoped to clean up the worst examples of racial stereotypes and to introduce positive black characters if that could be done without too much trouble. But the agency would not go beyond these minimal steps, and it often fell short even of these."[48]

The revue format presented an ideal platform by which to make limited concessions to Black performers, as it facilitated their inclusion in films without offending white Southern audiences' sensibilities. Racially segregated specialty numbers ensured a policy of racialized visual containment, enabling Black performers to appear briefly onscreen without requiring them to interact with their mainly white colleagues. As noted in the previous chapter, Baker was able to dance sensually with white men in French cinema, but her attempt to do so on the U.S. stage ended in failure. Sean

Griffin cites *Star Spangled Rhythm* as a specific example of the specialty number, which could be cut without affecting a film's plot.[49] Hence, Black performers could be removed when productions were shown in the racially segregated South. The potential for excision reflected the wider policy of racial exclusion in the South, where the law mandated segregated movie houses and film censors banned films that depicted Black and white people as social equals. Thomas Cripps identifies what he terms "the myth of the Southern box office," which held that the region's response to a film would impact significantly on its overall financial success, and which therefore allowed Southern racial attitudes to dictate movie content.[50]

Nevertheless, Griffin also reads these scenes as sites of cinematic autonomy that displaced conventional racial hierarchies by providing platforms for Black performers to display technical artistry and steal attention from less talented white stars: "In all likelihood . . . audiences flocked to these films more for the musical numbers than for the plot lines, and evidence indicates that the virtuoso talent of minority specialties often worked effectively to interrupt and supersede the white stars and the narrative trajectory."[51] Similarly, Arthur Knight argues that, "downplaying the specialty number may downplay a key mode of Black reception," and that, "However reluctantly, musicals—perhaps especially in their 'more randomized, more fragmentary forms' like the specialty numbers . . . offered African Americans access to these processes [of contestation] and remain as evidence of struggle."[52] These readings may risk recuperating the specialty number in ways that overshadow their function in containing and omitting African American artistry, but they highlight these scenes as important sites of onscreen authorship that held psychological significance for large numbers of Black filmgoers. As *Sirène*'s transatlantic reception has shown, many African American audience members were prepared to overlook subjugating plots in favor of seminal artistry and to recognize talented Black performers as their films' stars.

Star Spangled Rhythm marginalizes Dunham and Anderson in a number of ways. Bob Hope introduces the routine, describing it as a chance to watch "Rochester," which conflates Anderson with his servant persona on the *Jack Benny Program*. Dunham remains unidentified, although she is credited in the cast list. This lack of attribution devalues Dunham's artistry: she must appear onscreen as a nameless dancer. As in *Pardon My Sarong*, in which white dancers performed her choreography, Dunham is forced to engage with a racially subjugating cinematic framework.

Restricted to a single scene that is alienated from the rest of the film and performing merely as musical entertainers, Dunham and Anderson do little to structurally oppose Hollywood's negative representations of Black artists. Heavy-handed racial codes reassert derogatory assumptions about Black lives. A dancing toddler and a piano player who merely motions movements with his arms situate Black performance as innate and undermine the dancers' skills. Anderson is also unconvincing as a masculine hero and his dance performance verges on slapstick humor, while Dunham, who is his superior in height and posture, undermines his manliness still further. Anderson's version of the zoot suit exaggerates the costume's oversized shoulders, which were originally intended to signify physical power, reducing the costume and its wearer to ridicule.[53] Dunham is also forced to adapt her cross-cultural technique to more conventional notions of Black vernacular expression. Dunham was only a coauthor in the scene; she had to work with white dance director Danny Dare and coordinate her style to Anderson's steps. The result is a diminution of Dunham's art and a compromise to Hollywood notions of African American performance that speaks to her struggle for artistic control as a Black woman on the World War II–era screen.

But Dunham did make behind-the-scenes efforts to challenge the scene's degradations and create a more positive depiction of Black lives, which included changing her single line in the scene from "You *is*" to "*You're* Haile Selassie."[54] Anderson is also shown signing up for combat. In his consideration of Hollywood war-era representations of African Americans, James Nesteby referred to "a dominant Hollywood concept of the Afro-American as entertainer . . . rather than as a serious participant in the war effort."[55] Similarly, in their consideration of a sequence in Warner Brothers' *This Is the Army* featuring zoot suit–wearing African Americans "made up for a minstrel show," Koppes and Black maintain that the Harlem street setting "exemplifies white impressions of the Black capital as an *entertainment mecca*," and that "Here was the Black man not as worker, father, or solid citizen but as lover, playboy, and flashy dresser—and the war as fashion show."[56] However, Dunham and Anderson's *Star Spangled Rhythm* sequence complicates these tropes, as it serves as a cinematic acknowledgment of African American men's military participation in World War II.

The scene does still foreground African Americans as entertainers, but in so doing it provides a platform for Black artistry. The Harlem setting simplifies Black lives, but it celebrates the urban street as a site of communality and artistic innovation. Marking the street's location is a sign for the "Happy Feet" dance hall, white patrons' condescending nickname for the Savoy Ballroom in Harlem, where many early-twentieth-century popular dance styles originated. Such a setting allows Dunham to celebrate onscreen historically disregarded Black dance practices even within the scene's choreographic confines. Although the dance routine physically straitens her by requiring her to dance toe-to-toe with Anderson, her performance nevertheless is centered on the hip and incorporates pelvic gyrations, which suggests that she exercised some creative influence over the scene. Pelvic movement, which Dunham observed in the Caribbean and which would become a key component of Dunham Technique, was extremely unusual in mainstream U.S. culture at this time. Millicent Hodson claimed that Dunham "established for the modern dance a new vocabulary of movement for the lower body," a claim that Dunham substantiated in an interview before her death.[57] Dunham's use of the pelvis in her dance sequence thus represents a rare midcentury Hollywood tribute to Caribbean dance practices.

At the end of the sequence, Dunham and Anderson perform a variation on Truckin', a one-step that became fashionable in the 1930s United States in which the feet shuffle and the pointed right index finger shakes in the air. Instead of waving their forefingers over their heads as in traditional Truckin', Dunham and Anderson wave their wrists, with Anderson simulating a salute (see figure 12). The scene appropriates Black vernacular dance for propaganda purposes, but it also serves as a rare cinematic tribute

FIGURE 12. Eddie "Rochester" Anderson and Dunham performing a variation on Truckin' in *Star Spangled Rhythm* (Paramount Pictures, 1942).

to a historical Black dance practice. Truckin' was a pre–World War I Black Southern leisure activity.[58] The gesture also bears striking similarities to Baker's finger actions before the spotlight in *Zouzou* and Truckin's' history has been held to resemble the foot shuffle and wagging finger of Jump Jim Crow.[59] Truckin' can therefore be read as an African trace in North American dance culture that was crudely appropriated by white dancers and practiced concurrently by African American working-class communities. The movement illuminates the complex ways in which dance forms moved between cultural locations and allows for a multiplicity of significations. Like much of Baker's work, it may be read as a derogatory gesture or as a celebration of African American artistry.

Contemporary African American newspapers confirm the performance's celebratory potential. Listed as a "high poin[t]" in the picture by the *New York Times*, Susan Roper asserts that, while *Star Spangled Rhythm* received mixed reviews, "most of the praise went to a patriotic number choreographed by Danny Dare for Katherine Dunham and Eddie 'Rochester' Anderson."[60] Several Black newspapers foregrounded Dunham and Anderson over the film's other well-known names, emphasizing their achievements and imbuing them with stardom merely hinted at in the film itself. In a noteworthy parallel with *Sirène*'s U.S. reception, *Atlanta Daily World* recorded the audience's excitement when the film premiered at a local Black cinema. The reporter emphasized the fact that the "clamoring" audience had arrived to see Dunham and Anderson by noting that the queue consisted "mostly of jitterbugs," and concluded that, "our stars put a touch of art in 'Star Spangled Rhythm' and they are the ones, at least in our opinion, who put the 'star' in the title."[61]

Such anticipation for the "Sharp as Tack" sequence suggests that specialty performers such as Dunham were important identifiers for large numbers of Black cinemagoers, who chose to celebrate their artistry and read them as their films' stars despite their marginal roles. Although she questions their overall effectiveness, Megan E. Williams notes the frequency with which women entertainers such as Dunham appeared on the cover of African American magazine *The Crisis* to argue that "many Black spectators viewed African American players like dancer Katherine Dunham (March 1941) as signifying a dazzling, respectable, and imitable Black femininity never before represented on the stage and screen."[62] Williams's reading recalls African American cinemagoers' excited response to Baker's star performance in *Sirène* and highlights the psychological significance of Dunham's screen image for many war-era Black viewers, for whom her persona presented a marked contrast to minstrelsy-derived representations of Black womanhood.

Yet the African American press was clearly aware that the jive scene might invite readings of Black spontaneity and worked to negate such interpretations by pointing up Dunham and Anderson's artistry. The *New Journal and Guide* maintained that, while "it will all look so spontaneous, fast and breathtaking that audiences may feel that it was all done on the spur of the moment," the scene had in fact been "plotted like the building of a ship."[63] Similarly, the *Baltimore Afro-American* stressed that the performance "took ten days of the most intensive rehearsing with the complete routine being *tediously* worked out by Rochester, Miss Dunham and the chorus with Danny Dare, dance director."[64] The *Afro-American* noted that a recording orchestra had to "practice for a day to get in all details to match the fast action as Rochester's singing and dancing had to be coordinated with Miss Dunham's sensational style of dancing and singing."[65] These newspapers' emphasis on the scene's technical complexity highlights classical Hollywood's persistent depiction of Black dance as instinctive. Paradoxically, they also uncover Dunham and Anderson's authorial contributions to the sequence and encourage readers to celebrate their onscreen achievements.

A comparison of Dunham's role with Balanchine's ballet number also shows that, despite its potential significance for Black audiences as an assertive expression of Black womanhood, it remained heavily circumscribed by racial codes. Balanchine's scene, like Dunham's "Sharp as a Tack" performance, positions a woman's body as a site of war propaganda: a soldier in an army barracks dreams of Vera Zorina as she performs a snow-set ballet. The sequence creates an aestheticized fantasy of white womanhood, allowing Zorina to reveal technical proficiency and "cultured" artistry that displays a female form while making it appear intangible and unearthly (see figure 13). Dunham is positioned as more overtly sexual: she is the flirtatious and therefore attainable object of an African American man's attention. Dunham's dance is presented as a spontaneous act, playing into notions that musicality is a racial trait. The two scenes establish fixed contrasts between "earthy" and "low-brow" Black street life and romantic and "high-brow" white creative artistry.

However, this structural division elides the performances' stylistic similarity. Dunham claimed that her "blatant use of the pelvic girdle" in *Cabin in the Sky*, a physical movement popular in African and Black Caribbean dance cultures but held to be suggestive and risqué in European and American societies, encouraged Balanchine to reconfigure the rigidly upright form of the traditional ballerina.[66] As discussed in the study's introduction, evidence suggests that Baker and Dunham inspired Balanchine to incorporate

FIGURE 13. Vera Zorina's snow-set ballet scene in *Star Spangled Rhythm*.

African-derived dance movements into his art. Both sequences emphasize the hip and hint at sexual suggestiveness, although Zorina's scene does so in more subtle ways. Susan Roper quotes Zorina's recollection that her training with Balanchine "mostly involved the hip—as if I were learning to move sideways after having kept my body up and down" as proof that her "'makeover' [by Balanchine] involved a reposturing that accentuated body curves."[67] Zorina's hip movements reveal Balanchine's authorial control and disempower her character as the subject of a man's fantasy. By contrast, Dunham's assertive gesture places her on an equal footing with Anderson's zoot-suited suitor and signals her choreographic influence.

Balanchine reshaped the ballerina's body, diminishing her individuality and propagating an artificial vision of womanhood. Although Beth Genné has argued persuasively that Balanchine's feminine ideal was modeled on Baker, I propose that it also bore striking similarities to the standardized myth of femininity depicted in chorus lines such as those seen in the *Ziegfeld Follies*, on which Baker and Balanchine jointly worked. Peter Stoneley argues that Balanchine "set a new, modern style for the dancer—tall, and so thin as to be almost breastless," and that "Some of Balanchine's alleged comments on weight have become legendary: 'Don't eat less, Gelsey—eat nothing!'"[68] Zorina is reduced to a soldier's dream, and as Roper notes, "The barefoot Zorina chaînés, arabesques, and leaps through a forest, often pausing to pose with hip thrust forward and back arched, a body use that suggests sexual submissiveness."[69] Conversely, Dunham's performance resists the male gaze by placing the woman in a position of power. Dunham is the leader in the game of courtship as she is able to choose her suitor. The film therefore places Dunham's dancing body at odds with Balanchine's ballerina in ways that highlight apparently fundamental differences in their social status. But it also positions Dunham's protagonist as a strong, independent woman while Zorina's dancer is forced to remain passive.

Star Spangled Rhythm presents a multifaceted vision of African American identities. Hollywood racial codes reduce a Harlem street to a series of derogatory props, while African American fashions and art forms are appropriated as war propaganda. In a visually and creatively constraining scene, Dunham's intercultural dance style and glamorous image are reworked to appeal to white fantasies of Black urban culture and to persuade African American audiences to enlist in warfare. But the "Sharp as a Tack" number nevertheless is a rare cinematic celebration of midcentury African American performance venues, fashions, and artistry and it allows Dunham to assert her authorship and present a dance performance that challenges restrictive gender conventions. Through self-assured performances, Dunham and Anderson construct a vision of African American experience that can be read either as subversive or conservative, but which created a means by which World War II-era Black audiences could and did celebrate African American artistry onscreen.

Dunham's final war-era film, *Stormy Weather*, expands the "Sharp as a Tack" sequence's propaganda themes into a feature-length picture. Produced by 20th Century Fox, *Stormy Weather* was one of only two Black-cast Hollywood musicals made during the 1940s and was the result of lobbying by the National Association for the Advancement of Colored People (NAACP) for more positive African American screen roles. It is a rare cinematic platform for leading African American artists of the age, including tap dancer Bill "Bojangles" Robinson, jazz singer Cab Calloway, and singer Lena Horne. Together with *Cabin in the Sky*, it featured the largest employment of African American talent yet seen in Hollywood. The film provides Black actors with major screen roles and is set in a credibly modern urban environment, a decisive break from the romanticized rural depictions of Black communities seen in similar films of the period. But in other ways it is a utopian depiction of African American lives. Director Andrew L. Stone and his production team were all white, but white society's impact on the film's characters is never mentioned. The NAACP and Bureau for Motion Pictures criticized the film for racial separation and derogatory iconography that recalls minstrelsy and insinuations of musical spontaneity are pervasive. Moreover, *Stormy Weather*'s general emphasis on the cakewalk and tap, styles widely identified by mainstream U.S. culture as traditional Black forms, situates the film as a nostalgic celebration of African American folk culture.

The film begins with a World War I victory party and ends with a revue for World War II troops preparing for combat. Lauren Rebecca Sklaroff observes that *Stormy Weather* appeared at a time when certain African American performers were believed to have "great value in any propaganda program."[70] This propaganda positions the film as part of a developing humanization of African American characters on screen. However, a key rationale of such positive representation was to foster patriotism among Black audiences rather than to effect meaningful representational change, as *Star Spangled Rhythm* has shown. Dunham's sequence plays into such a purpose because it forms part of a troop revue. But her performance challenges this framework insofar as it provides her with artistic self-determination and independence from the film's other scenes. Griffin asserts that, unlike *Cabin in the Sky*, whose musical numbers are "integrated" into the narrative, affording performers little autonomy from its white production framework, "the looser vaudeville structure of *Stormy Weather creates more leeway for individual creativity*."[71] Similarly, dance historian Richard A. Long maintains that the film's "revue format" presents a golden opportunity for multifarious African American performers to show off their skills.[72] These interpretations suggest that, as in *Star Spangled Rhythm*, the film's performers had some control over their cinematic representations. I contend that Dunham's self-choreographed dance scene is a key moment of artistic experimentation and therefore a rare instance in which a Black woman artist was able to shape a studio-era film's aesthetics.

Dunham's dance temporarily interrupts Horne's emotive rendition of the film's title song, taking the place of a traditional break in a jazz number in which lyrics are replaced by instrumental improvisation, thereby positioning her scene as a site of experimentation. Horne has been performing on an elaborate stage whose scenery includes a set of steps and a window, from which can be seen a rain-soaked street. Distracted halfway through the song when the rain turns to wind and thunder, she runs up the steps to close the window. The camera pans out onto the street, which is inhabited by a group of African American sex workers and their clients sheltering under a train platform. There is no dialogue; instead, with the exception of Dunham's character, the men and women all join up in close embraces and begin a slow drag, a dance rooted in the historical musical forms of the blues and ragtime, in time to jazzy but somber music. The dancers' costumes are highly theatrical stylizations of urban poverty. As in *Star Spangled Rhythm*, the men wear zoot suits, and both the men and women display large, angular patterns on their clothing.

It is possible to read the setting as an autobiographical reference to the impoverished Chicago South Side that Dunham experienced as a child, and there is a striking description of her impressions of the city's South Side train platform in her childhood memoir *A Touch of Innocence*. Adopting a third-person narrative, she writes that, "At the bottom of the steps there was a new world. The train rumbled away overhead to lose itself in the far South Side, and the impact of Negro sounds and smells hit the child with such force that she nearly melted with fear, clinging close to her Aunt Lulu and drawing as far away as she could from the dark stares and sullen laughter and bold flaunting, the dust and litter of the pavement, the weariness and sickness."[73] Dunham's recollection calls attention to her class difference from Baker; she is merely an observer and not a participant in the scene. Nevertheless, *Stormy Weather* shows that African American vernacular dance traditions played an important role in Dunham's as much as Baker's work. As with her choreography of Caribbean and Brazilian dance cultures, it also demonstrates that she employed these forms to celebrate the lives and artistry of their practitioners.

In this short section, historical depictions of African American identities are both performed and subtly undermined. The dancers' roles as sex workers and their clients visually reinscribe a history of Black bodies as salable commodities. Halifu Osumare claims that Stone planned for the whole scene to focus on the sex workers, but that Dunham replied, "nothing doing!"[74] According to African American composer William Grant Still, Fox producers wanted to degrade Black performers by presenting Dunham's scene as "lowbrow."[75] Still quit the production rather than score such a sequence. Yet the scene also stylizes these dancing figures. The fact that the troupe performs on the street, which is where tap dance developed, marks the scene as referential of African American vernacular expressions. The performance may be read as a rupturing of white audience perceptions of African Americans as "natural" performers, because, like *Star Spangled Rhythm*, it openly acknowledges the "street" as an important site of dance formation and by extension artistic invention.

The scene's inclusion of zoot suits situates it as an ambiguous zone of identity contestation. Robin D. G. Kelley considers the zoot suit to have been a means by which African American men living in urban environments during the 1940s were able to construct a positive and autonomous vision of Black masculinity. He argues that, "Seeing oneself and others 'dressed up' was enormously important in terms of constructing a collective identity based on something other than wage work, presenting a public challenge to the dominant stereotypes of the black body, and reinforcing a sense of dignity that was perpetually being assaulted."[76] Jazz singer Cab Calloway wears a zoot suit throughout *Stormy Weather* both to highlight his individuality and to emphasize his stylishness. Kathy Peiss argues that *Stormy Weather* made the outfit "integral to the history of Black performance and part of a confident African American culture on the home front."[77] Yet, as in *Star Spangled Rhythm*, the suits in Dunham's scene invite a counter-reading. The costumes' weather-beaten stripes link the figures to their surroundings, hinting at their entrapment within their urban environment. The suits can also be interpreted, not only as self-assertive display, but also as visual disorder that hints at misrule. Widely perceived as signs of defiance against military participation in World War II, negative attitudes toward zoot suiters descended into violence in Los Angeles just a month before *Stormy Weather* was released. While the causes of what became known as the "Zoot Suit Riots" hint at racial tensions as much as issues of patriotism because suit wearers were mainly Mexican and African American youths, the visual link between the suits and sex work plays into contemporary notions that the wearing of the outfits signified immorality. The scene can thus be read as a statement on urban vice rather than as an artistic validation of Black youth culture.

But a clap of thunder breaks the scene's bleak mood, causing Dunham's character to look up sharply and the camera to cut to a cloudy sky that is then merged with an ethereal, dreamlike stage, as shown in figure 14. In this transformative moment, the figures escape their urban poverty. Stage effects convey wind, mist, and lightning and inform the audience that the scene has moved from the street to the sky. Gone is the jazzy guitar music; instead, a chorus of heavenly female voices introduces the troupe as it emerges from the mist onto what is now a concert dance stage. In this section, the performers take on new roles. The men no longer wear zoot suits but rather tight-fitting Arabesque costumes, while the women wear delicate, trailing skirts over bare legs. The cultural incongruity of the costumes could appear to indulge white fantasies of the performers as exotic spectacles; conversely,

FIGURE 14. The ethereal setting of Dunham's "ballet" sequence in *Stormy Weather* (20th Century Fox, 1943).

they position the scene as intangible and unearthly and in this sense recall Zorina's performance in *Star Spangled Rhythm*. Propelled by the wind effects, the tattered, trailing skirts accentuate the scene's sense of emotional fragmentation while simultaneously emphasizing the precision of the dancers' movements, positioning the performance as an embodied signification of complex human experience conveyed through physical grace. The scene's effect is to allow an impoverished Black community a moment of imagined flight from their grim surroundings and to visualize alternative possibilities.

This section counteracts the heightened sexuality of the street scene and opens up a space for imaginative contemplation, for social commentary, and for artistic experimentation. The sequence's employment of orchestral music—woodwind, brass, and string sections operate in counterpoint to perform an instrumental variation of the title song—and its concert dance setting connects it to European notions of high art. Shane Vogel recognizes this sequence as a citation of Ethel Waters's original "Stormy Weather" rendition at Harlem's Cotton Club in 1933, which was also followed by a dance sequence featuring synchronized chorus dancers.[78] Yet as Vogel also observes—and in stark contrast to the *Blackbirds* reference identified at the beginning of this chapter, which capitulates to white fantasies—Dunham offers a "modernist revision of the racial aesthetic of the black nightclub tradition" that reveals its technical complexity and places it in conversation with European dance practices.[79] The scene is established early on as a ballet sequence. As dance historian Ramsay Burt notes, "the stage smoke . . . along with gauze curtains and a wind machine are the sine qua non of filmed dream ballets."[80] The choreography too is rooted in balletic influences. As she emerges from the mist, Dunham performs a developpé, a gradual leg extension, and a rond de jambe en l'air, a circular leg action. Her dancers also perform ballet movements. Burt observes that, "the women sail forwards with a beautiful balletic port de bras"; upon entering the scene, they also perform a pirouette in the arms of their male partners.[81] This deliberate recourse to ballet elevates the dancers as physically refined and graceful, situating the scene as an attempt to intervene in and reconfigure Eurocentric notions of beauty. In a signal of Dunham's authorial contribution to the film, it can be read as her response to her exclusion from *Star Spangled Rhythm*'s ballet, a self-reflexive effort to challenge derogatory conceptions of African American performers by demonstrating that Dunham and her troupe are highbrow artistes. Notably, the scene marks the first cinematic representation of Black dance on a concert stage.

Dunham's engagement with ballet provoked criticism, which underscores the prejudices against African American claims to "cultivated" artistry. *New York Times* dance critic John Martin reviewed Dunham's production *Tropics and Le Jazz "Hot"* in 1940 as follows: "The group as a whole is handsome and competent, though there is among certain of the male dancers . . . a distressing tendency to introduce the technique of the academic ballet. What is there in the human mind that is so eager to reduce the rare and genuine to the standard and foreign?"[82] This reference to ballet as "foreign" nods to elitist notions of the genre as an authentically European and culturally valuable dance style beyond the artistic and physical reach of peoples of African descent. Martin's reaction underscores perceptions of a binary separation, among white critics at least, of white and Black bodies and performance cultures. Yet by incorporating ballet into *Stormy Weather*, Dunham goes some way toward destabilizing these categories. The scene stages its performers as embodiments of human emotion, effectively using the body to challenge problematic associations of African Americans with brute labor and primitive sexuality toward metaphysical and sensual experience. Like the song "Stormy Weather," which declares that "since my man and I ain't together, [it] keeps raining all the time," the performances mirror and augment the thunderous scene and are positioned as physical expressions of one woman's disappointment. Bodies leap and lean against each other to hint at a tempestuous world of confusion and even despair. The dreamlike sequence begins and ends with a close-up of Dunham's protagonist's face, the audience directed to her anxious expression. Such a focus emphasizes the scene's psychological aspect, hinting that the dreamlike sequence, whose location remains ambiguous throughout, is an interior shot of the protagonist's mind.

Dunham's choreography also inscribes Caribbean and African American vernacular dance techniques onto the concert dance stage and screen, and critics have read her work as a key site of cross-cultural amalgamation. Shane Vogel writes that, "Dunham brought gestures from 1920s Black social dance onto the same stage as classical dance movements"; pelvis-centered gestures begin to replace more formal ballet techniques toward the end of the piece, as seen in figure 15.[83] In an action that recalls Baker's popularization of African diasporic dances on the European stage and screen, some of

FIGURE 15. Dunham dancers performing pelvis-centered gestures in *Stormy Weather*.

the dancers perform Shimmylike shoulder movements. Joyce Aschenbrenner argues that Dunham "created a dance technique that blended African-based movement with ballet and modern dance to liberate the knees and pelvis, fundamentally changing American dance."[84] The originality of Dunham's method is underscored by the fact that it preceded Agnes de Mille's choreography for the Broadway show *Oklahoma!* (1943). *Oklahoma!* combined vernacular dance, ballet, and Broadway show dancing and has been held to be the first show to fuse these forms. However, Dunham claimed that de Mille borrowed her intercultural dance method without crediting her, noting in an interview that, "I was really annoyed with her because I think her idea [of combining dance forms] came from something . . . in our concerts . . . I feel we were the first to do that."[85]

As *Journey to Accompong* elucidates, Dunham's Jamaican fieldwork taught her that seemingly sexual movements in dance practices throughout African and Caribbean cultures rarely had direct sexual purposes; instead, they were being used to symbolize fertility and to celebrate community cohesion. Dunham's employment of the pelvis in *Stormy Weather* therefore serves as cinematic evidence of her wider effort to reconfigure associations of Black bodies with exotic sexuality toward sensual and communal experience. Drawing from her anthropological encounters, Dunham used her stage and screen roles to call attention to what she understood to be two key functions of dance in Caribbean folk cultures: the nonverbal articulation of the psychological and the representation of community relationships. However, paralleling Baker's experiences in Europe, contemporary U.S. audiences lacked the critical tools to interpret the psychological significances of Caribbean dance practices. If the scene appears to represent complex human emotions, it still can be viewed more superficially as a depiction of "exotic" sexuality. The fact that it has no geographical parameters means it can be read equally as spiritually elevating or alienating: there are no visual markers with which ordinary African American viewers, whom Dunham believed formed 10 percent of her stage audiences, could hope to identify.

Dunham worked to convey onstage the emotional and spiritual significance of international dance cultures, but producers and critics in the 1930s and 1940s did not have the analytical skills to comprehend the social meanings behind the dances she performed. In her consideration of Dunham's impact on contemporary white audiences, Susan Manning concludes that, "Although it's clear that many black and white critics learned to read Dunham's performance of diaspora, it's equally clear that many spectators were drawn to (and some critics put off by) the eroticism of Dunham's performances. For some spectators, Dunham's dances reinforced stereotypical images of sexy black female bodies, what a reporter for *Time Magazine* described as a 'great scalawaggery of shimmying, shagging, rowdy flashing of black eyes and brown legs, a lively wigwagging of rumps.'"[86] Manning's statement points up a fissure between Dunham's choreographic practice and its reception. For some contemporary U.S. spectators at least, her emphasis on the sensuality of physical bodies upheld conceptions of Black people as sexually licentious, as demonstrated by William Grant Still's decision to quit the production.

The imaginative power of Dunham's *Stormy Weather* scene therefore is tempered by its overt engagement with sexuality and also via its status as war propaganda. Yet the ethereal staging of the sequence, its relaxed plot structure, and the permission that it grants to Dunham to stage her own choreography, enable her to construct an image of Black bodies on film that challenges minstrelsy-derived representations and is forward-looking in its emphasis on beauty, grace, and dignity. Like *Carnival of Rhythm*, it is a dignified depiction of men and women as equal partners in human interaction. As in Baker's film work and Dunham's other Hollywood performances, the *Stormy Weather* scene reworks traditional female roles of subjugation. Dunham is the leader in games of courtship, both on the street and in the sky. Her character is a sex worker with the power to reject her clients, and she shakes her head at a young man played by future choreographer Talley Beatty when he rests his hand on her shoulder. Other female characters initiate their own sales, suggesting that they retain some control over their bodies. The fact that Dunham's character does not pair up provides her with even greater autonomy, enabling her to resist the role of sex worker, at least until the rain stops. In the dream sequence too, Dunham, who is in almost every camera shot and leads the performance, remains sexually dominant. Halfway through the scene, she draws a male dancer to the front of the stage; here, the woman takes the lead in selecting a partner. The camera also follows her as she dances around the men, pausing to gaze at them before choosing a partner (played by Roger Chardieno), and then leaning her back against his in an engagement that is both extremely physical and emotionally distant. As Burt acknowledges, "If she was in control earlier by saying no, she is in control now as she unhesitatingly chooses to dance for a moment with one [male dancer] and then another and another man."[87] If Dunham plays a body on display in this scene, it is a body in control of its sexuality, and this is a woman-centered performance in which the men act as subsidiary supports to their woman dance leader.

Dunham's sequence in *Stormy Weather* is all the more significant because, as Horne noted of her Hollywood experiences in her 1961 memoir *Lena*, "Our little segregated sections were always cut out . . . from the basically white musicals in which we appeared. But the all-Negro pictures were shown in the South because there was no mixing of the races to which the whites could object. And the Negroes responded enthusiastically to *Cabin* [*in the Sky*] and *Stormy* [*Weather*]."[88] Horne highlighted *Stormy Weather*'s significance as a corrective to regional elisions of Hollywood's African American stars as it provided Black audiences in the South with access to their talents. Horne claimed that the film's success with Black Southern audiences and World War II troops played a key role in establishing her as a star.[89] Yet it would be a mistake to conclude that the response to *Stormy Weather* was unambiguously positive as audience attendance varied between U.S. cities, and Sklaroff speculates that minstrelsy-derived performances may have deterred some cinemagoers.[90]

Two letters from Black soldiers to the *Chicago Defender* shed useful light on the film's complex reception. Sergeant Elijah Brown called *Stormy Weather* "one of the greatest movie productions ever released," a "sensational musical triumph," and connected the production and war to a wider fight for equal rights, suggesting that he found the film psychologically inspiring.[91] Conversely, Sergeant Fred Thompson claimed that the production perpetuated derogatory representations of Black performers but held up Dunham, Horne, and Calloway as artists who ought to be afforded greater cinematic recognition.[92] Sergeant Thompson's letter expresses distaste for the film's nostalgic portrayal of Black lives but also shows that Dunham and other cast members were interpreted outside of this framework. Such positive responses to Dunham should be understood in light of the fact that, as VèVè Clark has argued, "every other dance idiom in this film is totally predictable" and thus rooted in white expectations of Black artistry.[93] Yet Dunham's performance avoids such a heritage by borrowing directly from Caribbean community dance forms and ballet to create an innovative vision of Black artistry.

Dunham's cinematic impact on non-U.S. Black audiences also deserves exploration. Stephanie Leigh Batiste celebrates Dunham's performance in *Stormy Weather* as a powerful assertion of African American national inclusion while noting that the international Black origins of Dunham's art are not clearly stated and get lost in the film's message of war-era domestic conformity.[94] Such analysis underscores the challenges of contesting racist ideologies in mainstream cinema and the ultimately ambiguous reception of Dunham's artistic vision, although it is worth stressing that Dunham's international Black cultural influences are explored more explicitly in *Carnival of Rhythm*. Moreover, the film appears to have spoken to non-U.S. Black filmgoers even if it did not speak directly for them. Robert Farris Thompson has claimed that *Stormy Weather* and *Cabin in the Sky* inspired Cuban mambo practitioners to add African American dance patterns to their movements.[95] Thompson's observation demonstrates that not only was the film marketed to African diasporic audiences, but it also had a psychologically positive and culturally influential effect on them. Thus, if *Stormy Weather*'s chief goal was to foster social conformity among World War II–era African American audiences, its international cultural impact exceeded such a purpose.

Dunham's early films demonstrate the extent to which classical Hollywood straitened, segregated, and subjugated Black performers. And yet they also show how the choreographer mediated cinematic representations to create a vision of Black corporeal artistry that was rooted in African diasporic rituals and psychological experience, allowing for scenes that communicated and reinterpreted Black cultural expressions. The films serve as cinematic documents of the intellectual underpinnings of Dunham's work, which were centered on celebrating Black cultures as a means of defying artistic binaries and humanizing their subjects. Like Baker before her, Dunham succeeded in creating visions of Black experiences within limiting production frameworks that contemporary African American audiences could and did celebrate. The films are examples of a meaningful challenge to classical Hollywood's racial politics. They represent rare but significant instances in which studio-era Hollywood created a platform for the beauty, artistry, and social-scientific credentials of a Black woman performer-choreographer and serve as crucial documents for understanding the relationship between Dunham's performance-based anthropology and choreography. Although Dunham admitted frustration with the manner in which her company was represented, her engagement with Hollywood cemented her status as a leading U.S. choreographer, enabling her to pursue a lengthy international career, beginning in 1940s Europe, in which she situated dance performance at the heart of a global struggle for racial equality.

CHAPTER SIX

Navigating Primitivism's Persistent Gaze

Dunham in Postwar European Cinema

As the first major U.S. dance company to perform in postwar Europe, Dunham and her troupe enjoyed a level of acclaim comparable to Baker's success two decades earlier. Dorothea Fischer-Hornung observes that Dunham's fame in Paris was "second only to Josephine Baker's triumph in the 1920s," and London newspapers reported that she was more popular in England than dance icon Isadora Duncan at the height of her fame.[1] Like Baker, Dunham inspired fashion lines in London and Paris.[2] Dunham in turn suggested that her Parisian reception encouraged Baker to revitalize her career. In a 1979 interview, she concluded that, "our presence in Paris created a psychological reaction in her" with the result that "I think that Josephine's immediate reaction was to accept us as a challenge in her own field."[3] Baker had in fact been battling ill health since World War II and was bedridden for five months in 1946.[4] However, she admitted to having been so moved by Dunham's company that she returned "three times" and would soon plan her own Haiti-themed show.[5] She likened their performances to the artistic innovations of the Ballets Russes, praising "our grand Katherine."[6] She declared, "Here is what we [Black people] are capable of," suggesting that Dunham's combination of European and African diasporic dance forms had caused white audiences to take Black art seriously, a status that Baker had earlier worked to attain through her adoption of ballet techniques and French music hall traditions.[7] Also like Baker, Dunham's

European success precipitated an enduring international career, and Dunham's company spent the next eleven years touring fifty-seven countries as the world's largest unsubsidized dance troupe.

This chapter examines Dunham's interventions in European cinema to show that Black art was still perceived through a racist lens on the continent, despite Baker's optimistic interpretation of Dunham's work, but also to highlight the substantial creative freedom that midcentury European cinema granted to a Black choreographer. Dunham's European reception has led scholars of her work to read the continent as offering an escape from U.S. racism. As with Baker, Dunham was afforded a level of cinematic recognition in Europe that she was unable to achieve in Hollywood. However, close scrutiny of her European films shows that the reality of her transatlantic cultural encounter was complex. In contrast to Baker's interwar career, Dunham's performances did not engender negative reactions; instead, her artistry was almost universally praised. Yet the primitivist iconography that haunted Baker's films resurfaced in Dunham's European cinematic work. In the West German revue film *Die Große Starparade* (The Big Star Parade) (1954), Dunham and her company appear briefly to perform snippets of *Choros #1*, a stylized version of a Brazilian quadrille, and *Shango*, a staged translation of a Vodou ritual. Here, Dunham's art is decontextualized, reduced to fast-paced fragments, and presented as an exciting contrast to Bavarian village life. But this chapter shows that Dunham was able to showcase her art more extensively and contest such reductive portraits of her work in her other two European films, *Botta e risposta* (also known under the French title *Je suis de la revue*) (1950) and *Mambo* (1954). Here, too, the company's onscreen treatment suggests that its European welcome was filtered through the same crude ideas about Black cultures that informed Baker's work. And yet within such a framework, Dunham was afforded authorial control over her dance scenes to an extent not possible in Hollywood and, like Baker, used these scenes to present a culturally complex vision of Black womanhood that countered racist misconceptions. Like Baker, therefore, Dunham highlights the need to look beyond U.S. borders to more meaningfully recover African American artists' contributions to midcentury cinema. I establish *Botta e risposta*'s historical significance as a filmic record of work by Dunham and other leading African American artists and argue that Dunham should be understood as a coauthor of *Mambo*, whose narrative is framed around her company and which situates her choreography as central to its aesthetics.

Shortly after arriving in Europe, Dunham deplored cinema's power to shape U.S. racial attitudes. In a 1949 letter to British film critic Peter Noble, she wrote, "Hollywood is controlled by a very small group of people who have an extremely far-reaching influence on the entire body of American thinking."[8] She claimed that these same people were promoting racism by treating minority groups with "as little dignity as possible."[9] Recognizing that Black performers had secured more extensive film roles as a result of World War II, she nevertheless concluded that this achievement was undercut by the fact that "Hollywood still doesn't consider Negroes as people."[10]

The Dunham troupe's last Hollywood film had been *Casbah* (1948), a remake of *Algiers* (1938), which in turn was a version of the French movie *Pépé le Moko* (1937), a starring vehicle for Baker's *Zouzou* costar Jean Gabin. *Pépé le Moko*, and subsequently *Casbah*, reasserted the *doudou* trope of Baker's European films: as Dina Sherzer has shown, *Pépé le Moko* echoes Baker's cinema narratives in its depiction of a white French man's rejection of a racial Other.[11] But *Casbah* also reinscribed the visual subjugations of Hollywood. The film's exotic Other was played by Yvonne de Carlo, an actress of Scottish and Italian descent. Dunham's company appeared merely as "Algerian" dancers and much of their work was cut.[12] Two scenes include brief Dunham company performances. Both dances feature Dunham Technique hip and shoulder isolations combined with dervish turns, a meditative exercise practiced by Mevlevi orders in Turkey as a means of achieving religious ecstasy.[13] This blurring of styles could be read as an assertion of psychological equivalences between Caribbean and Islamic dance rituals. Yet the spiritual significance of such movements is obscured; instead, they are employed at one stage to evoke and another to invoke the male lead's sexual desires. Singer and former Dunham company member Eartha Kitt made her film debut in *Casbah* and described the troupe's appearance at a Ramadan Festival as "a frenzied thing where everyone, including Miss Dunham, went out of his head."[14] The *Los Angeles Times* interpreted the company's dancing as "the sensuous writhings of the Casbah's dark-skinned 'natives.'"[15]

Casbah was Dunham's final Hollywood screen role. Her frustrations with its racial codes led her to abandon mainstream U.S. cinema, and she returned only years later to choreograph *Green Mansions* (1959), directed by Mel Ferrer and starring Audrey Hepburn and Anthony Perkins, and John Huston's *The Bible: In the Beginning . . .* (1966). However, even these later films were sites of negotiation and omission that denied Dunham full creative freedom. She admitted to taking these opportunities out of financial necessity and found that she was unable to work with her own dancers and that her choreography barely featured in her final two Hollywood movies.[16] There is little evidence of Dunham Technique in these films. Instead, Dunham's art is reduced to a series of basic and rapid movements, including leaps and spins, which function as background color to "primitive" birth and masculine rituals to signify the emotional uninhibitedness of "pre-civilized" societies. The misuse of Dunham's art highlights the distortion of Black cultures and denial of meaningful creative opportunities to Black artists in midcentury U.S. cinema.

By the early 1950s, Dunham had become politically engaged in challenging Hollywood's derogatory representations of Black performers. Along with Paul and Eslanda Goode Robeson, Richard Wright, and Langston Hughes, she was a consultant on the Committee for Mass Education in Race Relations, which was formed with the intent to "produce films that combine entertainment and purposeful mass education in race relations."[17] She also turned to Europe, expressing the hope that, "filmmakers in Mexico and Europe will have the foresight to make use of the great quantity of Negro talent in their countries, and that once this has been done the resultant films are somehow released in the United States."[18] Echoing Baker's optimism that with *Zouzou* and *Princesse Tam-Tam* she could launch a U.S. career, Dunham believed that by building a reputation in European cinema she could circumvent the racist restrictions of Hollywood. She anticipated that translating new Black subjectivities onto the European screen would defamiliarize perceptions, forcing audiences to resee Black identities, and that these new representations could be imported to the United States to wear down Hollywood's racial codes. She affirmed that, in terms of their respective depictions of Black performers, "Hollywood can certainly take a leaf out of Europe's book."[19] Her decision to relocate was also motivated by financial need, however. The Katherine Dunham School of Dance in New York, which she ran between 1945 and 1957, was self-funded and depended entirely on her company's commercial success. In conversation in 1978, Dunham claimed, "Without Europe we couldn't have survived."[20] Nevertheless, Dunham's actions were not just driven by expediency, as she felt that European commentators understood her material far better than did U.S. critics. She claimed that her work was appreciated as a new theater form and that her company was "admired as people that knew something [about art]."[21]

Dunham's statement articulates her concern with exploring aestheticism as a way out of objectification and also hints that the European imaginary idealized Black performers and continued to hold many of the primitivist perceptions detailed in Baker's memoirs even as it provided a liberating contrast to U.S. racism. Julie Robinson Belafonte, the former wife of singer Harry Belafonte and the company's only white dancer, appeared in both *Botta e risposta* and *Mambo*. She recalled that the company's European popularity was "incredible," but that racist beliefs undermined its artistic aims.[22] Describing postwar England and France, she noted that, "They're both colonial powers, and I think in those days—as well as probably today—they found black people exotic and fantastic, as long as they weren't too cerebral."[23] As Baker's memoirs have demonstrated, paradigms of racial essentialism worked differently in different national contexts. Like Baker, the company encountered a European cultural legacy dating back to Sara Baartman, in which racial difference was made spectacular but which allowed African Americans a measure of physical freedom not possible back home. Debuting in England just three weeks before the arrival of the *SS Empire Windrush*, whose passengers became the first sizable group of African Caribbeans to settle in the U.K. after World War II, the company was so successful that its three-week performance at the Prince of Wales Theatre was extended to three months.[24] However, company members were forced to move five times due to housing discrimination when they returned to England in 1952, which suggests that they encountered a post-*Windrush* rise in racism.[25] A Black dance company was no longer seen as a novelty in Britain, but instead perceived as a social threat. In Paris, on the other hand, they were indulged with champagne and treated as stars. But Robinson Belafonte attributed this acceptance to the fact that they were "exotic and in the theater."[26] In her opinion, Dunham's company's success was based at least partly on a colonial ideology that held Black performers to be foreign spectacles.

Robinson Belafonte's recollections suggest that, like Baker before her, Dunham encountered a white European mindset that was largely unable to conceive of Black performers as social equals, and her efforts to translate her art to the screen were mediated by racial prejudices. Critics treated Dunham favorably. Ramsay insists that, "her work received unqualified approval of a kind that critics in the United States seem never to have been able to grant her," observing that "the eroticism of Dunham's dancing and choreography was not used by either the English or French press to criticize or slight her in the way a number of U.S. critics had done."[27] Unlike Baker's work in 1920s Europe, Dunham's performances did not generate protests and did not "immediately divide the public into two camps: those who love [her] and those who do not."[28] Her universal critical acceptance signals that she came across a better-informed and more cosmopolitan Europe than did Baker twenty years earlier, in which "Blackness" was deemed either a moral threat or a site of spiritual rejuvenation. Dunham also negotiated her European career differently from Baker, which may have bolstered her approval. Baker encouraged readings of her early performances as spontaneous while Dunham emphasized the studied nature of her art and the diverse cultural origins of her sources.

However, some newspapers did repeat racist assumptions about Black dance. London's *News of the World* called the dancers "uninhibited to the point of abandonment."[29] The city's *Star* newspaper commented on what it saw as the "shoulder-shaking prancing and shuffling of negroes [*sic*]."[30] Most frequently, critics tried to marry preconceived ideas about Black cultures with the dancers' carefully rehearsed performances. An article in the Birmingham *Picture Post* entitled "Miss Dunham's Witchery" applauded the dancing as "an affair of high artistic quality," but it also stressed its "exciting" quality.[31] A reviewer for Italy's *La Stampa* emphasized Dunham's company's "refined" choreography and "prodigious" music but also referred to her "African witchcraft" and described her work as "the evocation of an earthly paradise from which we all feel exiles."[32] The article also perceived that Dunham found in Paris, like Baker before her, "that sympathy the French capital has always had for people of color" and that, as an artist who "expressed the sensibility of her race," Dunham was in fact "grander" than Baker.[33] Such a reading reveals a pseudo-ethnographic fascination with Dunham's work as an expression of an "authentic" racial self. It connects her to the *Negrophilia* movement that influenced Baker's career, whose adherents saw Black bodies as symbols of a culturally "pure" preindustrial age. As with Baker, European critics therefore responded ambivalently to Dunham, recognizing her artistry while continuing to equate Blackness with spontaneity and sexuality. Also like Baker, however, Dunham presented a culturally complex vision of Black womanhood in response to such misconceptions that enabled her to achieve a measure of control over her cinematic representation.

Botta e risposta exemplifies postwar Europe's contradictory attitudes to Dunham's work. The French-Italian coproduction restates lurid fascinations with Black artistry that were apparent in Baker's films. Cropped camera angles and heavy lighting present leading African American jazz artists as threateningly unruly and innately musical; when rehearsing offstage, Dunham's troupe is portrayed as sexually provocative. Yet within this framework, Dunham creates a geographically and culturally diverse depiction of Black dance onscreen. *Botta e risposta* underscores an enduring fascination with racial Otherness in the postwar European imagination but at the same time affords space to an international choreographic method that sought to contest exotic depictions of Black womanhood. The film is both a historical record of mid-twentieth-century European racial mindsets and, in Dunham's performance scenes, a cinematic challenge to primitivist ideologies and celebration of Black Atlantic dance practices.

Botta e risposta adopts a basic plotline involving a stolen dress to foreground a range of dancers and musicians. Like *Revue*, *Zouzou*, and *Star Spangled Rhythm*, the majority of the movie takes place against the backdrop of a stage revue in Rome. Among the acts are three sets of African American musicians and dancers: Dunham and her company, Louis Armstrong and His All-Stars, and the Nicholas Brothers. The film was the immediate follow-up to *I pompieri di Viggiù* (*The Firemen of Viggiù*) (1949), which launched leading Italian producer Dino De Laurentiis's career.[34] Previously, De Laurentiis had been a struggling producer in postwar Italy. Short of finances and film ideas, he traveled to Rome, where he witnessed three all-star shows. Noticing that theater performers enjoyed tremendous popularity in the capital but that Italy's war-torn infrastructure made it difficult for them to tour the country, De Laurentiis realized that placing them onscreen could bring them to a national audience and enable him to profit from their talents.[35] He decided to commit star acts to a single film, bound together by a threadbare plot in which actors playing firemen were inserted between performance numbers, a decision he described as "a gimmick to hold the [musical] pieces together."[36] His efforts echoed the Baker short *Le Pompier des Folies-Bergère* (The Fireman of the Folies-Bergère) (1928), whose drunken fireman narrative was a front for promoting the Folies-Bergère's naked feminine displays. The low-budget result, which De Laurentiis was forced to self-distribute, was a critical flop but a commercial hit.[37] It provided him with financial security and enabled him to produce a range of other films, including the neorealist production *Bitter Rice* (1949), which starred his future wife and *Mambo* star Silvana Mangano.[38] *Botta e risposta*, released a year after *Bitter Rice*, copied *I pompieri*'s formula to repeat its commercial success.

Botta e risposta is culturally significant as a visual document of popular icons such as Armstrong and Fernandel, who was 1950s France's biggest cinema star, and it is perhaps one of the only filmic records of Dunham's postwar European stage performances. The production's inclusion of a sizable number of African Americans presents a significant contrast to the racial elisions of midcentury Hollywood and helps to shed light on their presence in postwar Europe, much of which centered on the U.S. State Department's sponsorship of jazz artists. The film is particularly important for helping to delineate the artistry and reception of Dunham, who performed alongside

State-sponsored jazz artists such as Armstrong but whose gender and radical politics placed her outside of this framework—much like Baker, who used her international tours during this period to speak out against racism. Dunham's popularity in Europe at this time was such that she and Armstrong share third billing after Fernandel and singer Suzy Delair. In newspaper advertisements Dunham was even listed above Armstrong, who had recently become the first jazz musician to feature on the cover of *Time* magazine.[39] Moreover, the film's commercial success and circulation beyond the major cities in which Dunham performed suggests that it was the means by which most French and Italian cultural consumers encountered her work.[40] *Botta e risposta* is a historical record of Dunham's company at the height of its European fame, and as such it provides a measure of her celebrity status as well as a visual record of her performances.

There are no critical texts on *Botta e risposta*, let alone on Dunham's scenes. The film does not fit into "New Wave" or neorealist categories of European cinema and did not enjoy a global circulation. Instead, it was one of many low-budget films produced specifically for French and Italian audiences between the signing of the Franco-Italian coproduction agreement in Rome in October 1949 and the early 1970s. Coproductions were extremely popular during this period as such films could rely on two nations' financial support and audiences. However, their lack of a clear cultural identity made them hard to market elsewhere and *Botta e risposta* does not appear to have been screened outside of Europe. Coproductions such as *Botta e risposta* are exemplars of what Jean-Pierre Jeancolas identifies as 1950s European cinema's many "inexportable" films.[41] Jeancolas suggests that such productions were frequently "unintelligible" to international audiences. He concludes that such movies were "in all respects of poor quality and [had] no artistic ambitions"; their appeal rested on their identifiable local signifiers such as a well-known show, actor, or musician, and it was often these signifiers "alone which justified the making of a film commercially."[42] Notably, *Botta e risposta* (which translates roughly as "repartee," "sharp reply to the point," or "witty retort") is framed partly around the Italian radio show from which it takes its title.

Jeancolas recognizes that these films may be "of interest to cultural historians insofar as they are 'multi-media'" and feature a variety of cultural forms.[43] But his chapter-length study claims only to "touch on its subject in the hope of initiating a more comprehensive, European-wide examination" and so does not analyze films in detail and thus does not uncover the authorial contributions that talented performers brought to movies such as

Botta e risposta.[44] Italian newspaper *La Stampa* described the production as a "tentative" attempt by a film industry emerging from war to rival Hollywood musicals.[45] As such, the newspaper highlighted *Botta e risposta*'s inclusion of stars such as Armstrong and Dunham, both of whom it located as central to the film's appeal.[46] The opening credits feature jazz music and silhouettes resembling Dunham and Armstrong, acknowledging African American artistry as a key aesthetic and thematic device.

But the silhouettes reduce the performers to one-dimensional images. They recall Baker's shadow dance in *Zouzou* and Paul Colin's *La Revue Nègre* posters. Colin in fact designed the poster for Dunham's 1948 Parisian staging of *Rhapsodie Caraïbe*, which depicts a dancer who vaguely resembles Dunham with pointed toes and an erect posture but gives her a barefoot and faceless male partner who appears merely to be leaping in the air, suggesting that his movements are unstructured and inviting readings of the company's dancing as "raw." Like Colin's work, *Botta e risposta*'s imagery reduces Dunham to an anonymous silhouette. Yet paradoxically it also captures her elegance. The representation is based on Dunham's performance in her ballet *L'Ag'Ya* (1938) and depicts her with her arms rounded and raised above her head, evoking the high fifth position in ballet (see figure 16). The silhouette therefore acknowledges Dunham as a practitioner of a dance style traditionally associated with Eurocentric notions of beauty even as it obscures her humanity. More troubling is the subsequent silhouette of a trumpeter, presumably intended to symbolize Armstrong, which depicts a crudely drawn head and lips as well as an elongated body, invoking physiognomic theories of racial difference and also recalling minstrelsy-derived iconography.

Such imagery demonstrates the endurance of derogatory representations of Black performers in postwar Europe, as the Armstrong and the All Stars sequence substantiates. Matthew F. Jordan argues that jazz was so ingrained in postwar France that it was no longer seen as a cultural threat. He claims that, "After the liberation, public debates about jazz and its meaning for French culture were marked by the absence of anti-jazz voices," and that, "Satchmo [Armstrong] was now a received master in France, an almost classical figure for older fans."[47] French fears of Americanization grew in the postwar era, but jazz was not associated with these anxieties because, Jordan posits, it "became congruous with postwar notions of Frenchness and representative of a 'true' France grounded in the wartime experience of resistance."[48] This is significant because African American bands introduced jazz to France during World War I. Originally a musical expression of the lived experience of the Great Migration and urbanization as well

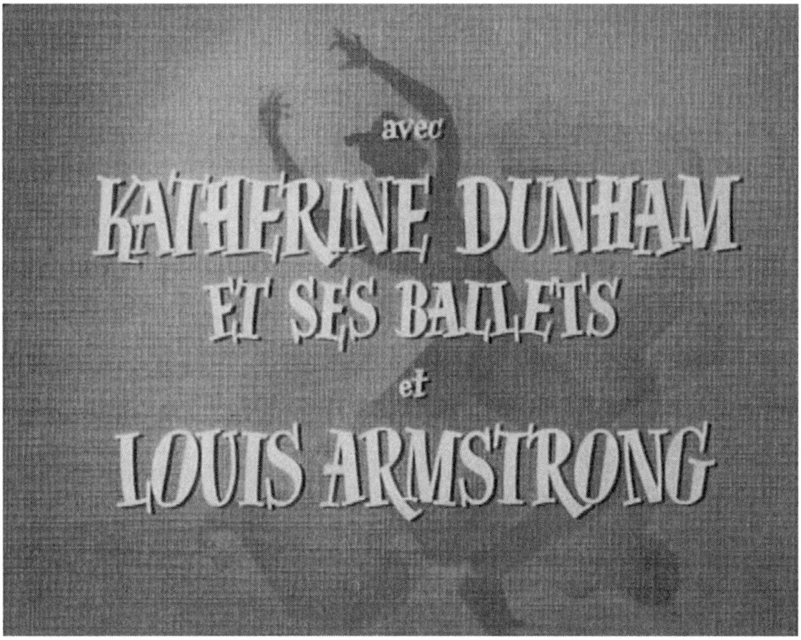

FIGURE 16. A title card showing Dunham in silhouette in *Botta e risposta* (Cosmopolis Films/ Les Films Georges Muller, 1950).

as Black soldiers' European battlefield encounters, jazz spoke to a French nation scarred by warfare. As Chad Louis Williams observes, "When the black military bands played, they invoked historical memories of the war and infused them with symbolic and ritual meaning in the context of the present."[49] Jazz became a cultural means for French citizens to recover psychologically from the conflict.

However, *Botta e risposta* shows that, although jazz was now part of French mainstream culture and once again held psychological significance for a continent recovering from warfare, primitivist representations of Black performers endured. The All Stars' performance features fast-paced solos by double bass player Arvell Shaw and pianist Earl "Fatha" Hines. Close-up shots of seemingly unfocused facial expressions encourage readings of mind-body divisions, positioning their art as mindless despite their technically complex musicianship. Even more troublingly, close-up shots of drummer Cozy Cole performing a fast-paced solo represent him as frenetic, and he is deliberately placed in heavy shadow and shot from below to add a frightening quality to his apparently "wild" playing style (see figure 17). Louis Armstrong and singer Velma Middleton also perform a highly animated vocal duet that emphasizes their facial expressions. Armstrong made his work a physical as well as a musical spectacle because he saw himself as a showman.[50] However, as Arthur Knight observes, the image of the grinning Black man, "*especially as embodied in Louis Armstrong's performance persona*—was probably the most widely disseminated image of Black musicianship in the world, and it had become a key image in the reformulation of the look of mid-1940s jazz, an image associated with the 'tomming' that bebop formed itself against."[51] Such rejection highlights potential readings of the sequence as a reassertion of crude white fantasies of Black performance.

Racial iconography is absent from the Nicholas Brothers' scene, but the film also plays up their perceived Otherness. The brothers appear alongside white chorus girls and perform their acrobatic stair dance; younger brother Harold also executes a vocal solo. Their stage backdrop is a painted cityscape intended to symbolize Broadway's theater district, which equates their work with the glamour of New York and thus with U.S. modern life.

FIGURE 17. Cozy Cole shot in deep shadow in *Botta e risposta*.

The pair's physically elevated performance, which combines synchronized tap steps, upper body movement, and balletic turns with a daring execution of jumping splits on a model skyscraper, invokes and associates them with their urban environment. Like Baker in her sound films, the brothers are afforded white dance partners, which breaks with the elisions and subjugation that they experienced in Hollywood, where they were typically consigned to racially segregated specialty numbers.[52] Such emasculating treatment began when the pair first appeared on Broadway in *Ziegfeld Follies of 1936*; their routines previously included chorus girls.[53] As discussed in the previous chapter, the Nicholas Brothers escaped the harsh critical reception that Baker endured for her *Follies* performance because their tap-based style was felt not to threaten racialized artistic hierarchies. But while *Botta e risposta* allows Harold, then the husband of Dorothy Dandridge, to sing a love song, it ultimately positions the duo as unsuitable male leads, suggesting that Black male sexuality was equally taboo on the European screen. The principal woman dancer towers over the diminutive pair; Harold's attempt to reach her arms to dance with her presents a comic moment, and the brothers spend much of the sequence leaping over or sliding under the legs of the chorus girls rather than dancing with them, which deprives them of sexual chemistry.

The film's ambivalence to Black sexuality is also apparent in Dunham's scenes. Her troupe performs twice and is also shown warming up backstage. Dunham's dancers have few lines and instead appear mainly as extras, which echoes the subjugation that they endured in Hollywood, although this production does negate possible readings of Black dance as spontaneous by acknowledging the training involved. In their first scene, a dresser (Nino Taranto) interrupts a Dunham company rehearsal to deliver Delair's outfit, only to find that it has been stolen. Arriving with the package, he encounters Dunham singing troupe members Gordon Simpson and Harriet Jackson and a seminaked Vanoye Aikens, Dunham's dance partner.

This scene dictates audience perceptions of Dunham's company. First, Aikens's nakedness positions him as sexually uninhibited, a construction that recalls the primitivist ideologies circulating around Baker in the 1920s. Second, the singers call attention to the training behind Dunham's art: they are undertaking vocal warm-ups. When Fernandel, playing a Frenchman stranded in Rome, arrives at the theater, Aikens and other troupe members perform Dunham Technique stretching exercises in the background, which underscores the method's similarities to ballet and demonstrates that dance is a carefully developed skill. But the scene simultaneously sexualizes the dancers and turns their art into comedy by contrasting their physical confidence with the Frenchman's sexual inadequacy. Earlier in the film, when Fernandel's character gazed on a woman in a state of undress, his wallet was stolen. In this scene, Dunham company member Dolores Harper approaches him wearing only a bikini top and skirt. When he instructs her to cover herself, she raises her skirt to her chest, exposing her legs. The Frenchman, intimidated by the sight, falls over a pair of equally scantily clad Dunham dancers as he attempts to flee. Tellingly, light-skinned Dunham company members such as Lenwood Morris and Julie Robinson Belafonte are not featured in this exchange. The scene therefore expresses contradictory attitudes to Black performers by acknowledging Dunham and her company's artistry while capitalizing on their perceived exotic appeal. It serves as visual evidence that postwar Europe read Dunham's company through the same exoticizing lens that Baker endured.

Yet much like Baker, Dunham asserts her authorship onscreen by presenting a multifaceted vision of Black art that interrogates these degrading representations. The scene includes a dress rehearsal of Dunham's *Jazz in Five Movements*, an interpretation of African American vernacular dance styles that featured in the company's original European tour. The performance incorporates ballet with tap in a cross-cultural assemblage of dance forms that collapses racial hierarchies. Aikens and other male dancers perform synchronized routines that include tap moves and balletic *tours en l'air* at the same time that they adopt bent-knee stances more commonly seen in African and Caribbean dance. A series of women, including Robinson Belafonte, Lucille Ellis, and Harper, perform pirouettes, while close-up shots of Dunham's feet show her executing taplike movements. Aikens and Dunham also perform lifts most commonly seen in ballet and modern dance; they then dance in closed position and execute backward kicks. Back kicks were popular embellishments of the Black Bottom, a 1920s social dance featured in *Shuffle Along* and which Baker performed in her second Folies-Bergère show, *Un vent de folie*. The Black Bottom's rhythm was based on the Charleston, the dance that Baker helped to popularize in Europe and which Dunham believed to be linked to the Haitian *La Martinique*.

This scene is a visual record of Dunham's commitment to fracturing artistic and racial binaries. The rapid variation in speeds and styles defies a simplistic reading of her choreography. Like *Barrelhouse* (1938), her iconic celebration of mature female sexuality, *Jazz in Five Movements* is a nostalgic interpretation of the 1920s African American social dance scene. The sequence is a historical document, and perhaps the only firsthand cinematic evidence, of Dunham's commitment to showcasing the artistry of Black U.S. dance. The dancer's engagement with African American vernacular forms has received far less consideration than her Caribbean-influenced choreography, yet the third act of every Dunham show was devoted to what she termed "Americana," which included square dances and the cakewalk as well as jazz and blues numbers. Dunham stated that such numbers were inspired by her realization on returning from the Caribbean in the mid-1930s that "there was this [cultural] richness right there in our country."[54] Julia L. Foulkes observes that, "As an anthropologist, Dunham recognized the importance of restoring and highlighting these dances as a crucial part of American identity," and that, "Instead of thematic pieces about the plight of Black people in American society that concerned white modern dancers, Dunham focused on the cultural contributions of African Americans themselves."[55] Thus, Dunham's engagement with African American styles onscreen should be understood as part of a recuperative project aimed at redressing limiting cultural representations by pointing up their significance within a wider Black Atlantic sphere. Moreover, such work should be seen as speaking back not only to white modern dance, but also to minstrelsy-derived distortions.

Dunham and her troupe's demeanors deserve particular attention as self-reflexive attempts to challenge minstrelsy-informed representations and to foreground the social and cultural significance of Black dance forms. Dunham voiced frustration with the forced and unnatural facial expressions that she was forced to adopt while filming *Carnival of Rhythm*. Daphne Lamothe argues that the dancer affects an "almost aggressively wide and frozen smile" in the film's opening shot, which "undercuts the voice-over narration's celebration of Third World sexuality as a dance of seduction that might include the viewer."[56] The expressions of Dunham's company remain impassive in *Jazz in Five Movements*. Dunham's composure evokes the seemingly withdrawn behavior adopted by bebop musicians and therefore is readable as a deliberate reaction against Armstrong and his All-Stars' animated facial expressions. By undertelling, Dunham privileges the psychological over the physical, forcing the audience to engage actively with the performance. The dancers' faces reveal inner restraint, which offsets white fantasies by turning what might otherwise be read as a sexual encounter into a social exchange with ritualistic significance. The performers' synchronized movements also underscore the rehearsed, and hence controlled, nature of their work, which challenges readings of Black performers as sexually uninhibited still further. Equally, visualization of the dancers' labor acknowledges Dunham as a key author in the scene; the audience witnesses artistry in the process of creation.

Dunham and her troupe appear again onstage in a performance of *Batucada*. Seen previously in *Carnival of Rhythm*, *Batucada* shows how Dunham developed a cross-cultural aesthetic vision of Black Atlantic working-class cultures. Dunham's *Batucada* in *Carnival of Rhythm* played into World War II propaganda but also represented a rare cinematic acknowledgment of the beauty of Black Bahiana women who directly inspired the image of white Hollywood star Carmen Miranda. As in *Carnival of Rhythm*, Dunham uses restrained choreography to construct a glamorous and dignified representation of Afro-Brazilian rope-weavers. However, unlike *Carnival of Rhythm*, which complicated Dunham's artistic intentions with shadowy backgrounds, a condescending voice-over, and what Dunham termed "contrived" props to symbolize Latin American abundance, the *Botta e risposta* version represents a verbatim record of *Batucada* as it was designed by her husband John Pratt to appear on stage. Thus, Dunham enjoys greater authorial independence here than she did in Hollywood, as she is able to transfer her stage work directly to the screen.

Dunham's performance takes place on an almost bare stage set, with only a rope-net to indicate the dancers' occupation. This basic direction accentuates the beauty of African diasporic art forms and their practitioners. In *Carnival of Rhythm*, frenetic camera shots undercut Dunham's presentation of Afro-Brazilian workingwomen, but *Botta e risposta* glamorizes Dunham by filming her close-up shots in soft focus (see figure 18). As in Baker's "Le Chemin de bonheur" performance in *Princesse Tam-Tam*, such a technique creates an ethereal quality that emphasizes Dunham's beauty and stardom in a striking distinction from Hollywood representations of Black performers. It also places her visually in contrast to Louis Armstrong's starkly lit All Stars. Dunham's dance is sensual and playful, and she employs rhythmic pelvic movements to attract the rope-weavers. As in *Jazz in Five Movements*, Dunham adopts suggestive rather than explicitly sexual movements. In this way, the scene reworks a history of white fantasies of Black eroticism, as explored in Baker's early music hall performances, into a dignified social encounter. *Batucada*'s inclusion alongside *Jazz in Five Movements*' cross-cultural exploration of African American vernacular forms alludes to the geographical breadth of styles from which Dunham drew inspiration. The film replicates the cultural diversity that audiences witnessed in her stage shows, and it acknowledges Dunham as an anthropological authority on dance.

Dunham's touring career coincided with a U.S. Government project to export a racially inclusive vision of America around the world. In the

FIGURE 18. Soft focus close-up of Dunham performing *Batucada* in *Botta e risposta*.

mid-1950s, the State Department began sponsoring Black artists to perform abroad to counter the nation's reputation for racism, which had become a prominent feature of Communist propaganda in the Soviet Union and elsewhere. As Penny Von Eschen asserts, these international tours were "Intended to promote a vision of color-blind American democracy . . . with blackness and race operating culturally to project an image of American nationhood that was more inclusive than the reality."[57] The government's oversight of such tours meant that performers were forced to work within dominant paradigms of representation. Yet they brought individuality to their roles and drew global attention to their art, positioning themselves as world-leading creative practitioners. Dunham believed that dance should play a key role in international cultural exchange, describing it as "more than any other art form the expression of the life of a people."[58] But she has not traditionally been considered as an ambassador alongside jazz artists because her company did not receive State Department support.

Dunham's cross-cultural Black aesthetic conflicted with the race-blind image that the State Department sought to convey, with its dance panel preferring instead to support the "universal" abstract style of white artists such as Martha Graham.[59] Dunham also drew State Department anger for *Southland*, an antilynching ballet that she staged in Santiago, Chile, in 1951 and again in Paris in 1953. The Government's lack of support for Dunham echoed its response to Baker, who was barred from appearing in the United States and Latin America throughout much of the 1950s for her outspoken criticism of U.S. racism. Sexual prejudice may also have prevented women such as Dunham from securing State Department funding. Although critics praised male jazz performers for their experimentation, they chose to speculate on whether Dunham was "producing art or 'catering to popular taste and producing cheap entertainment,'" which shows that Dunham was as constrained as Baker by benighted critical attitudes.[60] By contrast, by the mid-1960s Dunham was herself dismissive of the artistic and cultural value of U.S. jazz, which she referred to as "pure commercial exploitation," concluding that African Americans had "lost control over their contribution to music."[61]

More remarkably than her jazz musician contemporaries, however, Dunham forged an international career largely independently of the State Department. Like Armstrong and other artists, her global career enabled her to influence a Black international cultural agenda. As Joanna Dee Das observes, "Denied the opportunity to represent the United States as an official goodwill ambassador, she created a role for herself as an unofficial ambassador of the African diaspora."[62] Dunham in fact worked indirectly with the State Department as the U.S. representative to the First World Festival of Negro Arts in Senegal in 1966. Von Eschen contends that the festival "provided a forum for an international affirmation of African and African diasporic art, and was a catalyst for the State Department's shift toward a wider range of black music."[63] The Department's cultural dealings with Africa had previously been driven by chauvinism toward a continent that it considered culturally unsophisticated.[64] If Dunham could not exploit the Department's financial resources, she at least attempted to influence its adoption of a worldlier attitude to Black artistry. Her plans for a West African cultural arts academy on the Senegalese island of Gorée were to be developed as part of a six-month State Department assignment.[65] For Dunham, this would form part of a widening commitment to "deepening understandings and exchanging cultural patterns that [would] eventually result in the dissolution of social and racial prejudices."[66] Although her project was out of step with contemporary Senegalese concerns and ultimately unfulfilled, its conception underscores her commitment to intercultural education.

Botta e risposta shows that Dunham employed a choreographic method rooted in an international vision of Black artistry to challenge reductive readings of Black women's dancing bodies. It illustrates primitivism's endurance in postwar Europe, yet Dunham's tonally complex performances contest these conceptions. Affording her substantial freedom to showcase her artistic practice, the film serves as visual testimony to her commitment to educating audiences around the world about the diversity and social significances of African diasporic dance cultures. Dunham's next production, *Mambo*, grants even more space to her art. The film situates dance as a central narrative trope and relies on Dunham's choreography, allowing her to stylize and celebrate an African diasporic heritage to an extent not possible in studio-era Hollywood. Like *Botta e risposta*, *Mambo* is historically valuable as a rare cinematic dramatization of Dunham's choreography that evidences her popularity in Europe. The film does marginalize Dunham's troupe in its attempt to position Italian actress Silvana Mangano as its star attraction. The film's borrowing of Dunham's art for the purposes of elevating Mangano's image recalls a history of Euro-American appropriation of African American performance. Nonetheless, it also visualizes Dunham's contribution in a manner that complicates this history. By transposing Afro-Caribbean and Afro-Brazilian dance forms onto an Italian dancer's body, the film reenacts its cultural crossovers and facilitates Dunham's agenda of articulating intercultural exchange. In this case, unlike in many of Dunham's Hollywood films where white dancers performed her choreography, the film's dance authorship as well as its complex artistry and cultural origins are acknowledged.

Mambo was released in Italy in 1954 and enjoyed a limited U.S. release in 1955. Mangano plays Giovanna, a young woman who joins Dunham's dance company during its tour of Venice and becomes its star. But she abandons her career success in favor of two love rivals: hemophiliac count Enrico (Michael Rennie) and her former lover Mario (Vittorio Gassman). Anticipating the count's death, Mario persuades the reluctant Giovanna to marry Enrico so that the pair will inherit his fortune. The scheme ends in tragedy and the film concludes with Mangano's character returning to Dunham's company and to her career as a dancer.

In a memorandum to *Mambo*'s producers, Dunham outlined specific ideas about how her work should be staged, suggesting that she saw the production as a serious artistic enterprise but that she also felt she was being sidelined from the creative process.[67] Dunham received credit for her choreographic work and for the songs' lyrics, but she struggled to claim copyright for her musical contributions.[68] She also appeared in the film as "herself." Several scenes feature her leading her troupe in rehearsal, which contest myths of "authentic" Black performance by pointing to the carefully constructed nature of her work. *Mambo* acknowledges Dunham as a leading dancer-choreographer and positions her in the role of trainer of a successful touring company.

The film does not repeat the racist occlusions that led to the omission of Dunham's troupe from most of the Hollywood films that she choreographed. Instead, the production is built around the company and its performances and the dance style is specific to Dunham Technique. Significantly, *Botta e risposta* creator Dino de Laurentiis coproduced the film. De Laurentiis's practice of building a film around well-known stars suggests that the story may even have been conceived around Dunham and her company. Dunham and her troupe are given subsidiary roles, however. Aside from Mangano performing as the dance lead, actress and former Katherine Dunham School of Dance student Shelley Winters, as "Toni," takes on Dunham's real-life position as company manager. The effect of this delegation is to undermine Dunham's position; performance footage centers on Giovanna, with Dunham functioning mainly in the role of teacher. *Mambo* relies on Dunham's choreography but visually subjugates its author. It situates her dance work as central to the film's aesthetics and plot, affording her prominent cinematic authorship, but denies her full participation in her own contributions. Yet a close analysis of the film reveals that within its structural confines Dunham exercised a determining influence over the production's aesthetics, and *Mambo* should be recognized as an artistically and culturally significant treatment of her choreography.

Film critic Roy Thomas lists *Mambo* alongside *Carnival of Rhythm* and *Stormy Weather* as one of a "triptych of Dunham Technique in commercial films."[69] Thomas's reading overlooks *Botta e risposta*, but it underscores *Mambo*'s importance as a visualization of Dunham's artistry. Yet despite Dunham's presence and influence, the film's perceived shortcomings—Alan Casty calls it a "film *manqué*"—mean that it has been critically neglected.[70] Dorothea Fischer-Hornung remains the only scholar to afford serious attention to Dunham's work on the production. She argues that *Mambo* "marks a brave attempt to transcend the boundaries of the culturally racialized dancing body, a film that takes itself and, more significantly, Dunham's contribution to modern dance culture seriously."[71] Her reading complicates interpretations of Giovanna as simply perpetuating a history of white appropriation of African American artistic labor. Mangano adopts and masters Dunham's movements, but she does so in ways that acknowledge the complexities of Dunham's work and counter the notion that there are innate differences between Black and white bodies and artistries. Building on Fischer-Hornung's view that the film "marks a significant step in clearly recognizing African American agency in cultural production," I argue that Dunham Technique is in fact a key aesthetic and thematic device.[72] Consequently, Dunham is one of its chief visual authors, and even though the production displays contradictory attitudes to Black performers and artistry, it is a revealing dramatization of her cross-cultural dance philosophy. *Mambo*'s plot associates Dunham's choreography with exoticism, sexual liberation, and notions of "innate" Black performance. However, her strong creative influence and director Robert Rossen's experimental techniques muddle this narrative by presenting a visually challenging depiction of diverse forms of African diasporic artistry that situates Dunham Technique at the heart of the film's aesthetics.

Mambo had some Hollywood connections. The film was coproduced by Paramount Pictures, the studio responsible for *Star Spangled Rhythm*. It also boasted a Hollywood director in Rossen, who had been Oscar-nominated for *All the King's Men* (1949). Rossen was named as a Communist in 1951 and was blacklisted for two years before finally testifying about his Communist connections and naming fifty-three Party members. His participation in *Mambo* was precipitated by financial need following his blacklisting. However, it also substantiates Daniela Treveri Gennari's reading of the film as an example of "glocalization, where the use of local practices and traditions were employed to create an Italian movie that both derived from, and yet also acted as a response to, an American-made film."[73] Interviewed by the *New York Times* while shooting *Mambo*, Rossen expressed hope that the Italian film industry would maintain its independence, arguing that, "There is no need for Italy, with its wealth of native material and imagination, to imitate Hollywood. The industry here will prosper by continuing to be Italian in its approach to and execution of motion picture ideas."[74] Rossen had employed European cinematic techniques even before departing Hollywood for Italy. *All the King's Men* drew on Italian neorealist practices, including camerawork, cutting methods, and the employment of nonactors. Some of these techniques are evident in *Mambo*. In this way, the film can be read as a product of the flourishing U.S. art cinema movement of the postwar period, which authorized greater aesthetic experimentation than did Hollywood. *Mambo* capitalizes on this creative freedom. Although the film is fraught with themes of exotic sensuality, Dunham's choreography is central to its artistic vision. Unusually, a Black woman here is afforded significant creative influence over a mainstream midcentury film.

Mambo is a thematically and visually bold film that eschews convention and confounded contemporary critical opinion.[75] In a broken chronology—the film opens halfway into the narrative—the audience witnesses daring and sometimes confusing camera shots, most notably in the dance scenes. Situating dance, and Dunham Technique in particular, as a visual and narrative organizing principle, *Mambo* begins with a five-minute musical sequence choreographed by Dunham. The emotional intensity of this scene and its duration establish a heavy mood of love and jealousy that foreshadows the film's plot. The scene combines jazz with Black Atlantic cultural forms and ballet, fracturing artistic binaries, while skewed camera angles and rapid cuts evade straightforward readings. The audience therefore is challenged to make connections between different performance cultures and styles at the same time that it is called upon to identify the different art forms and, indeed, the racial identities of the performers. As with Baker's African American vaudeville-derived movements, which were esoteric to European audiences, such a complex aesthetic threatens to obscure Dunham's authorial intentions, but it also refracts reductive interpretations of her artistry.

In a call-and-response sequence, the opening shot reveals Afro-Cuban drummer Francisco Aguabella performing at a window before cutting to another Afro-Cuban artist, vocalist Xiomara Alfaro, who chants to the *orishas* (spirits of La Regla de Ocha or Santería) while dressed as a female pineapple vendor. Marta Moreno Vega contends that Dunham's work with sacred Cuban musicians such as Aguabella helped to expand the religion's presence in New York and influenced the city's mambo craze, and she points to this scene as evidence of Dunham's role in promoting both the dance and the religion.[76] Such a sequence consequently serves as an important cinematic record of Dunham's devotion to revaluing Black Atlantic artistry and to raising the visibility of its practitioners. Alfaro's white turban and gold earrings also recall *Batucada*'s Bahiana fruit vendor. As *Carnival of Rhythm* has shown, although Bahiana culture can trace its roots to Africa, only the intervention of Brazilian embassy officials could persuade Hollywood producers that Dunham was not too "Black" to perform a role that the pale-skinned Carmen Miranda had come to symbolize in U.S. cinema. Like *Carnival of Rhythm* and *Botta e risposta*, the scene's foregrounding of Alfaro and Aguabella therefore celebrates the beauty and sacred artistry of Black Latin American communities in a manner historically elided by Hollywood.

The camera then cuts to a white conductor, presumably the film's Italian conductor Franco Ferrara, and the call-and-response continues between the singer, a classical guitarist, and an orchestra, as a modest stage set, which features a stairwell, is revealed. Three women dancers emerge at the top of the stairs and execute angular hip and arm movements to the sound of the guitar before a reprise of the orchestra and camera cut to the orchestra pit signals another tonal shift. A white male dancer wearing a Mexican sombrero and white zoot suit then leaps onto the stage from the orchestra pit and performs an exaggerated jitterbug with a female dancer. The camera then shifts to Vanoye Aikens, abstractly attired in a striped jumpsuit. Aikens performs to a drumbeat a series of acrobatic high kicks, a balletic turn with a bent-knee stance, and what appears to be boxing jabs. Due to his commanding physique, Aikens was Dunham's dance partner from 1943 until the end of her career. His employment here suggests that Dunham wanted to emphasize the dance's physical power. The sequence echoes a stance that Aikens adopts in a video recording of Dunham's ballet, *L'Ag'Ya*.[77] In turn, it recalls the Ag'Ya fighting dance that Dunham recorded in Martinique in 1936. In this way, his performance may be read as a cinematic visualization of Dunham's concern to break down racialized artistic hierarchies and demonstrate the cultural value of Caribbean dance forms.

The sequence then becomes a danced narrative. Discordant, fragmented music and tense, sexually suggestive movements foretell in abstract visual language the film's themes of passion and tragedy. Dissonant music heralds Giovanna's arrival, and she adopts African American, South American, and Caribbean dance styles to enact the passionate love triangle on which she will embark. She approaches a light-skinned male dancer with movements borrowed from the *Cumbia*, a Columbian slave courtship ritual, combined with more balletic high kicks. Hip-centered and Shimmylike shoulder movements follow, and the male dancer joins her in rumba-style closeness before the pair jumps apart into a stylized Mambo, performing tempered attacking kicks that hint at Giovanna's tense relationship with Mario and again echo the Ag'Ya. This dance number mimics violence continually, as when the male dancer appears to strike Giovanna and as Mario does later in the narrative.[78] Another light-skinned dancer seemingly symbolizing Enrico appears and Giovanna dances with both men before coming to a sudden, passionate halt in the arms of Mario. After cutting away to Toni and Dunham, who are watching offstage, the music stops, and the audience hears a piercing descending scale from a woodwind instrument as the dancer playing Enrico falls to the floor, prefiguring the character's violent death. When the dancing resumes, Giovanna leaves the scene, as she will later turn away from Mario when he kills Enrico.

The scene is a vital record of Dunham's choreography and imbues her with authorial influence over the film, allowing her to foretell its plot. Yet it visually marginalizes Dunham and her dancers. Dunham is shown scrutinizing the performance from the wings (see figure 19), which acknowledges her as the choreographer, but a shot of the audience and the sound of their applause at Giovanna's appearance positions the white woman as the scene's star dancer. The foregrounding of Mangano facilitates readings of her performance as a European intervention in "innate" Black artistry. Her dance partners are also light-skinned. The film therefore appears to repeat a troubling history of white cultural appropriation. In particular, the central positioning of Mangano, a dancer with limited skills, reinforces perceptions of innate differences between Black and white dancing bodies. *Time* magazine suggested that, "Silvana mambos like a self-conscious tourist."[79] Fischer-Hornung goes so far as to argue that: "Unfortunately, Mangano's talent does not live up to the potential of the performance . . .

FIGURE 19. Shelley Winters, as "Toni," and Dunham, as "herself," watching Giovanna perform in *Mambo*'s (Dino de Laurentiis Cinematografica, 1954) opening sequence.

and the interpretive split between black body and white mind is reestablished despite the attempt at deconstruction of this very paradigm: what the viewer sees is 'white girls can't dance.'"[80] Mangano does appear to struggle in the sequence; her focused facial expression betrays a performance that is surprisingly stiff and lacking in confidence, and she relies heavily on her male partners' leads.

Although Giovanna becomes the dance company's star and so takes on most of the film's solos, subsequent sequences merely reinforce her physical limitations. The next staged musical sequence, "Baiao faz balancar" (Back to Bahia), takes place after Giovanna has joined and been trained by Dunham's company. "Baiao faz balancar" was part of a series of Brazilian-themed dances, eventually codified as "Brazilian Suite," which included *Batucada*, that were performed by the company throughout the 1940s and 1950s. As in the earlier *Batucada* film sequences, Dunham developed the music and choreography and Pratt designed the elaborate costumes. As *Carnival of Rhythm* has shown, *Batucada*'s purpose was to celebrate the Black Bahiana women whose beauty and artistry had been appropriated onscreen by the pale-skinned Carmen Miranda. However, *Mambo* employs Bahiana fashions to enhance Mangano's star image and the men she attracts are equally light-skinned, which elides the Caribbean and South American origins of Dunham's choreography. The film's appropriation of Dunham's material by a noncompany dancer also has negative implications for her artistry as it prevents company members from demonstrating their technical capabilities.

"Baiao faz balancar" is constructed as a duet, perhaps to hide the physical shortcomings of Mangano, who spends one part of the sequence in a hammock and another in the arms of her partner instead of dancing throughout the scene. *Mambo*'s focus on Mangano also allows Giovanna's association with the company to be read as a white woman's intervention in "exotic" and "primitive" performance. Upon first seeing the Dunham company rehearse, Giovanna is entranced. Attempting to describe the music, she falters, prompting Enrico to suggest that she is drawn to its "savage" appeal. Dance and atavistic sexuality are overtly linked in a complex interaction between Dunham's dance anthropology and primitivist thought. Like *Botta e risposta*, the scene provides cinematic evidence of the endurance of racist fantasies about Black sexuality in the postwar European imaginary.

Giovanna first encounters Dunham's company at a festival that blends elements of traditional Venetian and Caribbean carnivals in a hectic, trance-like visual display. In her only solo in the film, Dunham is shown singing in Spanish, kicking off her shoes, and discarding parts of her clothing to a rapid drumbeat to perform a seemingly primal dance. Fragmented camera shots capture Giovanna's confusion as she enters this world and proceeds to dance; as in *Princesse Tam-Tam*'s Conga and *Carnival of Rhythm*'s "Adeus Terras," the use of such a technique encourages readings of Black dance as an act of atavistic regression. Giovanna enters the scene wearing a Venetian mask; she "unmasks" during the Caribbean-themed festivities and discovers a more sensual self. Picking up the skirt that Dunham has thrown off, she begins to dance with it, drunkenly succumbing to the rhythms of Dunham's drummers and provocatively lifting her skirt and opening her legs. The scene ends with Giovanna being carried away by Enrico and, the film implies, forced to have sex with him. Dunham performs the Macumba in this scene, which she documented during a 1950 research trip to Brazil, and which illustrates the anthropological influences in her work. But, as with Baker's Conga in *Princesse Tam-Tam* and Dunham's experiences in Hollywood, the film frame prevents the choreography from being properly understood by reinforcing an apparent connection between African diasporic cultures and sex.

In the film's next scene, however, Toni invites Giovanna to join Dunham's company, positioning dance as an opportunity to escape the grip of male sexuality by offering a life independent of men. Thus, if *Mambo* presents dance as atavistic, it also recognizes its importance as a means of achieving financial independence, and of reconfiguring gender roles. In this regard, it visualizes a history of appropriation rooted in modern's dance's development, in which white women borrowed Black dance forms to achieve physical self-expression and forge successful careers. Perhaps what is most strikingly subversive about dance in the film is that it positions women as artists, succeeding independently in the world. One of a number of films banned by the Vatican from parish cinemas during this period, *Mambo* exuded a feminine independence that jarred with the Catholic Church's emphasis on female duty and motherhood. Alluding specifically to Mangano's performance in *Mambo*, Daniela Treveri Gennari argues that Gina Lollobrigida, Sophia Loren, and Mangano "not only embodied a form of sexuality that the Vatican dreaded, they also challenged the image of womanhood that the Catholic Church was eager to restore in postwar Italy: a woman totally dedicated to her children."[81]

Giovanna's final performance, a blues song entitled "New Love, New Wine" with lyrics by Dunham, positions her as a liberated woman. Performing subtle dance gestures based on the Mambo, which include those pelvic gyrations derived from her Cumbia movements at the beginning of the film, Giovanna is situated as a solo dancer for the first time. Dunham looks on again in a manner that alludes to her authorship and highlights her contribution to Giovanna's star image, but the performance also makes clear that Giovanna no longer depends on the Dunham dancers, nor on men, for success. She is now an autonomous star. Issues of authorship lie at the heart of the scene, especially when one remembers that Dunham, as the blues number's author, had to battle for copyright of the song. The scene's emphasis on an Italian performer in contrast to Black musicians who are barely visible in the background completes a gradual appropriation that takes place throughout the film.

However, reading Giovanna merely as a white appropriator of Dunham's material obscures a wider history of pseudoscientific racism to which Italian identities were in turn subjected. Paul Gennari describes how Southern Italians have historically been made victims of the "mythology of the Sicilian, the Calabrian, and the Neapolitan as lazy, morally corrupt, intellectually inferior Others, closer kin to the African savage than to the Florentine prince."[82] He notes that they were regarded as representatives of a "dangerous inbetweenness" that made them victims of Jim Crow legislation in the U.S. South during the late nineteenth century.[83] Such identity constructions informed the Hollywood career of *Casbah* actress Yvonne de Carlo, whose Italian heritage led her to be typecast as an "exotic" seductress. Critical Whiteness Studies scholar David Roediger demonstrates that working-class Irish immigrants also experienced racist treatment in nineteenth-century United States and attained "whiteness" by distancing themselves socially from African Americans.[84] In *Mambo*, however, a working-class Italian woman does exactly the opposite by accepting the schooling of an African American artist in a cinematic display of cross-cultural unity. *Mambo* is also careful to acknowledge Dunham's work by showing that Dunham Technique is a carefully developed "art" before Giovanna joins the company, and the film emphasizes the physical toil required to become a successful dancer. Giovanna's first words reveal the labor underpinning the film's opening performance, contesting popular readings of dance as pleasurable escapism. In a voice-over, she states, "For a year I'd done nothing but study and dance, dance and study, enduring the physical torment that was necessary before I'd be a machine living without a soul, just as Toni wanted." Such words emphasize the skill and precision involved in Dunham's work, countering readings of her material as spontaneous rhythmic movement.

Like *Botta e risposta*, *Mambo* devotes cinematic space to Dunham's dance rehearsals. In so doing, it allows Dunham to rupture the theatrical illusion and point to the carefully constructed nature of her art. In turn, it acknowledges her substantial creative contribution to the film and serves as an important site of midcentury Black screen authorship. *Mambo* features the only identified footage of Dunham teaching Dunham Technique during her performing career.[85] Dunham's company is shown in training four times, including in the final frame of the film, a visual trope that dramatizes the work that has been invested in staging the performances and developing the dancers' abilities.

The training scenes reveal the cross-cultural complexities of Dunham Technique, particularly the importance of ballet and Vodou in Dunham's choreography. In *Botta e risposta*, Dunham dancers perform balletlike stretching exercises. In *Mambo*, dancers are seen actually training at the barre, as shown in figure 20. Dunham used ballet in *Stormy Weather* to foreground her dancers as physically refined and graceful, thereby transforming Eurocentric notions of beauty in a self-reflexive effort to challenge perceptions of Black dance as lowbrow. Like *Stormy Weather*, this scene can be viewed as a self-reflexive appropriation of European art in which Dunham deliberately juxtaposes artistic forms to undermine racialized hierarchies of difference.

FIGURE 20. Dunham dancers training at the barre in *Mambo*.

After warming up at the barre, Giovanna undergoes a rigorous training regime that causes her to collapse from physical and mental exhaustion. It is possible to interpret this footage as an invocation of Dunham's anthropological research into Vodou and therefore as a cinematic articulation of her creative vision and a wider history of Black Atlantic cultural practices. Dunham Technique progressions, or training exercises, feature in the studio rehearsal scene. These movements were rooted in Dunham's fieldwork observations of Vodou rituals, specifically Yanvalou, which Dunham performed during her *lavé-tête*, and which she described as the "signature dance" of Vodou. The sequence therefore serves as visual evidence of the connection between Dunham's research and her choreography as it shows her scientific work in the process of transformation onto a commercial platform. As in *Botta e risposta*, in which Dunham dancers are presented warming up backstage, the film is able to go further than Dunham's stage performances in revealing the training and cultural crossovers involved in her artistry and in troubling assumptions about African Americans as merely "natural" entertainers.

The scene's incorporation of Vodou-inspired training exercises evidences Dunham's authorship as it provides a cinematic, albeit dramatized, record of her adaption of Haitian cultural forms. The sequence functions as a site of translation of Dunham's work for European audiences, as represented in the character of Giovanna. But in what ways are these translations represented, and how can they be perceived? Like the opening scene, the dance sequence is visually fragmented; sudden, jagged, and close-up camera shots alienate and disorient the viewer. Reflections and refraction in the studio's mirrors enhance this confusion and invoke Giovanna's "possession." Such cinematic effects recall *Princesse Tam-Tam* and *Carnival of Rhythm*'s rapid editing techniques, which invited Black dance to be read as sexually unrestrained. Yet the fragmented camera work also mirrors stylistically the fractured dance style of Dunham Technique and can be read equally as an endeavor to challenge racialized artistic binaries. Fischer-Hornung asserts that, "the highly disorienting camera work reflects Dunham's firm belief that a literal depiction of traditional African diasporic dance would not be adequate for comprehension by an audience outside the culture being depicted."[86] This suggests that Dunham may have influenced the framing of the sequence, and by avoiding "literal" depictions of racial identities she is able to move away from reductive representations. Training references and allusions to ballet undermine racist myths about Black performance still further. Consequently, the scene defamiliarizes racial identities, forcing the viewer to engage actively with the dancing and to interpret what it sees. Such a practice is analogous to Baker's intervention in African diasporic and European forms of artistry. It shows how both women retained creative independence by developing innovative configurations of Black female subjecthood that resisted commodification.

In his review of *Mambo*, *New York Times* film critic Bosley Crowther underscored the tensions between the perceived sexuality of Dunham's work and its artistic intentions. He chose to read Dunham and her dancers as sexually provocative entertainers. Overlooking the company's place in the film's plot, he claimed that, "Mr. Rossen has used the Dunham dancers and a riotous palazzo ball to establish a sense of degeneration in the dark byways of the lovely city of the canals," and that "Miss Dunham herself glitters gaudily a few times among her frenzied mambo cats."[87] Milan-based newspaper *Epoca* dismissed the film for its "erotic, satanic, mundane" aesthetic, echoing assumptions about Black cultures encountered by Baker on her first tour of Europe in the late 1920s, when Viennese detractors dubbed her "the Devil himself."[88] Such critics simply reasserted racial prejudices rather than engaging closely with Dunham's art, and their descriptions did not accurately reflect her company's performances. Their readings show how misleading could be the impressions of midcentury white male reviewers, who lacked the critical language properly to interpret Dunham, and equally Baker's work, and instead gave voice to the racial and sexual attitudes of their era. Close analysis of *Mambo* shows that cinematic visibility in fact enabled Dunham to challenge such racist assumptions about Black art. *Mambo* allows Dunham to present a widely circulated vision of her choreography that reveals that her dancers are not "wild" spectacles but technically accomplished artists. Although by participating in the film Dunham colluded in racially subjugating cinematic frameworks, such an intervention enabled her simultaneously to present a complex interpretation of African diasporic artistry onscreen.

At the film's end, Giovanna returns to Dunham's company. Her homecoming is constructed as atavistic. In her final voice-over, she expresses the hope that, "perhaps in my third world, the absorbing world of the Mambo, I could find forgetfulness of the past and in time peace and happiness." Seemingly a deliberate pun on "Third World" as a colonial definition of less economically developed societies, Giovanna's statement emphasizes the irreconcilability of her Italian life with her "exotic" career as a star dancer in a touring company. *Mambo* therefore presents a reductive vision of African diasporic cultures and identities, while offering few concessions to Dunham as a performer. Nevertheless, the film acknowledges and even relies on her artistic vision, affording her creative control over the dance performances. In contrast to Dunham's experiences of artistic subjugation in Hollywood,

Mambo makes her work central to its tone and plot. The result is a significant cinematic record of her dance practice and its anthropological influences. The film reveals the multiple representational tensions present in Dunham's postwar European career but also demonstrates that she was able to create a challenging depiction of diverse forms of African diasporic artistry even while caught within a production framework that sought to depict her choreography as exotic.

Botta e risposta and *Mambo* highlight the endurance of primitivist ideologies in postwar European cinema. They show how racist assumptions about Black Others shaped the ways in which African American performers were represented and perceived. However, both films seek to capitalize on Dunham's fame and artistry and in so doing afford her significant authorship over her dance scenes. Consequently, Dunham is able to speak back to racist perceptions by presenting a rich variety of Black dance and performance cultures onscreen. *Botta e risposta* grants Dunham space to construct a dignified depiction of Black artistry and thus to undercut derogatory racial iconography seen elsewhere in the film. By comparison, *Mambo* foregrounds Dunham's work in its narrative and visual style, which allows her to showcase the anthropological underpinnings of her choreographic practice. Both films enable her to emphasize the technical skill and labor involved in Dunham Technique. As with Baker's films, *Botta e risposta* and *Mambo* show that Dunham's French and Italian cinematic projects were sites of representational tension but also key sites of midcentury Black female cinema authorship. The two productions are vital records of Dunham's dance philosophy of cross-cultural exchange. They shed important light on European postwar racial ideologies while also revealing the importance of the continent's cinema in affording Dunham space to meaningfully showcase a dance practice that challenged these representations.

Conclusion

In *Josephine*, Baker declared that, "You never know how a film will turn out. None that I've ever appeared in has ended up the way I expected. After all, a director can do whatever he wants."[1] At the end of her performing career, Dunham acknowledged that, "The only satisfactory record of dance has been film."[2] But she also stressed the medium's "inadequacy," affirming that, "in my estimation the film is yet to be made which penetrates into the totality of the complex structure surrounding the dance."[3] She outlined plans to direct such a project, but her ambitions were never fulfilled. Baker and Dunham's frustrations exemplify the cinematic distortions of their art, and by extension, their battles as Black women to assert control over their work. As this study has shown, the idea of dance as cerebral artistry set against the commodification of Black female bodies is key to understanding both women's careers. In her consideration of European responses to Baker's art, Terri Francis goes as far as to argue that, "Aesthetically, the figure of Baker galvanized the transformation of nineteenth-century ethnological inquiry and the exotic human display that was part of colonial fairs into mass entertainment."[4] This claim could also be made for Dunham: through her anthropology and art, she entered into a distorted history that had dehumanized the Black Atlantic as a passive subject for the consumption of white European and U.S. spectators. Nevertheless, both women developed choreographies rooted in rich histories of Black dance to disrupt these same myths and imagine new aesthetic possibilities for Black women.

This study has investigated Baker and Dunham's films and writings to foreground their authorship despite such restrictions and to bring to light their important contributions to literature and cinema. It has privileged the dancers' literary voices both to highlight their place in an African American women's autobiographical tradition and to uncover the intellectual and psychological underpinnings of performance styles whose complexities were frequently elided by dance critics, but which were, in fact, built on a rich history of African diasporic artistry. Baker and Dunham were the first well-known African American women to write multivolume accounts of their lives, and their works document their interwar experiences and intellectual awakenings. Their memoirs show how they each used dance to engage self-reflexively with pseudo-ethnographic tropes and to contest dehumanizing attitudes to Black Atlantic cultures and identities. Such texts reveal the origins of their antiracist philosophies and call attention to their international contributions to the civil rights and Black Arts movements. Dunham wrote scientific texts and Baker coauthored her writings. Reclaiming the autobiographical significance of such work requires us to shift across traditional generic, geographical, and authorial boundaries. Yet the rewards are significant, for such texts contain valuable firsthand accounts of two African American women's midcentury transatlantic experiences and artistic practices.

In turn, the study has considered Baker and Dunham's films to underscore disjuncture between the artistic and social significance of Black dance techniques and the depiction of such practices on the European and U.S. stage and screen but also to recover the extensive authorship that they enjoyed as Black women stars and choreographers in mainstream cinema. It has adopted a transatlantic analytical approach to trace the physical freedoms and artistic and commercial appreciation afforded to Baker and Dunham outside the United States. The artists' screen careers in particular expand our understanding of African American film history by revealing key moments of early Black female stardom and authorship away from the strictures of Hollywood. The study acknowledges that Baker and Dunham's European success was framed by racial imaginaries in which Black women dancers were rendered hypersexual and their artistry innate. Yet it has also shown how their artistic interventions, which were frequently unscripted and typically located outside of plot boundaries, shaped their productions' aesthetics and allowed for resistant counter-readings.

Baker and Dunham's films represent vital visual records of their choreographies. The productions, many of which were circulated internationally, represent the platforms by which most audiences have—and continue to—appreciate their work. They show how both women's artistry was circumscribed by racial ideologies on both sides of the Atlantic while demonstrating how they each worked within such frameworks to reinterpret racist iconography and create new significations. Baker's silent films play into French colonial narratives and betray an intense ambivalence to Black women's sexuality. However, her dance scenes reveal a choreographic style marketed as "exotic" dance but fundamentally rooted in Black Atlantic performance traditions. Moreover, as the first Black actress to enjoy a leading role in a mainstream motion picture, Baker's work appealed to large numbers of African American cinemagoers. Her sound films deny her characters social acceptance, but they also celebrate her as a glamorous European *chanteuse* and screen star, a construction at odds with World War II–era Hollywood's subjugation of Black performers. Dunham's Hollywood films visually segregate the artist from film plots and at times replace her company with white dancers. They evidence the kind of cinematic mistreatment that Baker would have endured if her effort to break into the U.S. mainstream via the *Ziegfeld Follies* had been successful. But they also acknowledge Dunham's choreographic influence and allow her to showcase an artistic style, rooted in her anthropological work, which sought to elucidate the cultural and social significances of African diasporic dance forms. Equally, her European films illustrate the endurance of primitivist constructions of Black artists in postwar Europe. Yet, as with Baker's sound films, they celebrate her glamour and evidence the critical and commercial acclaim that she enjoyed on the continent. They also afford her a measure of authorial control over her cinematic representation and negate readings of Black dance as spontaneous by acknowledging the training behind her art.

This investigation has inevitably thrown up as many questions as it has answered. The films reveal that Baker and Dunham's performances often came across as esoteric: European audiences in particular would have had little understanding of the origins of their dance practices and thus of the cultural significances of their work. Such impressions were not helped by the performers' own actions, for Baker frequently played into her exotic image and Dunham failed to provide detailed information about the anthropological underpinnings of her performances, even though they were frequently rooted in firsthand encounters with African diasporic rituals. Baker and Dunham's films and writings also represent small and occasional components of careers that each spanned several decades. They are merely snapshots of their aesthetic practices. Yet the brevity of such sources is, paradoxically, useful for underscoring the extent to which Black women's artistry has been reduced to a footnote in mainstream cultural histories. And as tangible records of Baker and Dunham's intellectual philosophies and artistries, their films and writings serve as important correctives to contemporary European and Euro-American reviewers, who generally lacked the dance vocabularies to accurately describe their work and were instead prone to primitivist misinterpretations.

As the two most internationally celebrated Black women dancers of the twentieth century, Baker and Dunham's careers underscore the distortions and socially marginalizing effect of racist cultural imaginaries on both sides of the Atlantic in the three decades prior to the civil rights era. The limited opportunities that they enjoyed despite their statuses as dance icons call poignant attention to the wider devaluation and elision of Black women's artistry in twentieth-century transatlantic culture. Yet Baker and Dunham's accomplishments on the page and screen also demonstrate how they were able to rework and humanize such limited and demeaning narratives to the extent that they made significant authorial contributions to midcentury literature and cinema. Through their films and writings, we are able to see that, although racial ideologies have different sociopolitical origins and operate in different ways, white U.S. and European attitudes toward Black dance in the early- and mid–twentieth century heavily circumscribed the work of their practitioners. However, they also show how such talented performers used complex and self-referential artistry to challenge their subjugated status and achieve a measure of cultural recognition and creative autonomy.

Notes

Introduction

1. G. L. George, "Joséphine Baker revient à l'écran," *Paris-Jour*, September 27, 1934. Cited in Jules-Rosette, *Josephine Baker*, 92.

2. Cited in Hotchner, *Papa Hemingway*, 53.

3. France awarded women the right to vote in 1944, becoming one of the last Western European countries to do so.

4. Wood, *The Josephine Baker Story*, 138.

5. Baker was unable to stay in Paris when the Nazis occupied the city in June 1940 and relocated to North Africa with her French Resistance comrade Captain Jacques Abtey. However, her work as a military intelligence agent came to an end when she contracted peritonitis in Casablanca in June 1941. She was bedridden for the next nineteen months and suffered a lengthy relapse in spring 1944. Nevertheless, during a brief period of recovery in 1943, she performed for French, British, and American soldiers across North Africa and also worked to raise money for the Free French Forces.

6. See Baker and Bouillon, *Josephine*, 263. This study refers to the official English translation of *Josephine*; all translations of Baker's other writings and French and Italian primary sources are mine unless indicated as appearing in a secondary source.

7. Baker's dance style enjoyed critical acclaim only in Europe, but Dunham gained U.S. recognition, with *New York Times* dance critic John Martin declaring that, "With the arrival of Katherine Dunham on the scene, the prospects for the development of a substantial Negro dance art begin to look decidedly bright." Martin, "The Dance: A Negro Art," 114. Jayna Brown identifies Ada Overton Walker as one of the few other early-twentieth-century Black women dancers to achieve critical attention. She reads

her interpretation of *Salome* as a deliberate intervention in white modern dance and as a forerunner to Dunham's work. Brown, *Babylon Girls*, 180–82.

8. While Baker headed the event's French delegation, Dunham was its U.S. representative.

9. Genné, "Glorifying," 45.

10. See, for example, Beckford, *Katherine Dunham*; Rose, *Dunham Technique*; Aschenbrenner, *Katherine Dunham*; *Kaiso!*, a collection of writings by and on Dunham that Clark first published with Margaret B. Wilkerson in 1978 and revised and expanded with Sara E. Johnson in 2005; and Dee Das, *Katherine Dunham*.

11. See, for example, Ramsey, "Melville Herskovits," 196–216; Osumare, "Katherine Dunham," 612–23; Daniel, *Caribbean and Atlantic Diasporic Dance*; Chin, *Katherine Dunham*.

12. Townsend, "Un-Fixing Baker," 67.

13. See Burt, *Alien Bodies*, 49–71; Gottschild, *The Black Dancing Body*; McCarren, *Dancing Machines*, 159–91.

14. As of 2018, an unrestored version of *Die Große Starparade* can be found on YouTube.

15. Taylor with Cook, *Alberta Hunter*, 88.

16. Brown, *Babylon Girls*, 3.

17. Ibid., 204; Knowles, *The Wicked Waltz*, 143; Johnson, *Black Manhattan*, 190.

18. Wayburn, *The Art of Stage Dancing*, 60.

19. Brooks, *Bodies in Dissent*, 5.

20. Brown, *Babylon Girls*, 60.

21. Dunham, "Plan for an Academy," 408–9.

22. Desmond, "Embodying Difference," 50–51. Emphasis added.

23. Sharpley-Whiting, *Black Venus*, 119.

24. For studies of anthropology's relationship to early cinema, see, for example, Rony, *The Third Eye*, and Griffiths, *Wondrous Difference*.

25. Ezra, *The Colonial Unconscious*, 8.

26. Francis, "Embodied Fictions," 831.

27. See Manning, "Modern Dance," 487–503; Kraut, "Between Primitivism and Diaspora," 433–50.

28. As discussed in chapters five and six, only two of Dunham's films—*Stormy Weather* (1943) and *Mambo* (1954)—have received detailed critical analysis.

29. Thomas, "Focal Rites," 535–36.

30. Dreher, *Dancing on the White Page*, 4.

31. Baker and Bouillon, *Josephine*, 50, 58.

32. Beckford, *Katherine Dunham*, 105.

Chapter One. The Dancer in Translation

1. Colin overplayed his role in Baker's success, however. In an interview after her death, he claimed to have "spotted a girl in the chorus who had a beautifully propor-

tioned body" and to have lamented to *La Revue Nègre*'s director André Daven that she was not its star. Colin's recollection reduces Baker to a mindless body that was coaxed to stardom by European Svengalis. In fact, Baker's comic routine had already brought attention in the United States and made her highly conspicuous, even as a chorus dancer. See Baker and Bouillon, *Josephine*, 49. Subsequent references to *Josephine* in this chapter appear in parentheses.

2. *La Sirène des tropiques* was shot and released within weeks of *Les Mémoires de Joséphine Baker*'s publication; *Voyages et aventures de Joséphine Baker* concludes with a reference to the "two great films" that Baker is about to make; and movie extras from *Zouzou* interrupt the star's recollections in *Une vie de toutes les couleurs*, whose illustrations include a still from the movie. See Baker and Sauvage, *Voyages*, 150, and Baker, *Une vie*, 18.

3. Lupton, *Maya Angelou*, 98.

4. Baker's memoirs were published in French and sold only in Europe, which helps partly to explain their general absence from African American literary histories, although Joanne M. Braxton also identifies a wider distrust of the "authenticity" of coauthored texts by Black women performers. The *Oxford Companion to African American Literature* mentions but ultimately dismisses Baker's texts as "at moments autobiographical, but strongly biographical," suggesting that her authorial voice is fleeting. Braxton, "Autobiography and African American Women's Literature," 135; Sharon Carson, "Josephine Baker," 44.

5. Edwards, *The Practice of Diaspora*, 130.

6. Braxton, "Autobiography and African American Women's Literature," 135.

7. James Clifford, "Negrophilia," in *A New History of French Literature*, ed. D. Holier (Cambridge: Harvard University Press, 1989), 901. Cited in Burt, *Alien Bodies*, 71.

8. Critics have frequently compared Baartman and Baker's European receptions. See, for example, Sharpley-Whiting, *Black Venus*, esp. 105–17; Gottschild, *The Black Dancing Body*, esp. 148–65; Henderson, "Josephine Baker," 107–33; Francis, "Embodied Fictions," 824–45; Coly, "Housing," 259–76.

9. Living displays of non-European subjects at French Expositions can be traced as far back as 1867. Jean-Louis Paudrat points to the original aims of the 1878 *Exposition universelle*, the *Musée Africain*, and the *Musée d'ethnographie* to show that the rise of ethnography in late-nineteenth-century France was at least partly conceived as a means of bolstering French territorial desires by providing colonizers with knowledge about, and thus power over, African nations. See Henderson, "Josephine Baker," 109, and Paudrat, "From Africa," 126–28.

10. Clifford makes this observation. See Clifford, *The Predicament of Culture*, 122.

11. Burt, *Alien Bodies*, 71.

12. Ivy, "Sleep Naked," 9.

13. Baker and Chase, *Josephine*, 148.

14. Baker and Sauvage, *Mémoires* (1927), 33.

15. Baker and Chase, *Josephine*, 148. See also Baker and Sauvage, *Mémoires* (1927), 104.

16. Baker, Letter to Coward Mac Cann [*sic*], n.p.

17. Baker and Bouillon, *Josephine*, xii.

18. Smith and Watson, "Introduction," 11, 13–14. See also Fabian, *The Unvarnished Truth*, which examines the narratives of nineteenth-century beggars, convicts, fugitive slaves, and prisoners of war, many of whom were uneducated.

19. Robert Stepto terms emancipatory texts such as Henry Bibb's *Narrative of the Life and Adventures of Henry Bibb, An American Slave* (1849) "eclectic narratives" due to the numerous paratexts contained within them. Stepto, *From behind the Veil*, 6–10.

20. Baker also published *Les Mémoires de Joséphine Baker* in 1949, although this was chiefly a compilation of her previous work with Sauvage. She also inspired an antiracist novel, *Mon sang dans tes veines* (My Blood in Your Veins) (1931), which was a collaboration between her lover-manager Guiseppe "Pepito" Abatino and writer Felix de la Camara, and coauthored a children's book, *La Tribu arc-en-ciel* (The Rainbow Tribe) (1957), with her husband Jo Bouillon and illustrator Piet Worm, which celebrated her multicultural family.

21. See Haney, *Naked at the Feast*; Rose, *Jazz Cleopatra*; Baker and Chase, *Josephine*.

22. Jules-Rosette, *Josephine Baker*, 157. Claudine Raynaud, Tayana L. Hardin, and Zakiya Adair remain the only other scholars to reflect on Baker's authorship. Raynaud explores connections between *Mémoires* and *Princesse Tam-Tam* to unearth the film's biographical references to Baker. Hardin traces Baker's reliance on spectacle back to emancipatory narratives. Adair goes so far as to suggest that Baker's "writings, in connection with her stage performances and public spectacles, transformed twentieth-century performance styles and represented part of what made her a modern and transgressive performer" but does not elaborate on this fascinating claim in her brief study. See Raynaud, "Foil, Fiction"; Hardin, "Josephine Baker and the Shadow of Spectacle"; Adair, "Transgressive (Re)presentations," 81.

23. Humez, *Harriet Tubman*, 140. See also Humez, "Reading 'The Narrative,'" 29–52.

24. Humez, *Harriet Tubman*, 140.

25. Boittin, *Colonial Metropolis*, 15–16.

26. Baker and Sauvage, *Voyages*, 150. Subsequent references to *Voyages* in this chapter appear in parentheses.

27. My use of the term "mulatta" rather than "mulatto" follows the example of Eve Allegra Raimon, who argues that "mulatto" is a "misnomer" because the tragedy of such a character depends on her sexual vulnerability and hence her female gender. See Raimon, *The "Tragic Mulatta" Revisited*, 5.

28. Camara and Abatino, *Mon sang*, 143.

29. Baker, "Préface," 4–5.

30. "Josephine Baker and Black Power," F3.

31. Jules-Rosette, *Josephine Baker*, 4.

32. Baker and Sauvage, *Mémoires* (1927), 98–99.

33. "Vienna Police Guard," 10.

34. Atkinson, "Much Publicity," E51.

35. Haney, *Naked at the Feast*, 145.

36. Baker, *Une vie*, 9–10. Subsequent references to *Une vie* in this chapter appear in parentheses.

37. Jules-Rosette, *Josephine Baker*, 165.

38. See Hine, "Rape," 913.

39. See Carby, "Policing," 752.

40. See Drake and Cayton, *Black Metropolis*, 495–506, esp. 496, 497–99, 501–3.

41. Carby, "Policing," 752.

42. Forsyne made this assertion in an interview with Marshall and Jean Stearns in 1965. See Stearns and Stearns, *Jazz Dance*, 256.

43. See Baker and Bouillon, *Josephine*, 25.

44. Brown, *Babylon Girls*, 21.

45. Sweeney, *From Fetish to Subject*, 41–42.

46. Kraut, "Whose Choreography?" 2.

47. A more precise translation of *Verfremdungseffekt* is "defamiliarizing" or "distancing effect." Brooks, *Bodies in Dissent*, 4.

48. Ibid., 5.

49. Brooks, "The End of the Line," 2. Emphasis added.

50. See Baker and Bouillon, *Josephine*, 6, 10–11, 15.

51. Brown, *Babylon Girls*, 206.

52. Guterl, *Josephine Baker*, 19.

53. See Régnier, "Aux Champs-Elysées," 6, and Baker and Sauvage, *Mémoires* (1927), 16–27.

54. Gottschild, *The Black Dancing Body*, 208–9.

55. Michael Haggerty and Michel Leiris, "Jazz," *Sulfur* 15 (1986), 100. Cited in Jackson, *Making Jazz French*, 113.

56. Thirty-nine Black fatalities were recorded, yet local reports suggested that the real total might have been in the hundreds. Malcolm McLaughlin acknowledges, "The actual death toll is uncertain for the local authorities failed to account officially for many dead African Americans." See McLaughlin, *Power*, 3, 244, n.43, and Lumpkins, *American Pogrom*, 1–2. This limited figure nevertheless implies that it was even more deadly than the Chicago Race Riot of 1919, in which thirty-eight deaths were recorded. See Voogd, *Race Riots and Resistance*, 44.

57. Gates, "An Interview," 597.

58. Baker's sister Margaret admitted in an unpublished 1977 essay, "we never lived [in] East St Louis." Wallace, "The True Life," 4.

59. Dudziak, "Josephine Baker," 547.

60. Contemporary witnesses estimated seeing up to 7,000 people cross each of the Mississippi River's four bridges to escape the violence. See "The Looking Glass," 177.

61. Wallace, "The True Life," 4.

62. Extract from an interview in *National Observer*, 1964. Cited in Hammond and O'Connor, *Josephine Baker*, 209.

63. Cited in Martha Hursey, press release, n.p.

64. Dudziak, "Josephine Baker," 549.

65. “NAACP Praises Baker,” n.p.
66. Dudziak, “Josephine Baker,” 549.
67. Hill, “Katherine Dunham’s *Southland*, 348.
68. Remba, “A Variegated Life,” 6.
69. Dudziak, “Josephine Baker,” 569.
70. Hughes took an active interest in Baker’s humanitarian work. As Rose notes, he “collected every scrap of information he could find about her.” In a letter to the publisher and civil rights activist Dr. Carlton B. Goodlett, Hughes stated that, “I like her very much,” suggested that he was “grateful” to be asked to participate in her film project as such an idea had been discussed on previous occasions but never finalized and declared that he would write to Baker. See Rose, *Jazz Cleopatra*, 244, and Hughes, Letter to Dr. Carlton B. Goodlett, n.p.
71. Josephine Baker, Letter to Langston Hughes, n.p.

Chapter Two. The Dancer as Translator

1. Dunham, *A Touch of Innocence*, 178. Emphasis in the original.
2. Ibid., 177.
3. Ibid., 177–78.
4. Burt, *Alien Bodies*, 157.
5. See Marshall, “Notes on Floyd’s Guitar Blues,” 75.
6. Mazer, “Katherine Dunham,” 425.
7. Ibid.
8. Dunham, *A Touch of Innocence*, 312.
9. Aschenbrenner, *Katherine Dunham*, 156.
10. Lamothe, *Inventing the New Negro*, chapter 6. See, in particular, Knupfer, *The Chicago Black Renaissance*; Bone and Courage, *The Muse in Bronzeville*; Tracy, *Writers*; Hine and McCluskey, eds. *The Black Chicago Renaissance*; and Brian Dolinar, ed., *The Negro in Illinois*.
11. Batiste, *Darkening Mirrors*, 291, n.62.
12. Romero-Cesareo, “Travelers Possessed,” 133.
13. Jackson, “Katherine Dunham,” 242, and Braxton, “Autobiography and African American Women’s Literature,” 143–44.
14. Ramsey, “Vodou,” 358.
15. St. John, *Hayti*, vi.
16. Polyné, *From Douglass to Duvalier*, 155.
17. Ramsey, “Vodou,” 359.
18. “Dances of Haiti: Their Social Organization, Classification, Form, and Function” was submitted to the Department of Anthropology at the University of Chicago in 1937 in partial fulfillment of a master’s degree that Dunham did not immediately complete. It was translated and published in Spanish as *Las danzas de Haití* (1947), and in French as *Les Danses d’Haïti* (1950) before finally being published in English as *Dances of Haiti* in 1983. Dunham published throughout her career shorter ethno-

graphic writings and fictional works relating to Black dance, including two articles for *Esquire* (both 1939) and "The Negro Dance" for Sterling A. Brown's *The Negro Caravan* (1941). She also gave numerous lectures and performance-demonstrations based on her anthropological observations. Many of her published works can be found in Clark and Johnson, *Kaiso!*

19. Courlander, Letter to Katherine Dunham, n.p.

20. Ibid.

21. Ibid.

22. Clifford, "Introduction," 13.

23. Ibid.

24. Dunham, "Form and Function," 502.

25. Aschenbrenner, *Katherine Dunham*, 63.

26. Ibid.

27. *Vodou* is a common current spelling of the term, but it can also be spelled Vodoun, Vodun, Vaudou, Vaudoun, and Vaudun. The Anglicized spelling "Voodoo" is still used, but it is perceived by many to be pejorative given its roots in cultural distortions of the religion.

28. Osumare, "Katherine Dunham," 617.

29. Ibid.

30. Clifford, *The Predicament of Culture*, 24. Emphasis added.

31. Rao and Hutnyk, "Introduction," 2.

32. Köpping, *Shattering Frames*, 216.

33. Redfield, Letter to Katherine Dunham., n.p.

34. See Dunham, *Katherine Dunham's Journey to Accompong*, 1–2. Subsequent references to *Journey to Accompong* in this chapter will appear in parentheses.

35. Lloyd, *The Borzoi Book*, 252.

36. For detailed insights into Hurston's work in these areas, see Kraut's "Between Primitivism and Diaspora," and *Choreographing the Folk.*

37. Hurston's theories on Black dance and Black art in general can be found in her 1934 article "Characteristics of Negro Expression."

38. Murray, *Matter, Magic*, 88.

39. Braxton, *Black Women*, 154.

40. Ibid.

41. Ibid., 144.

42. Osumare, "Katherine Dunham," 615–16.

43. Aschenbrenner, *Katherine Dunham*, 51.

44. Hurston, "Thirty Days among Maroons," 272.

45. Ibid.

46. See Dunham, "Survival," 110.

47. Dunham, "The Anthropological Approach," 509.

48. Mackie, "Welcome The Outlaw," 58.

49. Perpener, *African-American Concert Dance*, 151.

50. Ibid., 151–52.

51. Beckford, *Katherine Dunham*, 35.

52. Dunham, "The Negro Dance," 997.

53. Fischer-Hornung, "'Keep Alive the Powers of Africa,'" 347.

54. Ibid.

55. Dunham, *Island Possessed*, 56. Subsequent references to *Island Possessed* in this chapter will appear in parentheses.

56. Murray, *Matter, Magic*, 89.

57. Ibid., 94.

58. Lamothe, *Inventing the New Negro*, 142.

59. Dunham, Manuscripts: *Island Possessed*, n.p.

60. Ibid.

61. Ibid.

62. LaMothe, *Nietzsche's Dancers*, 2.

63. Dayan, *Haiti, History*, 74. Emphasis in the original.

64. Largey, *Vodou Nation*, 202.

65. See Ramsey, "Katherine Dunham," 51–72.

66. Thompson, "Teaching the People," 343–44.

67. Dee Das, *Katherine Dunham*, 175.

68. Von Eschen, *Satchmo*, 150.

69. For a detailed discussion of this period of Dunham's career, see Dee Das, *Katherine Dunham*, 164–71.

70. Dunham, "The Performing Arts," 473.

71. Johnson, "Introduction," 10.

72. Foulkes, "Ambassadors with Hips," 81–97.

73. Beckford, *Katherine Dunham*, 60–61.

74. Ibid., 62.

75. Nettleford, "The Jamaican Connexion," 601.

76. Dunham, "The Dunham Schools," 479.

77. Nettleford, "The Jamaican Connexion," 599.

78. Ibid.

79. Scott, "'To Be Liberated," 138.

80. Polyné, *From Douglass*, 166.

81. Emery, *Black Dance*, 330.

82. Polyné, *From Douglass*, 171, 177.

83. Dunham, "Early New York Collaborations," 134.

84. Deren, *An Anagram of Ideas*, 20.

85. Dunham, "Plan for an Academy," 408–9.

Chapter Three. Performing within Primitivism

1. Baker and Bouillon, *Josephine*, 72.

2. Baker and Sauvage, *Voyages*, 140.

3. Ibid.

4. Ibid., 140–41.

5. Francis also observes that Baker's performance is at times shot theatrically rather than from the fireman's perspective, which affords her some visual independence from his sexual fantasy. Francis, "She Will Never Look," 113–14.

6. As Erin D. Chapman and Paula Massood observe, pioneering African American filmmaker Oscar Micheaux cast well-known theater performers and used press advertising to promote his actors as stars. Consequently, actress Evelyn Preer, who appeared in nine of his early films beginning with 1919's *The Homesteader*, was probably the first female star of Black independent cinema. The *Pittsburgh Courier* celebrated her as "the Colored Queen of the Cinema" in 1927, the year that *Sirène* was released. However, she was limited to uncredited work in short films when she subsequently transitioned to Hollywood. See Chapman, *Prove It on Me*, 31, and Massood, "African American Stardom," 233–35.

7. See, for example, Bogle, *Toms, Coons*, 33, and Regester, *African American Actresses*, 40.

8. See: Powrie with Rebillard, "Josephine Baker and Pierre Batcheff," 245–64; Powrie with Rebillard, *Pierre Batcheff*, 101–7; Habel, "To Stockholm, with Love," 125–38. Matthew Pratt Guterl also draws on *Sirène* to outline what he refers to as Baker's "colonial pastiche," an "over-the-top assemblage of a diversity of representations, parts, styles, and genres, a technique of performance that is implicitly parodic, if not deeply subversive in unsettling ways." Guterl points up Baker's physical resistance to racial frameworks, yet close analysis of her dance shows that it was not an amalgamation of diverse styles as he claims but instead was rooted in the movement patterns of Black vaudeville. Katherine Groo includes *Sirène* in a study suggesting that it is not the star but her films that construct her body as "indecipherable mixture" and thus "radical critique" of interwar racial frameworks. Groo censures recent recuperative readings of Baker for being lost in an "army of metaphors," but her reading of the dancer as an "ephemeral figure that cannot be pinned down or coherently defined" risks obscuring the albeit fragmentary literary and cinematic record of the art and lived experience of both a key Black presence in early film and, as her memoirs have shown, a rare explicator of the physical and psychological traumas of interwar racist poverty and violence. Guterl, "Josephine Baker's Colonial Pastiche," 26, and Groo, "Shadow Lives," 33, 11.

9. Francis, "The Audacious Josephine Baker," 238–59; Francis, "Embodied Fictions," 824–45; Francis, "She Will Never Look," 113–16.

10. Powrie with Rebillard, *Pierre Batcheff*, and Duckett, *Seeing Sarah Bernhardt*, are the only book-length studies of French silent film performance.

11. "Joséphine Baker dans 'Folie du Jour,'" 32. Her presence onscreen is impossible to verify as the film is lost, but Baker may also have appeared as a chorus girl alongside other *Runnin' Wild* cast members in Oscar Micheaux's *A Son of Satan* (1924).

12. Lareau, "Bitte einsteigen!" 82, n.2.

13. Henderson, "Josephine Baker," 118.

14. See Rony, *The Third Eye*, 199–203, and Griffiths, *Wondrous Difference*, xxix.

15. Ibid., 69.
16. Régnier, "Aux Champs-Elysées," 6; Levinson, "The Negro Dance," 74 (editors' translation).
17. Lemke, *Primitivist Modernism*, 97.
18. Ibid.
19. Stearns and Stearns, *Jazz Dance*, 96.
20. Ibid., 12.
21. *Un vent de folie* program, n.p.
22. Kraut, *Choreographing the Folk*, 76. See also Hurston, "Characteristics of Negro Expression," 24–31.
23. Levinson, "The Negro Dance," 74.
24. Edwards, *The Practice of Diaspora*, 159.
25. Ibid., 162.
26. Berliner, *Ambivalent Desire*, 124.
27. Edwards, *The Practice of Diaspora*, 162.
28. "A Note or Two," 6, and "Josie Baker's Portrait," 5.
29. Stovall, "No Green Pastures," 185.
30. See, for example, Rogers, "J. A. Rogers," 1; "'Jo' Baker offered $10,000 Contract," 9; and "Paris Theatre Crowded," 8.
31. Boittin, *Colonial Metropolis*, 30.
32. Jane Nardal, "Pantins exotiques," *La Dépêche africaine* 8 (October 1928), 2. Cited in Edwards, *The Practice of Diaspora*, 169.
33. Ibid.
34. Jordan, *Le Jazz*, 57.
35. See Blake, *Le Tumulte noir*, 56–57.
36. Ibid., 38.
37. Dayal, "Blackness as Symptom," 45.
38. "A Chorus Girl," 6.
39. Ibid.
40. Ibid.
41. Stearns and Stearns, *Jazz Dance*, 13.
42. Baker and Bouillon, *Josephine*, 27.
43. Jelavich, *Berlin Cabaret*, 186.
44. Brown, *Babylon Girls*, 98; Allen, *Horrible Prettiness*, 174.
45. Baker and Sauvage, *Voyages*, 138.
46. Ibid., 129.
47. Ibid., 141.
48. Ibid., 141–42.
49. Haney, *Naked at the Feast*, 138.
50. See Baker and Chase, *Josephine*, 152.
51. Baker and Sauvage, *Voyages*, 135–36.
52. Baker and Bouillon, *Josephine*, 73.
53. Ibid.

54. Ibid., 72.
55. Fronval, "À Mogador," 14.
56. Ibid.
57. Baker and Bouillon, *Josephine*, 72.
58. Baker and Sauvage, *Voyages*, 143.
59. See Baker and Sauvage, *Mémoires* (1927), 47.
60. Observing the "tragic mulatto/a" characters in Gustave de Beaumont's *Marie* (1835), Werner Sollors makes the case that such a figure could plausibly be traced to France. See Sollors, *Neither Black nor White yet Both*, 241.
61. Berliner, *Ambivalent Desire*, 148–50.
62. Cripps, *Slow Fade to Black*, 211.
63. Ibid.
64. "L'Activité Cinégraphique," 33; Spa, "Figaro Cinema," 4.
65. Jules-Rosette, *Josephine Baker*, 73.
66. See Sampson, *Blacks in Black and White*, 235.
67. Mulvey, "Visual Pleasure," 11.
68. Ibid., 7.
69. Powrie with Rebillard, *Pierre Batcheff*, 158.
70. Ibid., 105.
71. Ibid., 106.
72. Wood, *The Josephine Baker Story*, 99.
73. Jordan, *Le Jazz*, 106. As Marlene Spanger shows, critics in 1928 Copenhagen were equally taken aback by Baker's light complexion and performance style. Spanger, "Disturbance and Celebration," 111–29.
74. Gustave Fréjaville, "Chronique de la semaine," *Comœdia*, October 8, 1925, 2. Cited in Jordan, *Le Jazz*, 107. Emphasis added.
75. Levinson, "The Negro Dance," 73–74.
76. Specifically, Leiris described *Blackbirds* as "more pure and naïve." Michel Leiris, "Civilisation," *Documents 1* (June–September 1929), 221. Cited in Jordan, *Le Jazz*, 133.
77. Jordan, *Le Jazz*, 107. Emphasis added.
78. Ibid., 103. Emphasis added.
79. Kraut, "Whose Choreography?" 4.
80. Fronval, "À Mogador," 14.
81. Ibid.
82. See Wood, *The Josephine Baker Story*, 165.
83. Baker and Sauvage, *Voyages*, 147.
84. Manning and Millman, *Frankie Manning*, 46.
85. African American nightclub owner, Ada "Bricktop" Smith, and Euro-American *Ziegfeld Follies* dancer, Bee Jackson, both performed the Charleston in Europe before Baker's arrival in 1925. Bricktop first executed the dance at the suggestion of Cole Porter while performing at Le Grand Duc, a Montmartre nightclub frequented by leading artists and writers such as Ernest Hemingway, Pablo Picasso, and F. Scott Fitzgerald. She also gave private Charleston lessons to high-society individuals such as

Clark Gable and the Rothschilds. Bee Jackson, whose name is sometimes credited as the source for the Bee's Knees, performed the dance at the Music-Hall des Champs-Elysees in July 1925, three months before Baker's arrival in Paris.

86. Wayburn, *The Art of Stage Dancing*, 60.

87. Dunham, "The Negro Dance," 999.

88. Hurston, "Characteristics of Negro Expression," 29.

89. Stearns and Stearns, *Jazz Dance*, 29.

90. Banes, *Writing Dancing*, 163.

91. "Coming of Mayor Walker," 8.

92. See Cripps, *Slow Fade to Black*, 104–5.

93. "Baker Picture Now Looms," n.p.

94. Fabre, "International Beacons," 129.

95. "Josephine Baker, In 'Siren' Film," 8; "Josephine Baker Here Soon," 12; "Jo Baker's Great Cinema," A3.

96. "Girls Hold Million Dollar Film," A3; "Josephine Baker Here Soon," 12.

97. Ibid.

98. Magill, "Siren of the Tropics," 7, and "Doesn't Like the Baker Picture," 8.

99. "Jo Baker Film," 7.

100. "Josephine Baker, In 'Siren' Film," 8.

101. Ibid.

102. "Doesn't Like the Baker Picture," 8.

103. Magill, "'Siren of the Tropics," 7.

104. Ibid.

105. "Screen Review," A9.

106. Ibid.

107. Ibid. Emphasis added.

108. Rogers, "Josephine Baker," 9.

109. Ibid.

110. Ibid.

111. "Jo Baker Picture," 16, "Baker in 'Siren,'" 15, and "Josephine Baker, In 'Siren' Film," 8.

112. "Coming of Mayor Walker," 8.

113. Ibid.

Chapter Four. Cinematic Stardom

1. Pierre Lazareff, "Joséphine Baker sage est revenue a Paris," *Paris-Midi*, April 20, 1929. Cited in Rose, *Jazz Cleopatra*, 140, 287 (my translation).

2. Bernard, "Les Nouveaux Films," 6.

3. Fatimah Tobing Rony describes Baker in *Zouzou* as a "visible fetish of racism" and a "colonial stereotype," T. Denean Sharpley-Whiting argues that both films "allow certain ideas of the self and the Other to be validated," Elizabeth Ezra reads the productions as symptoms of a "colonial unconscious in twentieth-century France,"

and Eileen Julien sees them as "vehicles for *French* exploration of racial identity and national belonging" (emphasis in original). Conversely, Samir Dayal reads them as self-reflexive colonialist narratives, Scott Balcerzak explores *Zouzou*'s showcasing of Baker as "star," and Claudine Raynaud unearths *Princesse Tam-Tam*'s biographical references to Baker. Rony, *The Third Eye*, 202; Sharpley-Whiting, *Black Venus*, 7; Ezra, *The Colonial Unconscious*, 99; Julien, "Now You See It," 48, emphasis in the original; Dayal, "Blackness as Symptom," 47–48; Balcerzak, "Nationalizing," 27; Raynaud, "Foil, Fiction," 1–10.

4. McCarren, "The Use-Value," 1–5; Bâ and Taylor-Jones, "Affective Passions," 53–66; and Hill, *Black Soundscapes*, 74–96.

5. Although the Nazi invasion of France in June 1940 prevented *Fausse alerte* from being screened widely until 1945, Bennetta Jules-Rosette records that it premiered at Paris's Théâtre Français on May 7, 1940, and Impérial Pathé on May 27, 1940. See Jules-Rosette, *Josephine Baker*, 290.

6. Baker and Sauvage, *Voyages*, 135.

7. See chapter three for Baker's frustration with her early films. Balcerzak asserts that *Zouzou* was devised to counter *Sirène*'s mistakes and establish Baker as a star. Balcerzak, "Nationalizing," 14.

8. Ibid., 16. Half of the films made in France in the early 1930s were independent. Following the collapse in 1935 of France's two major studios, Pathé and Gaumont, this figure actually rose to around 90 percent for the rest of the decade, with the remainder produced by German companies. See Hayward, *French National Cinema*, 46.

9. Anon. (but presumed to be Abatino), Preliminary *Zouzou* screenplay, n.d., 1. Cited in Bergfelder, Harris, and Street, *Film Architecture*, 194. Bergfelder, Harris, and Street note that, "The final page of the outline reiterates that much of the film will be taken up with song and dance rather than plot detail." Ibid., 291, n.46.

10. Driskell, *The French Screen Goddess*, 7.

11. Baker and Bouillon, *Josephine*, 93, and Balcerzak, "Nationalizing," 19.

12. See Dyer, *Stars*, 12.

13. "Cinémas," 5.

14. The state of Ohio banned Black film distributor Sack Amusement from screening *Princesse Tam* in 1941, which Ellen C. Scott attributes to the production's interracial themes. Scott, *Cinema Civil Rights*, 76.

15. Buss, "Josephine Baker," 38.

16. "Nouveaux Films," 4, and Bernard, "Les Nouveaux Films," 6.

17. Balcerzak, "Nationalizing," 19, and Baker and Bouillon, *Josephine*, 94.

18. Stovall, "The New Woman," 5.

19. Jules-Rosette, *Josephine Baker*, 83.

20. Julien, "Now You See It," 51.

21. See Jules-Rosette, *Josephine Baker*, 81, and "Nouveaux Films," 4.

22. Baker, *Mémoires* (1949), 162.

23. Ibid.

24. Ibid., 158.

25. Ibid.
26. Sheridan, *André Gide*, 401.
27. Geiger, "Sightseeing," 120.
28. Ibid.
29. See Balcerzak, "Nationalizing," 19, and Ezra, *The Colonial Unconscious*, 110.
30. Willis and Williams, *The Black Female Body*, 2.
31. Conway, *Chanteuse in the City*, 142, and Julien, "Now You See It," 56.
32. See Shaw, *Seeing the Unspeakable*, 20–22.
33. Ibid., 22–27.
34. Brooks, "The End of the Line," 5.
35. G. L. George, "Joséphine Baker revient a l'écran," *Paris-Jour*, September 27, 1934, n.p. Cited in Jules-Rosette, *Josephine Baker*, 80 (author's translation).
36. Brooks, "The End of the Line," 5.
37. Ezra, *The Colonial Unconscious*, 112. See Berliner, *Ambivalent Desire*, 10.
38. Flanner, *Paris Was Yesterday*, xxix.
39. Thomas, *The French Empire*, 2, and Ezra, *The Colonial Unconscious*, 112–13.
40. Polyné, *From Douglass to Duvalier*, 155.
41. See Jeff and Simmons, *The Dame in the Kimono*, 288.
42. Allen, *Horrible Prettiness*, 245.
43. Barbara Stratyner traces the inspiration for *Follies* dance director Ned Wayburn's precision dancers to the New York appearance of the Original English Pony Ballet, a group trained by the John Tiller School in London. See Stratyner, *Ned Wayburn*, 15.
44. Castle, *The Folies Bergère*, 110, and Baker and Bouillon, *Josephine*, 61.
45. Mizejewski, *Ziegfeld Girl*, 3.
46. Baker and Bouillon, *Josephine*, 61.
47. Genné, "Glorifying," 39.
48. Baker and Bouillon, *Josephine*, 101.
49. Atkinson, "The Play," 17.
50. "The Theatre," n.p.
51. Atkinson, "The Play," 17.
52. Duke, *Passport to Paris*, 311. Cited in Genné, "Glorifying," 54, n.17.
53. Baker and Sauvage, *Mémoires* (1949), 24.
54. Genné, "Glorifying," 54, n.17.
55. Dyer, *Heavenly Bodies*, 78.
56. Horne and Schickel, *Lena*, 105–6.
57. Ibid., 165.
58. Lucius Beebe, *New York Herald Tribune*, 1936, n.p. Cited in Rose, *Jazz Cleopatra*, 170.
59. Rose, *Jazz Cleopatra*, 170.
60. See Frith, *Performing Rites*, 170. Emphasis in the original.
61. Jules-Rosette, *Josephine Baker*, 89.
62. "Les Nouveaux Films—*Zouzou*," 4.
63. Baker and Bouillon, *Josephine*, 93.

64. Lanzoni, *French Cinema*, 74.
65. Kennedy-Karpat, *Rogues, Romance*, 104.
66. Baker and Bouillon, *Josephine*, 100. Emphasis added.
67. Lahs-Gonzales, "Josephine Baker," 40.
68. Raynaud, "Foil, Fiction," 9–10.
69. Baker, *Une vie*, 115.
70. Jules-Rosette also observes a double-pun in "Coton" (with cotton and colon, the French word for colonizer), and notes that Coton describes himself as a "nègre," a French colloquial term for a ghostwriter. See Jules-Rosette, *Josephine Baker*, 93.
71. Raynaud, "Foil, Fiction," 3.
72. Sharpley-Whiting, *Black Venus*, 111.
73. See Stearns and Stearns, *Jazz Dance*, 12–13, 104–5.
74. Marguet, "Le Miroir," 6.
75. "Princesse Tam-Tam," *L'Ouest-Éclair*, 7.
76. Bernard, "Les Nouveaux Films," 6.
77. Kalinak, "Disciplining," 324.
78. "Les Nouveaux Films—'Princesse Tam-Tam.'" 4.
79. Jules-Rosette, *Josephine Baker*, 98.
80. Ibid.; Sharpley-Whiting, *Black Venus*, 113.
81. Dyer, *The Matter of Images*, 164.
82. Ibid., 145.
83. Ibid., 165–67.
84. Raynaud, "Foil, Fiction," 5.
85. See Baker and Bouillon, *Josephine*, 100. Emphasis in the original.
86. Sharpley-Whiting, *Black Venus*, 117.
87. Moore, *Nationalizing Blackness*, 78–79.
88. Cheng, "Josephine Baker," 122.
89. Kalinak, "Disciplining," 331.
90. Baker and Bouillon, *Josephine*, 100–101.
91. "Le Cinéma,'" 4.
92. See Genné, "Glorifying," 46, and Gottschild, *Digging*, 59–79.
93. Root, *Cabin in the Sky*, Act One, n.p.
94. Dunham, "Survival," 121.

Chapter Five. Cinematic Segregation

1. According to New Yorker correspondent Janet Flanner, Baker arrived on Alex's back. See Flanner, *Paris Was Yesterday*, xxix.
2. Pryor, "Stormy Weather," 15.
3. Dee Das, *Katherine Dunham*, 78–79; Lamothe, *Inventing the New Negro*, 138; Cripps, *Making Movies Black*, 95.
4. See Clark, "Performing the Memory," esp. 195; Burt, *Alien Bodies*, 153–58; Vogel, "Performing 'Stormy Weather,'" 93–113; Lamothe, *Inventing the New Negro*, 139–40;

Batiste, *Darkening Mirrors*, 248–54; Chin, "Michael Jackson's Panther Dance," 59–63.

5. As a young child, Dunham saw leading vaudeville artists such as Bessie Smith, Florence Mills, and Ethel Waters. She also witnessed family members' unsuccessful efforts to enter the profession, which she later speculated had a subconscious influence on her choice of performance as a career. See Dunham, *A Touch of Innocence*, 59–60, 53–54.

6. Gomez makes this comment in Clark, Dunham Technique Seminar.

7. Foulkes, *Modern Bodies*, 76.

8. For Dunham's response to her omission from *Cabin in the Sky*, see Fischer-Hornung, "The Body Possessed," 102.

9. The film attributes its direction to writer Stanley Martin, but Dunham recalled that Negulesco oversaw the production.

10. Lloyd, *The Borzoi Book*, 349.

11. Ibid.

12. Dee Das, *Katherine Dunham*, 79.

13. Thomas, "Focal Rites," 535.

14. George Balanchine introduced the term *choreographer* to Broadway in 1936 to boost the dance author's prestige in the United States. See Taper, *Balanchine*, 180.

15. See "First Run Films," 16.

16. See Jackson, *Fade In, Crossroads*, 90.

17. Dunham, "Thesis Turned Broadway," 216.

18. Ibid., 214–16.

19. Lamothe, *Inventing the New Negro*, 138.

20. Mendible, "Introduction," 8.

21. Stovall, Dunham Technique Seminar.

22. For accounts of war-era Hollywood's crude and homogenizing treatment of Latin Americans, see Welky, *The Moguls and the Dictators*, esp. 173–74 and 222–23; Roberts, "The Lady in the Tutti-Frutti Hat," 3–23; Ovalle, *Dance and the Hollywood Latina*, esp. chapters two to three.

23. Dunham, Letter to Martin Sobelman, n.p.

24. Ibid.

25. Ibid.

26. Sobelman, Letter to Katherine Dunham, n.p.

27. For an account of Miranda's adoption of Bahiana fashions and performance cultures, see Stam, *Tropical Multiculturalism*, 84–87.

28. *Katherine Dunham and Ensemble*, n.p.

29. Courlander, *A Treasury of Afro-American Folklore*, 249.

30. Stam, *Tropical Multiculturalism*, 82.

31. See Freire-Medeiros, "Hollywood Musicals," 54.

32. See Ovalle, *Dance and the Hollywood Latina*, 66.

33. Ibid.

34. Stam, *Tropical Multiculturalism*, 84.

35. See Beckford, *Katherine Dunham*, 47. Orson Welles endured similar mistreatment from RKO when he traveled to Brazil in 1942 to film the Samba documentary *It's All True*. RKO's publicist described the film as "black as a storm cloud" and "full of jigiboos," causing the studio to terminate its contract before the production could be completed. See Denning, *The Cultural Front*, 397. See also Stam, *Tropical Multiculturalism*, chapter four.

36. Beckford, *Katherine Dunham*, 47.

37. Dee Das, *Katherine Dunham*, 78.

38. Perpener, *African-American Concert Dance*, 152–53.

39. Dunham, Letter to Sobelman, n.p.

40. Ibid.

41. Sobelman, Letter to Dunham, n.p.

42. Dunham, Letter to Sobelman, n.p.

43. Of the eight Abbott and Costello films produced in quick succession at Universal, *Pardon My Sarong* was the most successful. See Crowther, "Way of All Flashes," X3. A *Time* magazine article listed *Star Spangled Rhythm* as an example of unprecedented cinema attendance in the United States. The article observed that it had just "finished an eight-week run, longest in [New York's] huge Paramount Theater's history." See "Cinema: Boom," n.p.

44. Roper, "Balanchine in Hollywood," 69.

45. Jenkins, "Say It with Firecrackers," 320–321. See Altman, *The American Film Musical*, 238.

46. "Rochester and Katherine Dunham," 11.

47. See Sklaroff, "Constructing G. I. Joe Louis," 969.

48. Koppes and Black, *Hollywood Goes to War*, 79.

49. Griffin, "The Gang's All Here," 43.

50. Cripps, "The Myth," 128, 121.

51. Griffin, "The Gang's All Here," 36.

52. Knight, *Disintegrating the Musical*, 17, 20.

53. See Peiss, *Zoot Suit*, 93.

54. Beckford, *Katherine* Dunham, 47.

55. Nesteby, *Black Images*, 165.

56. Koppes and Black, *Hollywood Goes to War*, 182. Emphasis added.

57. See Hodson, "How She Began Her Beguine," 498, and "Katherine Dunham on Her Influence."

58. Hazzard-Gordon, *Jookin'*, 87.

59. Stearns and Stearns, *Jazz Dance*, 41.

60. Crowther, "Star-Spangled Rhythm," 20; Roper, "Balanchine in Hollywood," 71.

61. Calvin, "Eddie," 2.

62. Although Williams refers specifically to Dunham's appearance on the front of *Crisis* in March 1941, she was also its cover girl in March 1940 and June 1950. See Wil-

liams, "The 'Crisis' Cover Girl," 210. See also the following *Crisis* covers: 47.3 (March 1940); 48.3 (March 1941); and 57.6 (June 1950).

63. "Rochester," B21.
64. "Rochester and Katherine Dunham," 11. Emphasis added.
65. Ibid.
66. See Hill, "Collaborating," 235–47.
67. Roper, "Balanchine in Hollywood," 70.
68. Stoneley, *A Queer History*, 117.
69. Roper, "Balanchine in Hollywood," 69–70.
70. Sklaroff, "Constructing G. I. Joe Louis," 969.
71. Griffin, "The Gang's All Here," 38. Emphasis added.
72. Long, *The Black Tradition*, 47.
73. Dunham, *A Touch of Innocence*, 41–42.
74. Interview with Halifu Osumare in *Free to Dance.*
75. Schuyler, "Views and Reviews," 13.
76. Kelley, *Race Rebels*, 169.
77. Peiss, *Zoot Suit*, 94.
78. Vogel, "Performing 'Stormy Weather,'" 102.
79. Ibid., 109.
80. Burt, *Alien Bodies*, 154.
81. Ibid., 155.
82. Martin, "The Dance," 114.
83. Vogel, "Performing 'Stormy Weather,'" 108.
84. Aschenbrenner, *Katherine Dunham*, 1.
85. Hill, "Collaborating," 242–43.
86. Manning, "Modern Dance," 499.
87. Burt, *Alien Bodies*, 155.
88. Horne and Schickel, *Lena*, 172.
89. Ibid.
90. Sklaroff, *Black Culture*, 220.
91. Brown, "What I Am Fighting For," 14.
92. Thompson, "What the People Say," 12.
93. Clark, Dunham Technique Seminar.
94. Batiste, *Darkening Mirrors*, 251–52.
95. Thompson, "Teaching the People," 338.

Chapter Six. Navigating Primitivism's Persistent Gaze

1. Fischer-Hornung, "Jungle in the Spotlight?" 53.
2. Ibid., 53. Fischer-Hornung records that Dunham's presence in London "even influenced hat styles, the spring collection including the 'Dunham line' and 'Caribbean Rhapsody,' featuring vivid colors, large bows, and flowers." Burt reports that, "A

clipping from a [Parisian] newspaper fashion column notes the Dunham company's influence on the new season's hats—particularly checked cotton sun hats with wide straw brims, and the use of knotted kerchiefs." Burt, "Katherine Dunham's Floating Island," 99.

3. Beckford, *Katherine Dunham*, 106.

4. See Baker and Bouillon, *Josephine*, 147–48.

5. Baker, *Mémoires* (1949), 289. Plans for this ultimately unrealized musical show were announced in January 1951. Jose Ferrer and Richard Condon conceived the production and Ernest Hemingway was reported to be involved in the outline. Hammond and O'Connor, *Josephine Baker*, 163.

6. Baker, *Mémoires* (1949), 290.

7. Ibid.

8. Noble, *The Negro in Films*, 94.

9. Ibid.

10. Ibid.

11. Sherzer, "Race Matters," 232.

12. Lloyd, *The Borzoi Book*, 253.

13. During her initiation into Vodou in *Island Possessed*, Dunham described seeing the hounci, whose function it is to serve the loa, "whirling like dervishes." See Dunham, *Island Possessed*, 132.

14. Kitt, *Thursday's Child*, 115.

15. Scheuer, "Casbah," 23.

16. Dunham choreographed *Green Mansions* to pay the money she owed in back taxes. See Harnan, *African Rhythm*, 178.

17. Taylor, "New U.S. Black Cinema."

18. Noble, *The Negro in Films*, 94–97.

19. Ibid., 97.

20. Katherine Dunham, 1978 conversation with Joyce Aschenbrenner. Cited in Aschenbrenner, *Katherine Dunham*, 141.

21. Dunham, Dunham Technique Seminar.

22. Clark, "An Anthropological Band," 371.

23. Ibid.

24. See Dunham, "Address Delivered," 416.

25. Burt calls attention to the close temporal proximity between Dunham and the *Windrush*'s arrivals. See Burt, "Katherine Dunham's Floating Island," 99.

26. See Clark, "An Anthropological Band," 371.

27. Burt, "Katherine Dunham's Floating Island," 95, 98.

28. "La Revue Nègre," 4.

29. "Civilisation?" n.p.

30. "Jungle Artistry," n.p.

31. Lloyd, "Miss Dunham's Witchery," 11.

32. A. N., "Una mulatta," 3.

33. "Ibid., 3.

34. Interestingly, although Dunham was never granted a leading role in one of his films, she worked with De Laurentiis on three occasions: on *Botta e risposta* and *Mambo*, which are examined in this chapter, and *The Bible . . . In The Beginning*, for which she created two dance sequences.

35. Kezich and Levantesi, *Dino*, 70.

36. Ibid.

37. Ibid.

38. Ibid., 71.

39. See *La Stampa*, March 7–8, 1950, 2; *La Stampa*, March 11, 1950, 2; and the cover of *Time*, February 21, 1949.

40. The Vatican undercut *Botta e risposta*'s commercial success by excluding it from state-sponsored subsidies and awards because it took offense at a comic scene recorded in front of a poster announcing the Vatican's declaration of the Jubilee Year. Nevertheless, the film was commercially successful: one month after its Italian release, a comic story in the magazine *Spettacolo* imagined de Laurentiis in despair because he could not produce a failure. See Kezich and Levantesi, *Dino*, 73–74.

41. Jeancolas, "The Inexportable," 141.

42. Ibid., 141–42.

43. Ibid., 142.

44. Ibid., 141.

45. "Frank Capra," 4.

46. Ibid.

47. Jordan, *Le Jazz*, 233, 240.

48. Ibid., 234.

49. Williams, *Torchbearers*, 326.

50. For Armstrong's approach to performance, see DeVeaux, The Birth of Bebop, 74–75.

51. Knight, "Jammin'," 39. Emphasis added.

52. All of the brothers' studio-era Hollywood appearances were as specialties, and white women featured in just two of their musical sequences: "Mandy" from in *Kid Millions* (1934), and "Sheik of Araby" from *Tin Pan Alley* (1940). Harold also performed alone in front of white actress Gloria Jean in *Reckless Age* (1944).

53. Hill, *Brotherhood in Rhythm*, 107–8.

54. Hill, "Collaborating," 243.

55. Foulkes, *Modern Bodies*, 145.

56. Lamothe, *Inventing the New Negro*, 138.

57. Von Eschen, *Satchmo*, 4.

58. Dunham, "The Performing Arts," 473.

59. See Croft, *Dancers as Diplomats*, 114.

60. Von Eschen, *Satchmo*, 22.

61. Dunham, "The Performing Arts," 473.

62. Dee Das, *Katherine Dunham*, 124.
63. Von Eschen, *Satchmo*, 150.
64. See Davenport, "Jazz and the Cold War," 290–91.
65. Dunham, "Plan for an Academy," 408–10.
66. Ibid., 408.
67. See Fischer-Hornung, "The Body Possessed," 104, and Fischer-Hornung, "Giving Voice," 105–6.
68. Fischer-Hornung writes that, "Some of the music and many of the lyrics were provided by Katherine Dunham, and there is correspondence to indicate that she had difficulties in registering her copyright with the Italian musicians' union. This became particularly important after she learned that two of the songs, for example, the blues Mangano sings in the last third of the film, had been recorded for record production." Fischer-Hornung, "The Body Possessed," 108. Dunham ultimately did manage to register copyright of three of the film's songs. See *Catalog of Copyright Entries*, 11, 30, 156, 299.
69. Thomas, "Focal Rites,".
70. Casty, *Robert Rossen*, 181.
71. Fischer-Hornung, "The Body Possessed," 110. Casty is the only other scholar I have found who has examined the film, although he does not explore its dance elements or racial politics. See Casty, *Robert Rossen*, 175–81.
72. Fischer-Hornung, "The Body Possessed," 91.
73. Gennari, *Post-War Italian Cinema*, 146.
74. Hill, "Focus," X5.
75. See, for example, the negative reviews of *Mambo* in the British *Monthly Film Bulletin* (January 1955, 70–71); Italian newspapers *Il Contemporaneo* (December 15, 1954), *Epoca* (December 19, 1954), and *L'Europeo* (November 29, 1954), which are all extracted in Gambetti, *Vittorio Gassman*, 110–11; and U.S. publications *New York Times* (March 31, 1955, 23), *Newsweek* (April 18, 1955, 3), and *Time* (April 25, 1955).
76. Moreno Vega, "The Dynamic Influence," 328, 332, 333.
77. Dunham, "Ag'Ya Fight."
78. Contemplating a return to Mario in a voice-over later in the film, Giovanna concludes, "Mario had struck me, and I hadn't forgotten."
79. "Cinema: The New Pictures," n.p.
80. Fischer-Hornung, "Transbodied/Transcultured," 202–3.
81. Gennari, *Post-War Italian Cinema*, 124.
82. Gennari, "Passing for Italian," 40. Giovanna is Venetian, but Mangano was born in Rome, the border between northern and southern Italy, albeit to an English mother. More significantly, Stephen Gundle has noted that Mangano and fellow Italian stars Gina Lollobrigida and particularly Sophia Loren "were seen abroad as fiery and highly sexed," an image that was "not widely appreciated in Italy because it was an unwelcome reminder of past representations of Italian primitiveness." Gundle, "Miss Italia in Black and White," 262.

83. Gennari, "Passing for Italian," 40.

84. Roediger, *The Wages of Whiteness*, 133–37.

85. Fischer-Hornung, "Transbodied/Transcultured," 200.

86. Ibid., 202.

87. Crowther, "The Screen," 23.

88. Filippo Sacchi, *Epoca*, December 19, 1954. Cited in Gambetti, *Vittorio Gassmann*, 110; Baker and Sauvage, *Voyages*, 36.

Conclusion

1. Baker and Bouillon, *Josephine*, 230.

2. Dunham, "The World in Dance and Ritual," 530.

3. Ibid.

4. Francis, "Embodied Fictions," 829.

Selected Bibliography

Adair, Zakiya R. "Transgressive (Re)presentations: Black Women, Vaudeville, and the Politics of Performance in Early Transatlantic Theater." In *Understanding Blackness through Performance: Contemporary Arts and the Representation of Identity*, eds. Anne Crémieux, Xavier Lemoine, and Jean-Paul Rocchi. 75–90. Basingstoke, U.K.: Palgrave Macmillan, 2013.

Allen, Robert C. *Horrible Prettiness: Burlesque and American Culture.* Chapel Hill: University of North Carolina, 1991.

Altman, Rick. *The American Film Musical.* Bloomington: Indiana University Press, 1987.

A. N. "Una mulatta americana piu brava di Joséphine Baker." *La Stampa*, February 22, 1949, 3.

Aschenbrenner, Joyce. *Katherine Dunham: Dancing a Life.* Urbana: University of Illinois Press, 2002.

Atkinson, Brooks. "The Play; Fannie Brice in the 1936 Edition of the 'Follies' under Shubert Management." *New York Times*, January 31, 1936, 17.

Atkinson, Navarre. "Much Publicity for Josephine Baker." *New York Times*, March 4, 1928, E51.

Bâ, Saër Maty, and Kate E. Taylor-Jones. "Affective Passions: The Dancing Female Body and Colonial Rupture in *Zouzou* (1934) and *Karmen Geï* (2001)." In *De-Westernizing Film Studies*, eds. Saër Maty Bâ and Will Higbee. 53–66. Abingdon, U.K.: Routledge, 2012.

Baker, Jean-Claude, and Chris Chase. *Josephine: The Hungry Heart.* 1993; rpt. New York: Cooper Square Press, 2001.

Baker, Josephine. *Les Mémoires de Joséphine Baker*, recueillis et adaptés par Marcel Sauvage, avec 30 dessins inédits de Paul Colin. Original edition. Paris: Kra, 1927.

———. *Les Mémoires de Joséphine Baker*, recueillis par Marcel Sauvage, avec 29 dessins de Paul Colin. 1949; Paris: Éditions Dilecta, 2006.

———. Letter to Coward Mac Cann [*sic*] Inc., August 3, 1959, n.p. Box 1, folder 8. Josephine Baker Papers, Manuscript, Archives, and Rare Book Library, Emory University, Atlanta, Ga.

———. Letter to Langston Hughes, December 2, 1958, n.p. Box 1, folder 5. Josephine Baker Papers, Manuscript, Archives, and Rare Book Library, Emory University, Atlanta, Ga.

———. "Préface." In Felix de la Camara, and P. Abatino, *Mon sang dans tes veines: Roman d'après une idée de Joséphine Baker*. 3–6. Paris: Editions Isis, 1931.

———. *Une vie de toutes les couleurs*, souvenirs recueillis par André Rivollet. Grenoble: B. Arthaud, 1935.

Baker, Josephine, and Jo Bouillon. *Josephine*, trans. Mariana Fitzpatrick. London: W. H. Allen, 1978. (Originally published as *Joséphine* [Paris: Robert Laffont-Opéra Mundi, 1976]).

Baker, Josephine, and Marcel Sauvage. *Voyages et aventures de Joséphine Baker*. Paris: Marcel Seheur, 1931.

"Baker in 'Siren of the Tropics' at Elmore Next Week." *Pittsburgh Courier*, November 9, 1929, 15.

"Baker Picture Now Looms: Feverish Effort Now on after 'Hallelujah' Success at Lafayette." *New York Amsterdam News*, September 4, 1929.

Balcerzak, Scott. "'Nationalizing and Segregating Performance': Josephine Baker and Stardom in *Zouzou* (1934)." *Post Script: Essays in Film and the Humanities* 26.1 (2006): 13–31.

Banes, Sally. *Writing Dancing in the Age of Postmodernism*. Middletown, Conn.: Wesleyan University Press, 1994.

Batiste, Stephanie Leigh. *Darkening Mirrors: Imperial Representation in Depression-Era African American Performance*. Durham: Duke University Press, 2011.

Beckford, Ruth. *Katherine Dunham: A Biography*. New York: Marcel Dekker, 1979.

Bergfelder, Tim, Sue Harris, and Sarah Street. *Film Architecture and the Transnational Imagination: Set Design in 1930s European Cinema*. Amsterdam: Amsterdam University Press, 2007.

Berliner, Brett A. *Ambivalent Desire: The Exotic Black Other in Jazz-age France*. Amherst: University of Massachusetts Press, 2002.

Bernard, Gilbert. "Les Nouveaux Films—'Princesse Tam-Tam.'" *Le Matin*, October 21, 1935, 6.

Blake, Jody. *Le Tumulte noir: Modernist Art and Popular Entertainment in Jazz-Age Paris, 1900–1930*. University Park: Pennsylvania State University Press, 1999.

Bogle, Donald. *Toms, Coons, Mulattoes, Mammies, and Bucks: An Interpretation of Blacks in American Films*, 4th ed. New York: Continuum, 2001.

Boittin, Jennifer Anne. *Colonial Metropolis: The Urban Grounds of Anti-Imperialism and Feminism in Interwar Paris*. Lincoln: University of Nebraska Press, 2010.

Bone, Robert, and Richard A. Courage. *The Muse in Bronzeville: African American Creative Expression in Chicago, 1932–1950*. New Brunswick, N.J.: Rutgers University Press, 2011.

Braxton, Joanne M. "Autobiography and African American Women's Literature." In *The Cambridge Companion to African American Women's Literature*, eds. Angelyn Mitchell and Danille K. Taylor. 128–49. Cambridge: University of Cambridge Press, 2009.

———. *Black Women Writing Autobiography: A Tradition within a Tradition*. Philadelphia: Temple University Press, 1989.

Brooks, Daphne A. *Bodies in Dissent: Spectacular Performances of Race and Freedom, 1850–1910*. Durham: Duke University Press, 2006.

———. "The End of the Line: Josephine Baker and the Politics of Black Women's Corporeal Comedy." *Josephine Baker: A Century in the Spotlight*. Spec. issue of *The Scholar and Feminist Online* 6.1–6.2 (Fall 2007/Spring 2008): 1–6. http://sfonline.barnard.edu/baker/brooks_01.htm. Accessed November 30, 2018.

Brown, Jayna. *Babylon Girls: Black Women Performers and the Shaping of the Modern*. Durham: Duke University Press, 2008.

Brown, Sgt. Elijah. "What I Am Fighting For." *Chicago Defender*, August 21, 1943, 14.

Burt, Ramsay. *Alien Bodies: Representations of Modernity, "Race" and Nation in Early Modern Dance*. London: Routledge, 1998.

———. "Katherine Dunham's Floating Island of Negritude: The Katherine Dunham Dance Company in London and Paris in the Late 1940s and Early 1950s." In *Rethinking Dance History: A Reader*, ed. Alexandra Carter. 94–106. London: Routledge, 2004.

Buss, Robin. "Josephine Baker: An American in Paris." *Sight and Sound* 17.3 (March 2007): 36–38.

Calvin, Dolores. "Eddie, Katy Star in New Picture." *Atlanta Daily World*, January 18, 1943, 2.

Camara, de la, Felix, and P. Abatino. *Mon sang dans tes veines: roman d'après une idée de Joséphine Baker*. Paris: Editions Isis, 1931.

Carby, Hazel V. "Policing the Black Woman's Body in an Urban Context." *Identities*. Spec. issue of *Critical Inquiry* 18.4 (Summer 1992): 738–55.

Carson, Sharon. "Josephine Baker." In *The Oxford Companion to African American Literature*, eds. William L. Andrews, Frances Smith Foster, and Trudier Harris. 44. Oxford: Oxford University Press, 1997.

Castle, Charles. *The Folies Bergère*. London: Methuen, 1982.

Casty, Alan. *Robert Rossen: The Films and Politics of a Blacklisted Idealist*. Jefferson, N.C.: McFarland, 2013.

Catalog of Copyright Entries, Third Series. Vol. 8, Part 5B, No. 1 (Jan–Jun 1954) (Washington, D.C.: Copyright Office, The Library of Congress, 1954).

Chapman, Erin D. *Prove It on Me: New Negroes, Sex, and Popular Culture in the 1920s.* Oxford: Oxford University Press, 2012.

Cheng, Anne Anlin. "Josephine Baker: Psychoanalysis and the Colonial Fetish." *Psychoanalytic Quarterly* 75.1 (2006): 95–129.

Chin, Elizabeth, ed. *Katherine Dunham: Recovering an Anthropological Legacy, Choreographing Ethnographic Futures.* Santa Fe: School for Advanced Research Press, 2014.

———. "Michael Jackson's Panther Dance: Double Consciousness and the Uncanny Business of Performing while Black." *Journal of Popular Music Studies* 23.1 (2011): 58–74.

"A Chorus Girl Who Really Stood Out and Won Acclaim." *New York Amsterdam News*, May 13, 1925, 6.

"Cinema: Boom." *Time*, March 15, 1943, n.p.

"Cinema: The New Pictures." *Time*, April 25, 1955, n.p.

"Cinémas." *Le Matin*, September 21, 1935, 5.

"Civilisation? The Professor Takes It Away." *News of the World*, June 6, 1948, n.p.

Clark, VèVè A. "An Anthropological Band of Beings: An Interview with Julie Robinson Belafonte" (1983). In *Kaiso! Writings by and about Katherine Dunham*, eds. VèVè A. Clark and Sara E. Johnson. 364–81. Madison: University of Wisconsin Press, 2005.

———. Dunham Technique Seminar. East St. Louis. August 8, 1995. Video recording. Katherine Dunham Collection, Moving Image Section, Motion Picture, Broadcasting and Recorded Sound Division, Library of Congress, Washington, D.C.

———. "Performing the Memory of Difference in Afro-Caribbean Dance: Katherine Dunham's Choreography, 1938–87." In *History and Memory in African-American Culture*, eds. Geneviève Fabre, Robert O'Meally. 188–204. New York: Oxford University Press, 1994.

Clark, VèVè A., and Margaret B. Wilkerson, eds. *Kaiso! Katherine Dunham: An Anthology of Writings.* Berkeley: Institute for the Study of Social Change, University of California, 1978.

Clark, VèVè A., and Sara E. Johnson, eds. *Kaiso! Writings by and about Katherine Dunham.* Madison: University of Wisconsin Press, 2005.

Clifford, James. "Introduction: Partial Truths." In *Writing Culture: The Poetics and Politics of Ethnography*, eds. James Clifford and George E. Marcus. 1–26. Berkeley: University of California Press, 1986.

———. *The Predicament of Culture: Twentieth-Century Ethnography, Literature, and Art.* Cambridge: Harvard University Press, 1988.

Coly, Ayo Abiétou. "Housing and Homing the Black Female Body in France: Calixthe Beyala and the Legacy of Sarah Baartman and Josephine Baker." In *Black Womanhood: Images, Icons, and Ideologies of the African Body*, ed. Barbara Thompson. 259–76. Hanover, N.H.: Hood Museum of Art, Dartmouth College in Association with the University of Washington Press, 2008.

"Coming of Mayor Walker to Lafayette Last Sunday Night Furnished a Big Thrill." *New York Amsterdam News*, September 25, 1929, 8.

Conway, Kelley. *Chanteuse in the City: The Realist Singer in French Film*. Berkeley: University of California Press, 2004.

Courlander, Harold. Letter to Katherine Dunham. ca. 1943. Box 3, folder 5. Katherine Mary Dunham Papers, 1919–1968. Morris Library Special Collections Research Center, Southern Illinois University, Carbondale, Ill.

———. *A Treasury of Afro-American Folklore: The Oral Literature, Traditions, Recollections, Legends, Tales, Songs, Religious Beliefs, Customs, Sayings, and Humor of Peoples of African Descent in the Americas*. New York: Crown Publishers, 1976.

Cover image. *The Crisis* 47.3 (March 1940).

———. *The Crisis* 48.3 (March 1941).

———. *The Crisis* 57.6 (June 1950).

———. *Time* (February 21, 1949).

Cripps, Thomas. *Making Movies Black: The Hollywood Message Movie from World War II to the Civil Rights Era*. New York: Oxford University Press, 1993.

———. "The Myth of the Southern Box Office: A Factor in Racial Stereotyping in American Movies, 1920–1940." In *The Black Experience in America: Selected Essays*, eds. James C. Curtis and Lewis L. Gould. 116–44. Austin: University of Texas Press, 1970.

———. *Slow Fade to Black: The Negro in American Film, 1900–1942*. New York: Oxford University Press, 1977.

Croft, Clare. *Dancers as Diplomats: American Choreography in Cultural Exchange*. Oxford: Oxford University Press, 2015.

Crowther, Bosley. "The Screen: 'Mambo' Out of Step," *New York Times*, March 31, 1955, 23.

———. "'Star-Spangled Rhythm,' Bulky All-Star Variety Show, Makes Its Premiere Appearance at the Paramount Theatre." *New York Times*, December 31, 1942, 20.

———. "Way of All Flashes: A Word to Abbott and Costello Which Should, but May Not, Be Sufficient," *New York Times*, December 6, 1942, X3.

Daniel, Yvonne. *Caribbean and Atlantic Diasporic Dance: Igniting Citizenship*. Urbana: University of Illinois Press, 2011.

Davenport, Lisa E. "Jazz and the Cold War: Black Culture as an Instrument of American Foreign Policy." In *Crossing Boundaries: Comparative History of Black People in Diaspora*, eds. Darlene Clark Hine and Jacqueline McLeod. 282–315. Bloomington: Indiana University Press, 1999.

Dayal, Samir. "Blackness as Symptom: Josephine Baker and European Identity." In *Blackening Europe: The African American Presence*, ed. Heike Raphael-Hernandez. 35–52. New York: Routledge, 2004.

Dayan, Colin (as Joan Dayan). *Haiti, History, and the Gods*. Berkeley: University of California Press, 1995.

Dee Das, Joanna. *Katherine Dunham: Dance and the African Diaspora*. New York: Oxford University Press, 2017.

Denning, Michael. *The Cultural Front: The Laboring of American Culture in the Twentieth Century*. London: Verso, 1997.

Deren, Maya. *An Anagram of Ideas on Art, Form and Film*. Yonkers, N.Y.: Alicat Book Shop Press, 1946.

Desmond, Jane C. "Embodying Difference: Issues in Dance and Cultural Studies." In *Meaning in Motion: New Cultural Studies of Dance*, ed. Jane C. Desmond. 29–54. Durham: Duke University Press, 1997.

DeVeaux, Scott Knowles. *The Birth of Bebop: A Social and Musical History.* Berkeley: University of California Press, 1997.

"Doesn't Like the Baker Picture." *New York Amsterdam News*, November 20, 1929, 8.

Dolinar, Brian, ed. *The Negro in Illinois: The WPA Papers*. Urbana: University of Illinois Press, 2013.

Drake, St. Clair, and Horace R. Cayton. *Black Metropolis: A Study of Negro Life in a Northern City*, Rev. and enl. ed. Chicago: University of Chicago Press, 1993.

Dreher, Kwakiutl L. *Dancing on the White Page: Black Women Entertainers Writing Autobiography.* New York: State University of New York Press, 2008.

Driskell, Jonathan. *The French Screen Goddess: Film Stardom and the Modern Woman in 1930s France*. London: I. B. Tauris, 2015.

Duckett, Victoria. *Seeing Sarah Bernhardt: Performance and Silent Film*. Urbana: University of Illinois Press, 2015.

Dudziak, Mary L. "Josephine Baker, Racial Protest, and the Cold War." *Journal of American History* 81.2 (September 1994): 543–70.

Dunham, Katherine. "Address Delivered at the Dakar Festival of Negro Arts" (1966). In *Kaiso! Writings by and about Katherine Dunham*, eds. VèVè A. Clark and Sara E. Johnson. 412–17. Madison: University of Wisconsin Press, 2005.

———. "Ag'Ya Fight from 'L'Ag'Ya'" (1947). Video recording. Katherine Dunham Collection, Moving Image Section, Motion Picture, Broadcasting and Recorded Sound Division, Library of Congress, Washington, D.C.

———. "The Anthropological Approach to the Dance" (October 1942). In *Kaiso! Writings by and about Katherine Dunham*, eds. VèVè A. Clark and Sara E. Johnson. 508–13. Madison: University of Wisconsin Press, 2005.

———. "The Dunham Schools" (1964). In *Kaiso! Writings by and about Katherine Dunham*, eds. VèVè A. Clark and Sara E. Johnson. 479–80. Madison: University of Wisconsin Press, 2005.

———. Dunham Technique Seminar. East St. Louis. August 9, 1995. Video recording. Katherine Dunham Collection, Moving Image Section, Motion Picture, Broadcasting and Recorded Sound Division, Library of Congress, Washington, D.C

———. "Early New York Collaborations: Excerpt from 'Minefields,' Book II." In *Kaiso! Writings by and about Katherine Dunham*, eds. VèVè A. Clark and Sara E. Johnson. 125–49. Madison: University of Wisconsin Press, 2005.

———. "Form and Function in Primitive Dance" (October 1941). In *Kaiso! Writings by and about Katherine Dunham*, eds. VèVè A. Clark and Sara E. Johnson. 502–7. Madison: University of Wisconsin Press, 2005.

———. *Island Possessed.* 1969; rpt. Chicago: University of Chicago Press, 1994.

———. *Katherine Dunham's Journey to Accompong*. 1946; rpt. Westport, Conn.: Negro Universities Press, 1971.

———. Letter to Martin Sobelman, May 17, 1941, n.p. Box 2, folder 3. Katherine Mary Dunham Papers, 1919–1968. Morris Library Special Collections Research Center, Southern Illinois University, Carbondale, IL.

———. Manuscripts: *Island Possessed*—Original Notes, n.p. Box 51, folder 1. Katherine Mary Dunham Papers, 1919–1968. Morris Library Special Collections Research Center, Southern Illinois University, Carbondale, Ill.

———. "The Negro Dance." In *The Negro Caravan: Writings by American Negroes*, ed. Sterling Allen Brown. 991–1000. New York: Citadel Press, 1941.

———. "The Performing Arts of Africa." In *Colloquium: Function and Significance of African Negro Art in the Life of the People and for the People*. Dakar: 1st World Festival of Negro Arts, 1966. 473–80.

———. "Plan for an Academy of West African Cultural Arts" (1965). In *Kaiso! Writings by and about Katherine Dunham*, eds. VèVè A. Clark and Sara E. Johnson. 407–11. Madison: University of Wisconsin Press, 2005.

———. "Survival: Excerpt from 'Minefields,' Book I." In *Kaiso! Writings by and about Katherine Dunham*, eds. VèVè A. Clark and Sara E. Johnson. 85–124. Madison: University of Wisconsin Press, 2005.

———. "Thesis Turned Broadway" (August 1941). In *Kaiso! Writings by and about Katherine Dunham*, eds. VèVè A. Clark and Sara E. Johnson. 214–16. Madison: University of Wisconsin Press, 2005.

———. A Touch of Innocence. London: Cassell, 1959.

———. "The World in Dance and Ritual: World Dance Film Project" (January 1964). In *Kaiso! Writings by and about Katherine Dunham*, eds. VèVè A. Clark and Sara E. Johnson. 529–30. Madison: University of Wisconsin Press, 2005.

Dyer, Richard. *Heavenly Bodies: Film Stars and Society*. Basingstoke, U.K.: Macmillan, 1986.

———. *The Matter of Images: Essays on Representation*, 2nd ed. London: Routledge, 2002.

———. *Stars*, New Ed. With a Supplementary Chapter and Bibliography by Paul McDonald. London: British Film Institute, 1998.

Edwards, Brent Hayes. *The Practice of Diaspora: Literature, Translation, and the Rise of Black Internationalism*. Cambridge: Harvard University Press, 2003.

Emery, Lynne Fauley. *Black Dance from 1619 to Today*. 1972; rpt. Hightstown, N.J.: Dance Horizon Books, 1988.

Ezra, Elizabeth. *The Colonial Unconscious: Race and Culture in Interwar France*. Ithaca, N.Y.: Cornell University Press, 2000.

Fabian, Ann. *The Unvarnished Truth: Personal Narratives in Nineteenth-Century America*. Berkeley: University of California Press, 2000.

Fabre, Michel. "International Beacons of African American Memory: Alexandre Dumas père, Henry O. Tanner, and Josephine Baker as Examples of Recognition."

In *History and Memory in African-American Culture*, ed. Geneviève Fabre. 122–29. New York: Oxford University Press, 1994.

"First Run Films—'Sodom, Gomorrah' at the Regent." *Baltimore Afro-American*, February 9, 1963, 16.

Fischer-Hornung, Dorothea, "The Body Possessed: Katherine Dunham Dance Technique in *Mambo*" In *EmBODYing Liberation: The Black Body in American Dance*, eds. Dorothea Fischer-Hornung and Alison D. Goeller. 91–111. Münster: LIT VERLAG, 2001.

———. "Giving Voice and Vent to African American Culture: Katherine Dunham's Struggle for Cultural Ownership in *Mambo* (1954)." In *August Wilson and Black Aesthetics*, eds. Dana A. Williams and Sandra G. Shannon. 97–114. New York: Palgrave Macmillan, 2004.

———. "'Jungle in the Spotlight?' Primitivism and Esteem: Katherine Dunham's 1954 German Tour." In *Blackening Europe: The African American Presence*, ed. Heike Raphael-Hernandez. 53–72. New York: Routledge, 2004.

———. "'Keep Alive the Powers of Africa': Katherine Dunham, Zora Neale Hurston, Maya Deren, and the Circum-Caribbean Culture of Vodoun." *Atlantic Studies* 5.3 (December 2008): 347–62.

———. "Transbodied/Transcultured: Moving Spirits in Katherine Dunham's and Maya Deren's Caribbean." In *Recharting the Black Atlantic: Modern Cultures, Local Communities, Global Connections*, eds. Annalisa Oboe and Anna Scacchi. 197–211. New York: Routledge, 2008.

Flanner, Janet. *Paris Was Yesterday, 1925–1939*. 1972; rpt. London: Virago, 2003.

Foulkes, Julia L. "Ambassadors with Hips: Katherine Dunham, Pearl Primus, and the Allure of Africa in the Black Arts Movement." In *Impossible to Hold: Women and Culture in the 1960s*, eds. Avital H. Bloch and Lauri Umansky. 81–97. New York: New York University Press, 2005.

———. *Modern Bodies: Dance and American Modernism from Martha Graham to Alvin Ailey*. Chapel Hill: University of North Carolina Press, 2002.

Francis, Terri. "The Audacious Josephine Baker: Stardom, Cinema, and Paris." In *Black Europe and the African Diaspora*, eds. Darlene Clark Hine, Trica Danielle Keaton, and Stephen Small. 238–59. Urbana: University of Illinois Press, 2009.

———. "Embodied Fictions, Melancholy Migrations: Josephine Baker's Cinematic Celebrity." *Modern Fiction Studies* 51.4 (2005): 824–45.

———. "'She Will Never Look': Film Spectatorship, Black Feminism, and Scary Subjectivities." In *Reclaiming the Archive: Feminism and Film History*, ed. Vicki Callahan. 98–126. Detroit: Wayne State University Press, 2010.

"Frank Capra il ribelle domato." *La Stampa*, February 26, 1950, 4.

Free to Dance, Part II: The Steps of the Gods. Directed by Madison Davis Lacy. New York: National Black Programming Consortium, 2001. VHS.

Freire-Medeiros, Bianca. "Hollywood Musicals and the Invention of Rio de Janeiro, 1933–1953." *Cinema Journal* 41.4 (Summer 2002): 52–67.

Frith, Simon. *Performing Rites: On the Value of Popular Music*. Oxford: Oxford University Press, 1996.

Fronval, George. "À Mogador on tourne la Sirène des Tropiques." *Cinéa-ciné pour tous*, October 15, 1927, 14–15.

Gambetti, Giacomo. *Vittorio Gassmann*. Rome: Gremese Editore, 1999.

Gates, Henry Louis, Jr. "An Interview with Josephine Baker and James Baldwin." *Southern Review* 21.3 (1985): 594–602.

Geiger, Jeffrey. "Sightseeing: *Voyage au Congo* and the Ethnographic Spectacle." In *André Gide's Politics: Rebellion and Ambivalence*, ed. Tom Conner. 111–30. Basingstoke, U.K.: Palgrave Macmillan, 2001.

Gennari, Daniela Treveri. *Post-War Italian Cinema: American Intervention, Vatican Interests*. New York: Routledge, 2009.

Gennari, John. "Passing for Italian." *Transition* 72 (1996): 36–48.

Genné, Beth. "'Glorifying the American Woman': Josephine Baker and George Balanchine." *Discourses in Dance* 3.1 (2005): 31–57.

"Girls Hold Million Dollar Film." *Pittsburgh Courier*, August 3, 1929, A3.

Gottschild, Brenda Dixon. *The Black Dancing Body: A Geography from Coon to Cool*. New York: Palgrave Macmillan, 2003.

———. *Digging the Africanist Presence in American Performance: Dance and Other Contexts*. Westport, Conn.: Greenwood Press, 1996.

Griffin, Sean. "The Gang's All Here: Generic versus Racial Integration in the 1940s Musical." *Cinema Journal* 42.1 (Autumn 2002): 21–45.

Griffiths, Alison. *Wondrous Difference: Cinema, Anthropology, and Turn-of-the-Century Visual Culture*. New York: Columbia University Press, 2002.

Groo, Katherine. "Shadow Lives: Josephine Baker and the Body of Cinema." *Framework: The Journal of Cinema and Media* 54.1 (2013): 7–39.

Gundle, Stephen. "Miss Italia in Black and White: Feminine Beauty and Ethnic Identity in Modern Italy." In *Migrant Cartographies: New Cultural and Literary Spaces in Post-Colonial Europe*, eds. Sandra Ponzanesi and Daniela Merolla. 253–66. Lanham, Md.: Lexington, 2005.

Guterl, Matthew Pratt. *Josephine Baker and the Rainbow Tribe*. Cambridge: Harvard University Press, 2014.

———. "Josephine Baker's Colonial Pastiche." *Black Camera: An International Film Journal* 1.2 (Summer 2010): 25–37.

Habel, Ylva. "To Stockholm, with Love: The Critical Reception of Josephine Baker, 1927–35." *Film History: An International Journal* 17.1 (2005): 125–38.

Hammond, Bryan, and Patrick O'Connor. *Josephine Baker*. London: Jonathan Cape, 1988.

Haney, Lynn. *Naked at the Feast: A Biography of Josephine Baker*. London: Robson Books, 1981.

Hardin, Tayana. "Josephine Baker and the Shadow of Spectacle." *Dance Chronicle* 38.2 (2015): 179–203.

Harnan, Terry. *African Rhythm—American Dance: A Biography of Katherine Dunham.* New York: Alfred A. Knopf, 1974.

Hayward, Susan. *French National Cinema.* 2nd ed. Abingdon, U.K.: Routledge, 2005.

Hazzard-Gordon, Katrina. *Jookin': The Rise of Social Dance Formations in African-American Culture.* Philadelphia: Temple University Press, 1990.

Henderson, Mae Gwendolyn. "Josephine Baker and *La Revue Nègre*: From Ethnography to Performance." *Text and Performance Quarterly* 23.2 (April 2003): 107–33.

Hill, Constance Valis. *Brotherhood in Rhythm: The Jazz Tap Dancing of the Nicholas Brothers.* Oxford: Oxford University Press, 2000.

———. "Collaborating with Balanchine on *Cabin in the Sky*: Interviews with Katherine Dunham." In *Kaiso! Writings by and about Katherine Dunham*, eds. VèVè A. Clark and Sara E. Johnson. 235–47. Madison: University of Wisconsin Press, 2005.

———. "Katherine Dunham's *Southland*: Protest in the Face of Repression" (1994). In *Kaiso! Writings by and about Katherine Dunham*, eds. VèVè A. Clark and Sara E. Johnson. 344–63. Madison: University of Wisconsin Press, 2005.

Hill, Ed. "Focus on 'Queen of the Adriatic': Venice to Co-Star with Film Personalities In 'Mambo,'" *New York Times*, February 28, 1954, X5.

Hill, Edwin C., Jr. *Black Soundscapes White Stages: The Meaning of Francophone Sound in the Black Atlantic.* Baltimore: Johns Hopkins University Press, 2013.

Hine, Darlene Clark, and John McCluskey, eds. *The Black Chicago Renaissance.* Urbana: University of Illinois Press, 2012.

———. "Rape and the Inner Lives of Black Women in the Middle West." *Common Grounds and Crossroads: Race, Ethnicity, and Class in Women's Lives.* Spec. issue of *Signs* 14.4 (Summer 1989): 912–20.

Hodson, Millicent. "How She Began Her Beguine: Dunham's Dance Literacy" (1978). In *Kaiso! Writings by and about Katherine Dunham*, eds. VèVè A. Clark and Sara E. Johnson. 495–501. Madison: University of Wisconsin Press, 2005.

Horne, Lena, and Richard Schickel. *Lena.* London: Andre Deutsch, 1966.

Hotchner, A. E. *Papa Hemingway.* New York: Random House, 1966.

Hughes, Langston. Letter to Dr. Carlton B. Goodlett. October 23, 1958, n.p. Box 1, folder 5. Manuscript, Archives, and Rare Book Library, Emory University, Atlanta, Ga.

Humez, Jean McMahon. *Harriet Tubman: The Life and the Life Stories.* Madison: University of Wisconsin Press, 2003.

———. "Reading 'The Narrative of Sojourner Truth' as a Collaborative Text." *Frontiers: A Journal of Women Studies* 16.1 (1996): 29–52.

Hursey, Martha. Press release on Baker's visit to Fisk University, January 29, 1948, n.p. Josephine Baker Collection. James Weldon Johnson Collection in the Yale Collection of American Literature, Beinecke Rare Book and Manuscript Library.

Hurston, Zora Neale. "Characteristics of Negro Expression." In *Negro: An Anthology*, eds. Nancy Cunard, Hugh D. Ford. 24–31. Rev. ed. New York: Frederick Ungar, 1970.

———. "Thirty Days among Maroons" (1947). In *Kaiso! Writings by and about Katherine Dunham*, eds. VèVè A. Clark and Sara E. Johnson. 272–73. Madison: University of Wisconsin Press, 2005.

Ivy, James W. "Sleep Naked Is 'Jo' Baker's Beauty Secret." *Baltimore Afro-American*, July 14, 1928, 9.

Jackson, Gregory S. "Katherine Dunham." In *The Oxford Companion to African American Literature*, eds. William L. Andrews, Frances Smith Foster, and Trudier Harris. 242. Oxford: Oxford University Press, 1997.

Jackson, Jeffrey H. *Making Jazz French: Music and Modern Life in Interwar Paris*. Durham: Duke University Press, 2001.

Jackson, Robert. *Fade In, Crossroads: A History of the Southern Cinema*. Oxford: Oxford University Press, 2017.

Jeancolas, Jean-Pierre. "The Inexportable: The Case of French Cinema and Radio in the 1950s." In *Popular European Cinema*, eds. Richard Dyer and Ginette Vincendeau. 141–48. London: Routledge, 1992.

Jeff, Leonard J., and Jerold L. Simmons, *The Dame in the Kimono: Hollywood, Censorship, and the Production Code from the 1920s to the 1960s*. Rev. ed. New York: Grove Wiedenfeld, 2001.

Jelavich, Peter. *Berlin Cabaret*. Cambridge: Harvard University Press, 1993.

Jenkins, Jennifer R. "'Say It with Firecrackers': Defining the 'War Musical' of the 1940s." *American Music* 19.3 (Autumn 2001): 315–39.

"Jo Baker Film Shows Equality of Races." *Baltimore Afro-American*, September 28, 1929, 7.

"'Jo' Baker Offered $10,000 Contract," *Baltimore Afro-American*, February 11, 1928, 9.

"Jo Baker Picture Showing in Harlem." *Pittsburgh Courier*, January 25, 1930, 16.

"Jo Baker's Great Cinema Reaches States." *Pittsburgh Courier*, August 3, 1929, A3.

Johnson, James Weldon. *Black Manhattan*. New York: Atheneum, 1968.

Johnson, Sara E. "Introduction: Diamonds on the Toes of Her Feet." In *Kaiso! Writings by and about Katherine Dunham*, eds. VèVè A. Clark and Sara E. Johnson. 3–15. Madison: University of Wisconsin Press, 2005.

Jordan, Matthew F. *Le Jazz: Jazz and French Cultural Identity*. Urbana: University of Illinois Press, 2010.

"Josephine Baker, In 'Siren' Film, Scoring at Elmore." *Pittsburgh Courier*, November 16, 1929, 8.

"Josephine Baker and Black Power." *Washington Post*, October 4, 1970, F3.

"Joséphine Baker dans 'Folie du Jour.'" *Cinéa-ciné pour tous*, February 15, 1927, 32.

"Josephine Baker Here Soon in Film." *New York Amsterdam News*, July 31, 1929, 12.

"Josie Baker's Portrait Entered in Paris Salon." *Chicago Defender*, June 2, 1928, 5.

Jules-Rosette, Bennetta. *Josephine Baker in Art and Life: The Icon and the Image*. Urbana: University of Illinois Press, 2007.

Julien, Eileen. "Now You See It, Now You Don't: Josephine Baker's Films of the 1930s and the Problem of Color." In *Black Europe and the African Diaspora*, eds. Darlene

Clark Hine, Trica Danielle Keaton, and Stephen Small. 48–62. Urbana: University of Illinois Press, 2009.

"Jungle Artistry." *Star*, June 4, 1949, n.p.

Kalinak, Kathryn. "Disciplining Josephine Baker: Gender, Race, and the Limits of Disciplinarity." In *Music and Cinema*, eds. James Buhler, Caryl Flinn, and David Neumeyer. 316–35. Hanover, Conn.: Wesleyan University Press, 2000.

Katherine Dunham and Ensemble—Afro-Caribbean Songs and Rhythms. Decca Records (sleeve note). Theatre and Performance Biographical Files, V&A Theatre Museum, Blythe House Archive and Library Reading Room, London.

"Katherine Dunham on Her Influence on American Dance." September 2002. Video recording. Katherine Dunham Collection, Moving Image Section, Motion Picture, Broadcasting and Recorded Sound Division, Library of Congress, Washington, D.C.

Kelley, Robin D. G. *Race Rebels: Culture, Politics, and the Black Working Class*. New York: Free Press, 1996.

Kennedy-Karpat, Colleen. *Rogues, Romance, and Exoticism in French Cinema of the 1930s*. Plymouth, U.K.: Rowman and Littlefield, 2013.

Kezich, Tullio, and Alessandra Levantesi. Trans. from the Italian by James Marcus, *Dino: The Life and Films of Dino De Laurentiis*. New York: Miramax Books, 2004.

Kitt, Eartha. *Thursday's Child*. London: Cassell and Company, 1957.

Knight, Arthur. *Disintegrating the Musical: Black Performance and American Musical Film*. Durham: Duke University Press, 2002.

———. "Jammin' the Blues, or the Sight of Jazz, 1944." In *Representing Jazz*, ed. Krin Gabbard. 11–53. Durham: Duke University Press, 1995.

Knowles, Mark. *The Wicked Waltz and Other Scandalous Dances: Outrage at Couple Dancing in the 19th and Early 20th Centuries*. Jefferson, N.C.: McFarland, 2009.

Knupfer, Anne Meis. *The Chicago Black Renaissance and Women's Activism*. Urbana: University of Illinois Press, 2006.

Koppes, Clayton R., and Gregory D. Black. *Hollywood Goes to War: How Politics, Profits, and Propaganda Shaped World War II Movies*. London: I. B. Tauris, 1987.

Köpping, Klaus-Peter. *Shattering Frames: Transgressions and Transformations in Anthropological Discourse and Practice*. Berlin: Dietrich Reimer Verlag, 2002.

Kraut, Anthea. "Between Primitivism and Diaspora: The Dance Performances of Josephine Baker, Zora Neale Hurston, and Katherine Dunham." *Theatre Journal* 55.3 (2003): 433–50.

———. *Choreographing the Folk: The Dance Stagings of Zora Neale Hurston*. Minneapolis: University of Minnesota Press, 2008.

———. "Whose Choreography? Josephine Baker and the Question of (Dance) Authorship." *Josephine Baker: A Century in the Spotlight*. Spec. issue of *The Scholar and Feminist Online* 6.1–6.2 (Fall 2007/Spring 2008): 1–5. http://sfonline.barnard.edu/baker/kraut_01.htm. Accessed November 30, 2018.

"L'Activité Cinégraphique." *Cinéa-ciné pour tous*, September 1, 1927, 32–33.

Lahs-Gonzales, Olivia. "Josephine Baker: Modern Woman." In *Josephine Baker: Image and Icon*, ed. Olivia Lahs-Gonzales. 31–53. St Louis: Reedy Press, 2006.

Lamothe, Daphne. *Inventing the New Negro: Narrative, Culture, and Ethnography.* Philadelphia: University of Pennsylvania Press, 2008.
LaMothe, Kimerer L. *Nietzsche's Dancers: Isadora Duncan, Martha Graham, and the Revaluation of Christian Values.* Gordonsville, Va.: Palgrave Macmillan, 2006.
Lanzoni, Rémi Fournier. *French Cinema: From Its Beginnings to the Present.* New York: Continuum, 2002.
Lareau, Alan. "Bitte einsteigen! Josephine Baker's 1928 Return to Berlin." In *Topography and Literature: Berlin and Modernism*, ed. Reinhard Zachau. 69–86. Göttingen: V&R Unipress, 2009.
"La Revue Nègre." *L'Eclair*, October 8, 1925, 4.
Largey, Michael. *Vodou Nation: Haitian Art, Music and Cultural Nationalism.* Chicago: University of Chicago Press, 2006.
"Le Cinéma—'Princesse Tam.'" *Le Matin*, September 20, 1935, 4.
Lemke, Sieglinde. *Primitivist Modernism: Black Culture and the Origins of Transatlantic Modernism.* Oxford: Oxford University Press, 1998.
"Les Nouveaux Films—'Princesse Tam-Tam.'" *Le Matin*, October 18, 1935, 4.
"Les Nouveaux Films—*Zouzou.*" *Le Matin*, December 21, 1934, 4.
Levinson, André. "The Negro Dance: Under European Eyes," *Theatre Arts Monthly*, April 1927. In *André Levinson on Dance: Writings from Paris in the Twenties*, eds. Joan Acocella and Lynn Garafola. 69–75. Middletown, Conn.: Wesleyan University Press, 1991.
Lloyd, A. L. "Miss Dunham's Witchery." *Picture Post*, June 26, 1948, 11.
Lloyd, Margaret. *The Borzoi Book of Modern Dance.* New York: Alfred A. Knopf, 1949.
Long, Richard A. *The Black Tradition in American Dance.* New York: Rizzoli, 1989.
"Looking Glass: The Riot in East St. Louis, The." *The Crisis* 48.3 (August 1917): 175–78.
Lumpkins, Charles L. *American Pogrom: The East St. Louis Race Riot and Black Politics.* Athens: Ohio University Press, 2008.
Lupton, Mary Jane. *Maya Angelou: A Critical Companion.* Westport, Conn.: Greenwood Press, 1998.
Mackie, Erin. "Welcome The Outlaw: Pirates, Maroons, And Caribbean Countercultures." *Cultural Critique* 59 (2005): 24–62.
Magill, Charles T. "'Siren of the Tropics' Just Another Movie, Says Critic." *Chicago Defender*, October 12, 1929, 7.
Mambo (advertisement). *La Stampa*, March 7–8, 1950, 2.
Manning, Frankie, and Cynthia R. Millman. *Frankie Manning: Ambassador of Lindy Hop.* Philadelphia: Temple University Press, 2007.
Manning, Susan. "Modern Dance, Negro Dance and Katherine Dunham." *Textual Practice* 15.3 (2001): 487–505.
———. *Modern Dance, Negro Dance: Race in Motion.* Minneapolis: University of Minnesota Press, 2004.
Marguet, Jean. "Le Miroir des Films: La Critique." *Le Petit Parisien*, October 25, 1935, 6.
Marshall, Ronald. "Notes on Floyd's Guitar Blues: Katherine Dunham's Costumes and Musical Production." In *Katherine Dunham: Recovering an Anthropological Legacy,*

Choreographing Ethnographic Futures, ed. Elizabeth Chin. 73–78. Santa Fe: School for Advanced Research Press, 2014.

Martin, John. "The Dance: A Negro Art." *New York Times*, February 25, 1940, 114.

Massood, Paula J. "African American Stardom inside and outside of Hollywood: Ernest Morrison, Noble Johnson, Evelyn Preer, and Lincoln Perry." In *Idols of Modernity: Movie Stars of the 1920s*, ed. Patrice Petro. 227–49. New Brunswick, N.J.: Rutgers University Press, 2010.

Mazer, Gwen. "Katherine Dunham," *Essence* (December 1976). In *Kaiso! Writings by and about Katherine Dunham*, eds. VèVè A. Clark and Sara E. Johnson. 419–26. Madison: University of Wisconsin Press, 2005.

McCarren, Felicia M. *Dancing Machines: Choreographies of the Age of Mechanical Reproduction*. Stanford: Stanford University Press, 2003.

———. "The Use-Value of 'Josephine Baker.'" *Josephine Baker: A Century in the Spotlight*. Spec. issue of *The Scholar and Feminist Online* 6.1–6.2 (Fall 2007/Spring 2008): 1–5. http://sfonline.barnard.edu/baker/mccarren_01.htm. Accessed November 30, 2018.

McLaughlin, Malcolm. *Power, Community, and Racial Killing in East St. Louis*. New York: Palgrave Macmillan, 2005.

Mendible, Myra. "Introduction: Embodying Liberation, An Overview." In *From Bananas to Buttocks: The Latina Body in Popular Film and Culture*, ed. Myra Mendible. 1–28. Austin: University of Texas Press, 2007.

Mizejewski, Linda. *Ziegfeld Girl: Image and Icon in Culture and Cinema*. Durham: Duke University Press, 1999.

Moore, Robin Dale. *Nationalizing Blackness: Afrocubanismo and Artistic Revolution in Havana, 1920–1940*. Pittsburgh: University of Pittsburgh Press, 1997.

Moreno Vega, Marta. "The Dynamic Influence of Cubans, Puerto Ricans, and African Americans in the Growth of Ocha in New York City." In *Òrìṣà Devotion as World Religion: The Globalization of Yorùbá Religious Culture*, eds. Jacob Kẹhinde Olupona and Terry Rey. 320–36. Madison: University of Wisconsin Press, 2008.

Mulvey, Laura. "Visual Pleasure and Narrative Cinema." *Screen* 16:3 (Autumn 1975): 6–18.

Murray, David. *Matter, Magic and Spirit: Representing Indian and African American Belief*. Philadelphia: University of Pennsylvania Press, 2007.

"NAACP Praises Baker." *Dayton Express*, February 24, 1951, n.p. Josephine Baker Papers, Manuscript, Archives, and Rare Book Library, Emory University, Atlanta, Ga.

Nesteby, James R. *Black Images in American Films, 1896–1954: The Interplay between Civil Rights and Film Culture*. Lanham, Md.: University Press of America, 1982.

Nettleford, Rex. "The Jamaican Connexion (or *Journey from Accompong*)" (1988). In *Kaiso! Writings by and about Katherine Dunham*, eds. VèVè A. Clark and Sara E. Johnson. 598–602. Madison: University of Wisconsin Press, 2005.

Noble, Peter. *The Negro in Films*. London: Skelton Robinson, 1949.

"A Note or Two." *Chicago Defender*, March 31, 1928, 6.

"Nouveaux Films." *L'Humanité*, December 21, 1934, 4.

Osumare, Halifu. "Katherine Dunham, a Pioneer of Postmodern Anthropology." In *Kaiso! Writings by and about Katherine Dunham*, eds. VèVè A. Clark and Sara E. Johnson. 612–23. Madison: University of Wisconsin Press, 2005.

Ovalle, Priscilla Peña. *Dance and the Hollywood Latina: Race, Sex, and Stardom*. New Brunswick, N.J.: Rutgers University Press, 2010.

"Paris Theatre Crowded a Month for 'Jo' Baker Film." *Baltimore Afro-American*, February 18, 1928, 8.

Paudrat, Jean-Louis. "From Africa." In *"Primitivism" in 20th Century Art: Affinity of the Tribal and the Modern*, Vol. 1, ed. William Rubin. 125–75. New York: Museum of Modern Art, 1984.

Peiss, Kathy. *Zoot Suit: The Enigmatic Career of an Extreme Style*. Philadelphia: University of Pennsylvania Press, 2011.

Perpener, John O. *African-American Concert Dance: The Harlem Renaissance and Beyond*. Urbana: University of Illinois Press, 2001.

Polyné, Millery. *From Douglass to Duvalier: U.S. African Americans, Haiti, and Pan Africanism, 1870–1964*. Gainesville: University of Florida, 2010.

Powrie, Phil, with Éric Rebillard. "Josephine Baker and Pierre Batcheff in *La Sirène des tropiques*." *Studies in French Cinema* 8.3 (September 2008): 245–64.

———. *Pierre Batcheff and Stardom in 1920s French Cinema*. Edinburgh: Edinburgh University Press, 2009.

"Princesse Tam-Tam," *L'Ouest-Éclair*, May 2, 1936, 7.

Pryor, Thomas M. "'Stormy Weather,' Negro Musical with Bill Robinson, at the Roxy—'Hers to Hold' Opens at Criterion." *New York Times*, July 22, 1943, 15.

Raimon, Eve Allegra. *The "Tragic Mulatta" Revisited: Race and Nationalism in Nineteenth-Century Antislavery Fiction*. New Brunswick, N.J.: Rutgers University Press, 2004.

Ramsey, Kate. "Katherine Dunham and the Folklore Performance Movement in Post–U.S. Occupation Haiti." In *Katherine Dunham: Recovering an Anthropological Legacy, Choreographing Ethnographic Futures*, ed. Elizabeth Chin. 51–72. Santa Fe: School for Advanced Research Press, 2014.

———. "Melville Herskovits, Katherine Dunham, and the Politics of African Diasporic Dance Anthropology." In *Dancing Bodies, Living Histories: New Writings about Dance and Culture*, eds. Lisa Doolittle and Anne Flynn. 196–216. Banff, Alberta: Banff Centre Press, 2000.

———. "Vodou, Nationalism, and Performance: The Staging of Folklore in Mid-Twentieth-Century Haiti." In *Meaning in Motion: New Cultural Studies of Dance*, ed. Jane C. Desmond. 345–78. Durham: Duke University Press, 1997.

Rao, Ursula, and John Hutnyk. "Introduction." In *Celebrating Transgression: Method and Politics in Anthropological Studies of Culture: A Book in Honour of Klaus-Peter Köpping*, eds. Ursula Rao and John Hutnyk. 1–10. New York: Berghahn Books, 2006.

Raynaud, Claudine. "Foil, Fiction, and Phantasm: 'Josephine Baker' in *Princess Tam Tam*." *Josephine Baker: A Century in the Spotlight*. Spec. issue of *The Scholar and Feminist Online* 6.1–6.2 (Fall 2007/Spring 2008): 1–10. http://sfonline.barnard.edu/baker/raynaud_01.htm. Accessed November 30, 2018.

Redfield, Robert. Letter to Katherine Dunham, September 13, ca. 1936, n.p. Box 1, folder 4. Katherine Mary Dunham Papers, 1919–1968. Morris Library Special Collections Research Center, Southern Illinois University, Carbondale, Ill.

Regester, Charlene. *African American Actresses: The Struggle for Visibility, 1900–1960*. Bloomington: Indiana University Press, 2010.

Régnier, Pierre de. "Aux Champs-Elysées: *La Revue Nègre*." *Candide*, November 12, 1925, 6.

Remba, Michael. "A Variegated Life," NAACP Commemorative Program: Josephine Baker Day. May 20, 1951, 6–10. Josephine Baker Collection. James Weldon Johnson Collection in the Yale Collection of American Literature, Beinecke Rare Book and Manuscript Library.

"Review: *Mambo*." *Monthly Film Bulletin*, January 1955, 70–71.

"Review: *Mambo*." *Newsweek*, April 18, 1955, 3.

Roberts, Shari. "'The Lady in the Tutti-Frutti Hat': Carmen Miranda, a Spectacle of Ethnicity." *Cinema Journal* 32.3 (Spring 1993): 3–23.

"'Rochester,' Dunham Together in Feature Film Dance." *New Journal and Guide*, July 4, 1942, B21.

"Rochester and Katherine Dunham Head Colored in Paramount Film." *Baltimore Afro-American*, July 4, 1942, 11.

Roediger, David. *The Wages of Whiteness: Race and the Making of the American Working Class*. 1991; rpt. New York: Verso, 1999.

Rogers, J. A. "J. A. Rogers First to Interview Countess Pepito di Albertini." *New York Amsterdam News*, July 6, 1927, 1.

———. "Josephine Baker Acclaimed in Film in which She Plays a Leading Part." *Philadelphia Tribune*, February 9, 1928, 9.

Romero-Cesareo, Ivette. "Travelers Possessed: Generic Hybrids and the Caribbean." In *Between Anthropology and Literature: Interdisciplinary Discourse*, ed. Rose De Angelis. 133–57. London: Routledge, 2002.

Rony, Fatimah Tobing. *The Third Eye: Race, Cinema, and Ethnographic Spectacle*. Durham: Duke University Press, 1996.

Root. Lynn. *Cabin in the Sky (A Musical Play)*. Theater script, ca. 1940. Box 54, folder 10. Katherine Mary Dunham Papers, 1919–1968. Morris Library Special Collections Research Center, Southern Illinois University, Carbondale, Ill.

Roper, Susan. "Balanchine in Hollywood." *Ballet Review* 23.4 (Winter 1995): 48–73.

Rose, Albirda. *Dunham Technique: A Way of Life*. Dubuque, Iowa: Kendall/Hunt, 1990.

Rose, Phyllis. *Jazz Cleopatra: Josephine Baker in Her Time*. 1989; rpt. London: Vintage, 1991.

Sampson, Henry T. *Blacks in Black and White: A Source Book on Black Films*, 2nd ed. Lanham, Md.: Scarecrow Press, 1995.

Scheuer, Philip K. "'Casbah' Set to Music by Tony Martin." *Los Angeles Times*, April 15, 1948, 23.

Schuyler, George S. "Views and Reviews." *Pittsburgh Courier*, March 27, 1943, 13.

Scott, David. "'To Be Liberated from the Obscurity of Themselves': An Interview with Rex Nettleford." *Small Axe* 10.2 (2006): 97–246.

Scott, Ellen C. *Cinema Civil Rights: Regulation, Repression, and Race in the Classical Hollywood Era*. New Brunswick, N.J.: Rutgers University Press, 2015.

"Screen Review." *Baltimore Afro-American*, October 26, 1929, A9.

Sharpley-Whiting, T. Denean. *Black Venus: Sexualized Savages, Primal Fears, and Primitive Narratives in French*. Durham: Duke University Press, 1999.

Shaw, Gwendolyn DuBois. *Seeing the Unspeakable: The Art of Kara Walker*. Durham: Duke University Press, 2004.

Sheridan, Alan. *André Gide: A Life in the Present*. London: Hamish Hamilton, 1998.

Sherzer, Dina. "Race Matters and Matters of Race: Interracial Relationships in Colonial and Postcolonial Films." In *Cinema, Colonialism, Postcolonialism: Perspectives from the French and Francophone Worlds*, ed. Dina Sherzer. 229–48. Austin: University of Texas Press, 1996.

Sklaroff, Lauren Rebecca. *Black Culture and the New Deal: The Quest for Civil Rights in the Roosevelt Era*. Chapel Hill: University of North Carolina Press, 2009.

———. "Constructing G. I. Joe Louis: Cultural Solutions to the 'Negro Problem' during World War II." *Journal of American History* 89.3 (December 2000): 958–83.

Smith, Sidonie, and Julia Watson. "Introduction: Living in Public." In *Before They Could Vote: American Women's Autobiographical Writing, 1819–1919*, eds. Sidonie Smith and Julia Watson. 3–22. Madison: University of Wisconsin Press, 2006.

Sobelman, Martin. Letter to Katherine Dunham, May 20, 1941, n.p. Box 2, folder 3. Katherine Mary Dunham Papers, 1919–1968. Morris Library Special Collections Research Center, Southern Illinois University, Carbondale, Ill.

Sollors, Werner. *Neither Black nor White yet Both: Thematic Explorations of Interracial Literature*. New York: Oxford University Press, 1997.

Spa, Robert. "Figaro Cinema." *Le Figaro*, December 24, 1927, 4.

Spanger, Marlene. "Disturbance and Celebration of Josephine Baker in Copenhagen 1928: Emotional Constructions of Whiteness." In *Affectivity and Race: Studies from Nordic Contexts*, eds. Rikke Andreassen and Kathrine Vitus. 111–29. London: Routledge, 2016.

Stam, Robert. *Tropical Multiculturalism: A Comparative History of Race in Brazilian Cinema and Culture*. Durham: Duke University Press, 1997.

Stearns, Marshall, and Jean Stearns. *Jazz Dance: The Story of American Vernacular Dance*. 1968; rpt. New York: Da Capo Press, 1994.

Stepto, Robert B. *From behind the Veil: A Study of Afro-American Narrative*, 2nd ed. Urbana: University of Illinois Press, 1991.

St. John, Sir Spenser. *Hayti; Or, the Black Republic*. London: Smith, Elder, and Co., 1884.

Stoneley, Peter. *A Queer History of the Ballet*. London: Routledge, 2006.

Stovall, Jeanelle. Dunham Technique Seminar. East St. Louis, August 17, 1995. Video recording. Katherine Dunham Collection, Moving Image Section, Motion Picture, Broadcasting and Recorded Sound Division, Library of Congress, Washington, D.C.

Stovall, Tyler. "The New Woman and the New Empire: Josephine Baker and Changing Views of Femininity in Interwar France." *Josephine Baker: A Century in the Spotlight*. Spec. issue of *The Scholar and Feminist Online* 6.1–6.2 (Fall 2007/Spring 2008): 1–7. http://sfonline.barnard.edu/baker/stovall_01.htm. Accessed November 30, 2018.

———. "No Green Pastures: The African Americanization of France." In *Black Europe and the African Diaspora*, eds. Darlene Clark Hine, Trica Danielle Keaton, and Stephen Small. 180–97. Urbana: University of Illinois Press, 2009.

Stratyner, Barbara. *Ned Wayburn and the Dance Routine: From Vaudeville to the Ziegfeld Follies*. Madison, Wis.: Society of Dance History Scholars, 1996.

Sweeney, Carole. *From Fetish to Subject: Race, Modernism, and Primitivism, 1919–1935*. Westport, Conn.: Praeger, 2004.

Taper, Bernard. *Balanchine: A Biography*. Berkeley: University of California Press, 1996.

Taylor, Clyde. "New U.S. Black Cinema." *Jump Cut: A Review of Contemporary Media* 28 (April 1983; rpt. 2005). http://www.ejumpcut.org/archive/onlinessays/JC28folder/NewBlackCinema.html#3. Accessed November 30, 2018.

Taylor, Frank C., with Gerald Cook. *Alberta Hunter: A Celebration in Blues*. New York: McGraw-Hill, 1987.

"The Theatre: New Plays in Manhattan." *Time*, February 10, 1936, n.p.

Thomas, Martin. *The French Empire between the Wars: Imperialism, Politics and Society*. Manchester: Manchester University Press, 2007.

Thomas, Roy. "Focal Rites: New Dance Dominions" (1978). In *Kaiso! Writings by and about Katherine Dunham*, eds. VèVè A. Clark and Sara E. Johnson. 531–39. Madison: University of Wisconsin Press, 2005.

Thompson, Robert Farris. "Teaching the People to Triumph over Time: Notes from the World of Mambo." In *Caribbean Dance from Abakua to Zouk: How Movement Shapes Identity*, ed. Susanna Sloat. 336–44. 2002; rpt. Gainesville: University Press of Florida, 2005.

Thompson, Sgt. Fred. "What the People Say." *Chicago Defender*, August 5, 1944, 12.

Townsend, Julie. "Un-Fixing Baker: Against a Criticism of Stasis." *Modernist Cultures* 9.1 (2014): 62–79.

Tracy, Steven C. *Writers of the Black Chicago Renaissance*. Urbana: University of Illinois Press, 2011.

Un vent de folie program. Josephine Baker Collection. James Weldon Johnson Collection in the Yale Collection of American Literature, Beinecke Rare Book and Manuscript Library.

"Vienna Police Guard for Josephine Baker." *Chicago Defender*, February 11, 1928, 10.

Vogel, Shane. "Performing 'Stormy Weather': Ethel Waters, Lena Horne, and Katherine Dunham." *South Central Review* 25.1 (2008): 93–113.

Von Eschen, Penny M. *Satchmo Blows Up the World: Jazz Ambassadors Play the Cold War*. Cambridge: Harvard University Press, 2004.

Voogd, Jan. *Race Riots and Resistance: The Red Summer of 1919*. New York: Peter Lang, 2008.

Wallace, Margarette (Margaret). "The True Life of Josephine" (unpublished paper). February 8, 1977, 1–6. Series II, folder 162. Henry Hurford Janes-Josephine Baker Collection. James Weldon Johnson Collection in the Yale Collection of American Literature, Beinecke Rare Book and Manuscript Library.

Wayburn, Ned. *The Art of Stage Dancing: The Story of a Beautiful and Profitable Profession, A Manual of Stagecraft*. New York: Ned Wayburn Studios of Stage Dancing, 1925.

Welky, David. *The Moguls and the Dictators: Hollywood and the Coming of World War II*. Baltimore, Md.: John Hopkins University Press, 2008.

Williams, Chad Louis. *Torchbearers of Democracy: African American Soldiers in the World War I Era*. Chapel Hill: University of North Carolina Press, 2010.

Williams, Megan E. "The 'Crisis' Cover Girl: Lena Horne, the NAACP, and Representations of African American Femininity, 1941–1945." *American Periodicals: A Journal of History, Criticism, and Bibliography* 16.2 (2006): 200–18.

Willis, Deborah, and Carla Williams. *The Black Female Body: A Photographic History*. Philadelphia: Temple University Press, 2002.

Wood, Ean. *The Josephine Baker Story*. London: Sanctuary Publishing, 2001.

Index

Note: Page numbers in italics refer to images.

HANNAH DURKIN is a lecturer in literature and film at Newcastle University. She is a coeditor of *Visualising Slavery: Art Across the African Diaspora*.

The University of Illinois Press
is a founding member of the
Association of American University Presses.

Composed in 10.75/13 Adobe Garamond Pro
with Raleway display
by Kirsten Dennison
at the University of Illinois Press
Cover designed by Becca Alexander
Cover illustration: Josephine Baker, c. 1950s (Photofest);
Katherine Dunham, c. 1943 (Photofest)
Manufactured by Sheridan Books, Inc.

University of Illinois Press
1325 South Oak Street
Champaign, IL 61820-6903
www.press.uillinois.edu